DAVID OVASON is the author of ~
esoteric subjects. His most recent ˅
damus (1997), *The Zelator: A Modern ˌ*
(1998), *The Secret Architecture of Our*
Children: A Study of the Two Jesus Childrˌ
Secret Symbols of the Dollar Bill (2004)
(2005).

˷ʋ1), *The*
˷ʋry of the Horoscope

SHAKESPEARE'S
SECRET BOOKE

DECIPHERING MAGICAL AND
ROSICRUCIAN CODES

AD ÆTHERA VIRTVS

EX HIS

ORI—

DOCVIT QVÆ

OVID'S
METAMORPHOSIS
Englished
by
G . S.

Imprinted at
LONDON
MDCXXVI
Cum Privilegio

FORMANTVR ET

AMORE

SAPIENTIA

AFFIGIT HVMO DIVINÆ PARTICVLAM AVRÆ

VNTVR

CVNCTA

SHAKESPEARE'S SECRET BOOKE

DECIPHERING MAGICAL AND ROSICRUCIAN CODES

DAVID OVASON

CLAIRVIEW

Clairview Books
Hillside House, The Square
Forest Row, East Sussex RH18 5ES

www.clairviewbooks.com

Published by Clairview 2010

A catalogue record for this book is available from the British Library

ISBN 978 1 905570 26 3

Cover layout by Andrew Morgan Design. Cover image courtesy the Charles Walker
Collection, TopPhoto UK
Typeset by DP Photosetting, Neath, West Glamorgan
Printed and bound by Gutenberg Press Ltd, Malta

Mixed Sources

Product group from well-managed
forests, and other controlled sources
www.fsc.org Cert no. TT-CoC-002424
© 1996 Forest Stewardship Council

FSC

The paper used for this book is FSC-certified and
totally chlorine-free. FSC (the Forest Stewardship
Council) is an international network to promote
responsible management of the world's forests.

For my lovely wife.

Ma non eran da ciò le proprie penne...

Contents

Introduction

And now I will unclaspe a Secret booke,
And to your quicke conceyving Discontents,
Ille reade you Matter, deepe and dangerous
As full of peril and adventurous Spirit

[William Shakespeare, *The first Part of King Henry the fourth*, in the Folio
edition of 1623, *Histories*, p. 52, column 1.]

The title, *Shakespeare's Secret Booke,* is borrowed from the pen of the Bard
himself, and points to a hidden code that figures in the esoteric literature
of the Elizabethan and Jacobean periods. Shakespeare was a master of
numerology. The encoding methods that Shakespeare used in some of his
plays were continued into the printed plays that appeared in the post-
humous *First Folio* of 1623. This seminal source was edited by those who
had known Shakespeare during his lifetime, and who were quite clearly
familiar with his favoured method of encoding. Perhaps even more
remarkably, the identical codes were used later in the various funerary
lapidaries and monuments associated with the Bard – ranging from the
formal monuments and the curse-stone in Holy Trinity Church, Stratford-
upon-Avon, to the Shakespeare memorial in Westminster Abbey. What,
we must ask, is the secret behind the code or encodings that appear in
such monuments, and in this *Secret booke*? Was the matter hidden in the
codes really deep, dangerous, and full of peril, as Shakespeare had hinted?
Or was it more likely that Shakespeare and his near contemporaries were
attempting to deal with material that, if dealt with openly, might upset the
political and ecclesiastical powers that be?

There is considerable evidence to show that Shakespeare, and many
literary figures around him, employed a variety of numerological codes or
numbers.[1] Each number within this encoding was designed to point to
some specialist aspect of a hermeneutic system of beliefs. I have no
intention of surveying all these encodings, some of which are, to my mind,
invalid in terms of Shakespeare's *booke*. My own interest is presently
limited to the widespread use of the numerological encoding of the
number 33, which was certainly used by Shakespeare and many of his
associates in reference to the mystery of the Ego, or the higher, invisible

Self. This is mainly because, historically speaking, the 33 was used as a symbol of the interface between the familiar realm and the higher realm of spirit. The true Ego may be conceived as occupying that higher realm, and may therefore be conveniently symbolized by this number, 33. Here, I would like to reflect on the number 33 itself, which in the early seventeenth century was linked with Shakespeare by a number of writers and artists. An almost open link between Shakespeare and the 33 may be seen in the emblem book, *Minerva Britannia*, of 1612, which consisted of a series of emblems, each bearing an attached dedication above, and verses below.[2]

On page 33 of this Peacham work appeared an emblem (inadequately explained within the text) of a mailed hand holding a lance or spear. As the hand has no stability about it, this is a fair representation of a *shaking spear*.[3] Whatever sense one may extract from the two verses below the emblem, we may not doubt that this is a reference to Shakespeare, and that the 33 is being openly marked down as his number. Unlike any other page number within the book, this page number 33 is distinguished by a bold dot, as though designed to serve as an asterisk.

The 33 was a sort of esoteric leitmotif in literature and art. It was a sign, intended for those who had learned to recognize its presence in a work of art or literature, that there was something of deeper import in those works. The 33 stood as sentinel to the door that opened on a hidden world. We should not be surprised that the famous soliloquy of Hamlet, which is concerned with entry to

The undiscovered Countrey, from whose Borne
No Traveller returnes.[4]

is itself set out in exactly 33 lines (see page 63).

The earliest known use of the 33 encoding in colonial America is that which appeared in George Sandys' translation of Ovid's *Metamorphoses*. Sandys worked as treasurer of the Virginia colony between 1621 and 1631, writing this masterpiece partly in Virginia, partly in England, and partly during the terrible sea voyages between the two. Examples of the 33 encoding are found within the text of the work, but are also built into the ornate title-page of *Ovid's Metamorphosis, Englished*, which was published in 1626 (see frontispiece).

No fewer than four simple examples of the 33 encoding may be studied on this single title-page, which, graphically speaking, has all the appearance of being a doorway leading into another world. For example, a count of the number of all the words and part-words on the page reveals (provided one ignores the two single-letter abbreviations) exactly 33.[5]

Within this array of 33 titular words, there is a further inbuilt encoding of 33, in terms of letters. We find, in the simulated archway that bears the title proper, three words, one Roman numeral, and two abbreviations set in capital letters. These are,

OVID'S METAMORPHOSIS . G.S. . LONDON MDCXXVI.

A count reveals that, taken together, these six items consist of 33 letters.

The five words of Latin, circling the image of the enchantress, Circe, turning Ulysses' men into swine (page 4), consists of 33 letters.

This Latin is not lifted from Ovid's book. However, they do relate to a section in the *Metamorphoses*, where the narrator, Macareus, recalls the dramatic moment when Circe transformed him personally into the form of a pig. As he says, that part of him which had been designed to breath in the divine air was now thrust towards an earth burial.[6]

Yet another example of the 33 encoding upon this page may be seen in

the distinctive decorative lettering (it is not typeface, for it is written by the engraver) in the cartouches below the four images of the Elements, of Fire, Air, Earth and Water.[7] The word below the personification of Air has been hyphenated, thus *ORI-* and continues below Earth as *UNTUR*. This break is an essential part of the numerology, for Sandys was evidently inviting us to count the hyphen among the characters. The word-divisions in italic are:

EX HIS ORI- UNTUR CUNCTA

This must be counted in conjunction with the similar lettering, combining upper and lower case, at the bottom of the title: *Cum Privilegio,* thus:

EX HIS ORI- UNTUR CUNCTA Cum Privilegio

When we include the hyphen, we obtain 33 characters in the count.

Whilst the 33 encoding lent itself particularly well to literature – in letter-counts, word-counts and even line-counts – it was, at times, encoded in graphic forms. In such forms, it remained as more or less open symbols, albeit replete with hermeneutic content. For example, a triangle, representative of a single 3, was sometimes placed inside another triangle (which represented the second 3 of the numerological addition, 33) to obtain a magical figure, thus:

The figure encapsulated the number 33, yet at the same time, because the interaction of the two has created three new triangles within the One, this derived figure could be taken as a symbol of the Trinity. Another combination of the triangulated 3 + 3 = 33 is found in the magical symbol, the Seal of Solomon, which consists of two interpenetrating triangles, thus:

Related to this graphic symbolism, was the combination of two triadic sigils, intended to represent 3 + 3, and thus the 33.

Translated into words, the graphics read: an ascending triad (perhaps a supplicating or praying human) plus a descending triad, that might represent God reaching down a blessing towards the world, unite to form a six-pointed radiant. This stellar symbol is sometimes taken as a graphic statement of the old adage that, 'What is above, is like unto that which is below'.[8] Perhaps for this reason, as much as any other, the star has been adopted by many alchemists to symbolize their Art, the seeming six being a hidden 33. In this case, the symbolism so adopted was linked not only with the all-important 33, implicit within the star, but also with the notion that the descending triad represented Fire from Heaven. The patron of the alchemists was the pagan Vulcan, the smith among the ancient gods, who regulated his art by means of Fire. We shall see several examples of this hermetic star, of seeming six-points, in the following pages.

The triune nature of the 33 helps point to its Christian origins. It seems likely that the number was grafted into magical encoding because it was believed that Christ had lived on the earth for exactly 33 years. Whilst the 33 was later adapted for non-Christian and pagan art and literature, it was, in the medieval period, the supreme hermetic number. It is almost impossible to fully appreciate the depth of medieval art without some knowledge of the 33.

A single, well-chosen example from Christian art will help indicate how prevalent the 33 was, as a hidden form of symbolism, in the medieval period.

The encoded 33 is contained within the famous twelfth-century *Notre-Dame de la Belle Verrière*, in Chartres Cathedral (above, left). This glorious stained-glass window depicts the Christ child on the lap of his Mother. The secret encoding – if anything so openly on public display may be termed secret – is found on the inner concentric of her halo (above, right). Here, the alternate symbols of lozenge and roundel circuit the halo periphery in precisely 33 links.

Thousands of examples of this kind of 33 encoding may be found in medieval art. However, our own search is presently restricted mainly to the survival of this numerology in the sixteenth and seventeenth centuries.

When we turn to literature, the encoding of the 33 generally becomes far more inventive than the same code found in art forms. Indeed, the literated 33 plays a seminal role in the hermeneutic symbolism of alchemy, Rosicrucianism and all those arcane beliefs that touch upon the nature and mission of Christ, as well as the liminal realm between the material and spiritual world. In most cases, the encoding is fairly obvious. For example, a sentence that has been neatly crafted to contain 33 words, or 33 letters, may be taken as an encoded reference intended to alert a reader to the presence of, or the introduction to some hidden or esoteric idea. The 33 marked out for attention that liminal world of entrances – of ways up or down, and of doorways that open into rooms known or unknown.

It is for this reason that I intentionally phrased the opening sentence of this present Introduction so that it included precisely 33 words. It was to further emphasize this point that I constructed the second sentence so that it displayed 33 characters. In introducing these codes, I was announcing in an encoded way that the book would deal with hermeneutics or esoteric matters.

Like Shakespeare, Edmund Spenser was a subtle exponent of the 33, and like him, he linked the number with the idea of the human Spirit or Ego, as with the rarified realms of spirit. For this reason, an example from Spenser of the 33 encoding may be just as illuminating as one drawn from the plays or poems of the Bard.

If we turn for example to Book 3, Canto 3 (itself a sort of encoding of the 33) of *The Faerie Queene*, we find the first lines open with a vision of the celestial Spheres. In these lines, Spenser is pointing to the sacred fire that burns in the human frame, and which is itself born from the higher world:

Most sacred fyre, that burnest mightily
In living brests, ykindled first above
Emongst th'eternall spheres and lamping sky,
And thence pourd into men, which men call Love![9]

We note that the line opens this Book 3, Canto 3, itself consists of 33 characters. Spenser seems particularly intent on revealing, whilst hiding, that his poetic theme deals with the spaces of the spiritual realms, above the world of mankind.

This interesting example of a 33-letter line from the genius of Spenser should leave the reader in no doubt that I have no wish to mislead. I am not so foolish as to argue that Shakespeare was the inventor of this *Secret booke,* or of the 33 encoding, or that he was its sole exponent. Indeed, as we shall learn, other authors, who employed this encoding of 33 prior to Shakespeare, included the French savant Michel Nostradamus – without doubt the most famous esoteric writer and encoder in European history. The 33 code was in use long before Shakespeare was born: it just happens that his use of the code was so sophisticated, and so often beautifully framed.

My book is, then, not about Shakespeare, nor is it about his plays. Rather, it is partly about an intriguing numerological code, which was used from time to time in Elizabethan and Jacobean literature, and in certain later streams of esoteric tradition. As we shall see, our study of this encoding provides some evidence that the esoteric movement we now call Rosicrucianism was creatively active in those days.

Our search for the meanings of these encodings may begin with Shakespeare's *Secret booke* and with the encodings enforced upon the various memorials erected to the Bard after his death. However, the search soon leaves Shakespeare behind, as we follow a brilliant galaxy of alchemists, occultists and Rosicrucians of the seventeenth century. We shall encounter the astounding experiments of Michael Maier with a new triple form of literature, designed to reach the three human faculties of thinking, feeling and willing. We catch a glimpse of the influence of Jacob Boehme, who, like any good and learned alchemist, identified the Ego with the ancient 33 symbol called *The Seal of Solomon.* We see the dizzy wheels-within-wheels, motorized by the Rosicrucian, Heinrich Khunrath, anxious to display his truths by way of numerological symbols that interpenetrate a variety of languages. This complexity of his symbolism will be compared with the relative chastity of the symbolism of the alchemist, Andreas Libavius, before we move on, or backwards, to praise the quintessential magical master of them all – that misunderstood scholar, Dr. John Dee. With Dee, we witness the death of the old medieval approach to magical symbols, and the birth of an entirely new intellectual search for a universal esoteric archetypal symbolism. That Dee's new approach to symbolism has not been understood in modern times in no way diminishes his own achievement. His intelligently graded progression of theorems on the *Monas* (the word alone takes us back to Pythagoras) has excited scholars, but none so far has succeeded in understanding what he has to say.[10] Admittedly, Dee's language is difficult, his chosen subject recalcitrant, but his approach to symbols and encodings has deserved a better following than it has attracted. For us, at least, he will remain the supreme master of the 33 encoding, whilst his French counterpart, Nostradamus, must remain the master of general encoding.

One chapter presents Michel Nostradamus to our close gaze. Here, he is shown in his rightful guise as the greatest prophet of the medieval period, with almost two thousand prophetic verses to his credit. In this chapter, I treat him as a prophet who delighted in codes and encodings, and who seemed to be almost as keen as Shakespeare on the number 33. Nostradamus lived in that period that was at once *majestic, pious* and *sanctimonious* − to use three words introduced to the English language by Shakespeare. It was a time when the late medieval theological world clashed with the modern, to create not only the literature of Nostradamus, Ronsard and Rabelais, but also the wars of religion that shook their century and almost destroyed a world. These wars were born of the conflicts between the new-found independence of the Ego, with the old sense of selfhood − that selfhood of the old serpent in *Old Testament* lore − which mankind had yet to shake from its soul.

On the whole, conventional historians seem content to describe the conflicts of the sixteenth century in terms of religion and politics − and this is, indeed, a valid way of looking at history. However, the underlying truth about what happened in the sixteenth century must be found in the manifestation of tectonic tremors set up in society by the new feeling for the Ego, and the demands it made upon advanced members of society.

The reader may not be surprised by my hints that the number 33, whilst traditionally linked with the Christ, was adopted in the seventeenth century as a number symbol for the Ego. There is a particular magic about this word Ego, which so openly links the ancient worlds of Greece and Rome with modern times, and lends a Christian element to all Western thinking. The insistence upon the Christ element within the Ego (and thus in all men and women) is really a product of the activity of the Rosicrucian schools of the fifteenth and sixteenth centuries. Not surprisingly, then, the writings and symbols of the Rosicrucians deserve some mention in the following pages.

As a matter of fact, compelling examples of the relationship between the medieval Christ-number 33 and the modern Ego-word, the English I, are found in Rosicrucian literature. For example, we find such an image in the first few lines of the Preface to *The Fame and Confession of the Fraternity of the R: C: Commonly, of the Rosie Cross* (1652). The *Preface* to this early English work on Rosicrucianism was written by the alchemist, Eugenius Philalethes.[11] This was the pen-name of Thomas Vaughan, who evidently had more than a passing knowledge of the link between the Rosicrucians and the connected sacred numerological link between the 33 and the Ego, or I.

Below, I reproduce the first few lines of his *Preface*, to give some idea of the hermeneutics in which Philalethes indulged.

The Preface.

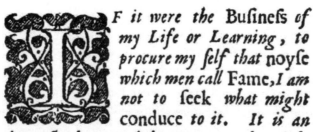

F *it were* the Bufinefs *of my Life or Learning*, *to procure my felf that* noyfe *which men call* Fame, *I am not to* feek *what might* conduce *to it*. *It is an* Age *affords many* Advantages, *and I might have* the choyce *of feveral* Foundations, *whereon to* build *my* felf. *I can fee withall*,

First, we should note the floriated, indented capital I, which is as open a reference to the Ego as one can reasonably expect in an English context. This is the I, or Ego, glorified in floriated print. Second, we should observe that the six lines of text incorporated in the indentation of this floriate capital consist of exactly 33 words. Third, we should note that the next two lines, following this indentation, each consist of 33 letters.

Here we encounter a compelling example of how the arcanist could make use of the sacred number 33, within a context of beginnings and the Ego. If we turn our attention from the hidden numerology to the sense of the text, we find that this deals with the nature of the Self, or Ego. The author has opened the *Preface* by reflecting upon his own reluctance to procure that 'noyse which men call Fame' — undoubtedly a reference to the title of the original Rosicrucian work, the *Fama*.[12] He then proceeds to link this with the building of his own self — the thing that he (and only he) may designate by the word I, which begins the *Preface*.

> It is an Age affords many Advantages, and I might have the choice of several Foundations, whereupon to build my self.

The entire sense, pertaining to this approach to the Ego, or **I**, or self, is bound within a hermeneutic numerology of 33 — whether it be in 33 letters or in 33 words. One suspects that if evidence were required of the connection between this 33 encoding and the Rosicrucians, one need turn only to these opening lines in Philalethes' masterly handling of the Rosicrucian *Fama*.

The importance of the Ego to our theme is such that, before I move on to the greater mysteries laid out in the following chapters, I must confess that I have no special visionary powers myself. I write as a historian, which is to say I am prepared to admit that I know nothing — that I merely look into things.[13] I cannot pretend to any deeply esoteric knowledge concerning the nature of the Ego, which seems now to underpin the mystery of the 33. The number underpins the Ego because, in a cosmic sense, the Ego is the doorway that facilitates entries and exits between the two worlds — in truth, between the three worlds, of heaven, earth and purgatory. One must be careful, here, for the 33 marks only the points of interface between these realms, not those realms themselves. The writers of old often distinguished their title-pages with a 33 encoding because they recognized the truth that when that title-page was opened, the reader would be plunged into a new world. It is so with the Ego: at each deathly exit from the world, it is hoped that one is plunged for further redemption into a new and better realm. This is one reason why we find so many tombs and memorials distinguished with this 33 encoding. As we shall see, the memorial to Shakespeare, in Holy Trinity Church, contains no fewer than seven examples of this 33 code.

That most perceptive of all modern esotericists, Rudolf Steiner, has said that it is possible, with higher vision, to look upon the Ego from outside, and that the experience involves seeing *twelve* different pictures of the Ego. Here, I have to confess my own ignorance of such things, and of such a visionary art.[14] Of course, it makes perfect intellectual sense to me that the higher spirit of the human being, which is so evidently derived from and linked with the zodiac or the *stellatum*, should express twelve phases, each linked with one of the zodiacal constellations. There is a sense in which Steiner was saying nothing new. A wide range of Rosicrucian and alchemical diagrams have portrayed this arcane teaching in graphic form. For example, the alchemist, Johann Daniel Mylius, invented an astounding roundel, centred upon a solar-faced Alchemical Star (below), which was itself surrounded by the twelve zodiacal images. This served as part of the arcane decoration for the title-page of his best-known alchemical work (figure 1).[15]

We should note that one of its concentrics incorporates a 33-letter phrase in Latin, which (incidentally) touches upon the secret nature of the Ego. Bounding this area is a pair of Ouroboros serpents, devouring each other – these are symbols of the Time-realm in which the Ego must dwell during its repeated earth lives. The outermost concentric band, freed of this serpentine limitation of Time, consists of a circle of twelve zodiacal images, depicting the twelve-fold zodiac, or life of ζωή, beyond the limits of Time.

There is a point where certain details of esoteric art become so open in their symbolism that they virtually relinquish their secret nature, becoming almost exoteric. This roundel design of Mylius is precisely such an example of an esoteric symbol that has become so open in its commentary on the Ego that it has almost ceased to be arcane. One almost feels that Steiner might have had this or some similar image in mind when he wrote about the twelvefold nature of the Ego — a truth which must itself remain one of the mysteries of modern arcane lore. This suggestion is not quite so wild as it may at first appear: Steiner was teaching, in a form adapted for a changed and modern world, many of the precepts and moral dicta of the medieval Rosicrucians. Whatever Mylius' personal affiliations might have been — whatever fed his esotericism and his alchemy — he was not far in spirit from those who are known to have belonged to that fraternity.

There is a sense in which the centuries we are about to investigate had no ending, for the streams of alchemy, esotericism and occult thought that sprang up in these glorious last days of the Renaissance, are, in a way, with us still. The great secret of modern occultism — and there is such a secret — is that, no matter which spiritual idea we seek to trace back to its roots, we at last find ourselves digging in the ancient loam and leaf-drift of the old Rosicrucian gardens. It was in these gardens where the *flos* flowers grew and the *ros* dew fell, that those anonymous wisemen worked, protected from myriad enemies by only a handful of symbols and numbers.

Broadly speaking, then, it is this encoded 33 that is the subject of the present work. Shakespeare's name may fade from these chapters, as we explore the encoding, but his *Secret booke* will remain: it was designed to serve impulses that will continue until the end of time.

Chapter 1

The Secret Number

...the greatest Matters, are many times carryed in the weakest Cyphars.

[Francis Bacon, *Of the Advancement of Learning*, 1605, Book II, p. 61.]

We may begin by opening our *Secret booke*. As we shall see, some of its texts speak with conviction of such things as faeries, of ghosts and of hauntings: others speak of even more subtle things, as the pathways to heaven. The interpenetration of the familiar realm by the spiritual, so often depicted by the 33 encoding, is no more dramatically illustrated than in the appearance of a ghost, which, almost by definition is an entity poised at the interface of two worlds. It is for this reason that, in *Hamlet*, Shakespeare has arranged for each of the three entries of the ghost of Hamlet's father to be linked with the 33 encoding.

The ghost is first seen by a number of Hamlet's friends, on a platform of Elsinore castle, at the striking of the clock, one hour after midnight. They had come to watch for the same spirit that had been seen walking abroad, on the previous night.

The initial entry of the ghost, as represented in this first scene, is set out in 33 characters:

Mar. Peace, breake thee of: *Enter the Ghost.*[1]

Marcellus, after calling for silence at the appearance of the ghost, recalls that Horatio is a scholar, and may declaim in Latin, believed to be the language of converse between men and spirits:

Thou art a Scholler; speake to it *Horatio*.[2]

Horatio addresses it in words of 33 characters, whereupon the spirit disappears:

Stay: speake: speake: I charge thee, speake.
                                        Exit the Ghost.[3]

Sometimes, the 33 encoding is linguistically subtle, as we see in the next appearance of the ghost, shortly afterwards, in the same scene:

Of this post-hast, and Romage in the Land,
Enter Ghost againe.
But soft, behold: Loe, where it comes again:[4]

The first of these lines consists of 32 characters, the third of 34: the implication is that the italicized direction-line should be conceived as being 33, in the sequence, even though the count is only half that number.

In Scene 3, Hamlet is taken by Horatio and Marcellus to see if the spirit will appear again, at the same time and place. Here, once again, we have a similar display of the 33 numerology. When Hamlet first sees the ghost (above), his astonished ejaculation consists of 33 characters:[5]

Angels and Ministers of Grace defend us:[6]

After the ghost has told Hamlet the truth about its own murder, and of the perfidy of his uncle and mother, it exits, begging Hamlet to remember him. In a state of shock, Hamlet falls into a soliloquy touching upon the terrible things he has just learned. The soliloquy ends when Horatio and Marcellus enter. The final line of the soliloquy reads:

It is; Adue, Adue, Remember me: I have sworn't.[7]

This line, which brings Hamlet back into the world of familiar experience, consists of 33 letters.

The interface with the spiritual world is similarly encoded in the play, *Julius Caesar*. Towards the end of Act 4, Brutus, whilst reading a book in his tent, is visited by the ghost of murdered Caesar. This preamble to the visitation is set in 33 letters:

> Where I left reading? Heere it is I thinke.
> *Enter the Ghost of Caesar.*[8]

When he first sees the apparition, Brutus first blames his own eyes, in a line of 33 letters:

> That shapes this monstrous Apparition.[9]

The initial shock over, he addresses the ghost, in a brief speech of 33 words:

> It comes upon me: Art thou any thing?
> Art thou some God, some Angell, or some Divell,
> That mak'st my blood cold, and my haire to stare?
> Speak to me, what thou art?[10]

Surprisingly little work has been done by scholars on the secret encodings of the sixteenth and seventeenth centuries. However, most of that little is brilliant. Among the brilliant, we must point with admiration to the researches of Kent Hieatt and Alastair Fowler, who revealed the secret encodings of Spenser, in his *Epithalamion* and *Faerie Queene*, respectively.[11] The encodings they reveal are complex, sophisticated, and replete with subtle meanings. However, this very complexity and variety implies that they are quite unlike the codes we are likely to encounter in Shakespeare's commodious *Secret booke*. The essence of this particular Shakespearean code is its simplicity. In view of this, one or two examples would not be out of place here, if only in order that we may learn the rules attached to this numerology.

For the moment, I will continue with examples from Shakespeare. I shall begin with a single line from *The Tempest*, and then move on to the Sonnets. Later still, I will move on to the literature of lesser poets and writers.

In Act 3 of *The Tempest*, the monster Caliban tells Stephano not to be afraid of this magical island on which he finds himself shipwrecked. This advice prefaces a wonderful description of the strangeness of the island, which, whilst it interfaces with the familiar world, is also part of a different spiritual realm. This is ideal material for the number 33, which (among other things) points to entrances and exits into a higher world. Caliban's opening line runs:

Be not affeard; the Isle is full of noyses...[12]

The line above is copied from the *First Folio* of 1623, which is, perforce, our fiducial in such matters. Not all versions of the line published in later times offer a count of 33. For example, one popular modern edition gives the line:

Be not afeard; the isle is full of noises.[13]

This version of the line displays only 32 characters: it lacks the encoding that interests us and which (I must emphasize) generally adds a certain learned quality to the line. One may see how even careful editing of such a line may eradicate some of the valuable significance of the original.

The following version of Caliban's speech is from the 1623 *First Folio*. It is a section that deserves more attention, in respect of the 33 encoding.

> *Cal.* **Be not affeard, the Iſle is full of noyſes,**
> **Sounds,and ſweet aires,that giue delight and hurt not:**
> **Sometimes a thouſand twangling Inſtruments**
> **Will hum about mine eares ; and ſometime voices,**
> **That if I then had wak'd after long ſleepe,**
> **Will make me ſleepe againe, and then in dreaming,**
> **The clouds methought would open, and ſhew riches**
> **Ready to drop vpon me, that when I wak'd**
> **I cri'de to dreame againe.**

One may, if so minded, editorially eradicate the illogical sequences of tenses that follow in Caliban's famous line about the music of the island. However, this very illogicality is essential to the suspension of time required, in this description of the interface between the familiar and the supersensible.[14] The dawning awareness, from the content of the speech, that Caliban is not quite the insensitive and materialistic monster he seems, becomes part of this supersensibility.

That the 1623 text retained a numerological integrity, which later editors and scholars have tended to ignore, may be seen almost poignantly from this sample text. Caliban's speech opens with a line of 33 characters. The next three lines retain no such symbolism. However, the next line also consists of 33 characters:

That if I then had wak'd after long sleepe,

Then follow a further three lines, devoid of the numerology. If we discount the final half-line (as we must), we find that, contiguous with the 33 character lines, are groups of 3 and 3 – surely another reference to 3 + 3 = 33. The 33 encoding within the passage may be schematized as follows:

[33 characters]
    3 lines ....↓
[33 characters]   33
    3 lines ....↑

By their very structure, the Sonnets are usually less complex in their encodings than speeches from the plays. Generally, the encoding in the Sonnets is used only to hint at some hidden element or esoteric strain within the verse. For example, the first four lines of Shakespeare's *Sonnet VI* have a mildly alchemical theme, and run:

Then let not winter's ragged hand deface
In thee thy summer, ere thou be distill'd:
Make sweet some vial; treasure thou some place
With beauty's treasure, ere it be self-killed.

A careful count, in accordance with simple rules, will reveal that the four lines encapsulate 33 words. The governing rules are that the word **winter's** which is possessive, and an abbreviation for **winter his**, should count as two words. For a similar reason, **beauty's**, in the fourth line, should also read as two words. On the other hand, the word **distill'd**, at the end of the second line, should count only as one word, for this is an abbreviation for **distilled**. These rules accord fully with the rules of grammar. Here, the encoding of the 33 seems to be linked with the idea of alchemical transmutation – another medieval realm of interface between the material and spiritual worlds.

What could well be Shakespeare's most glorious sonnet deals with death – with the doleful theme of the monumented departure from the world and entrance into the next. As we shall see, eventually, the 33 is often used to signal references to this exit from life as nothing more than an entrance to another life. Sonnet CVII is no exception, for the first four lines set out the mortuary thoughts in 33 perfect words:

Not mine own fears, nor the prophetic soul
Of the wide world dreaming on things to come,

Can yet the lease of my true love control,
Suppos'd as forfeit to a confin'd doom.

Sonnet CXXXV is Shakespeare's jesting play upon his own Christian name, William. As the Ego, or Self, is linked in the numerological tradition with 33, we may be surprised to find that the first four lines of this sonnet total only 32. That is, 32, unless one is prepared to read the single word **overplus** as really being the two words, **over plus**. Be that as it may, Shakespeare elected also to encapsulate the number 33 in the first line:

Whoever hath her wish, thou hast thy *Will*,
And *Will* to boot, and *Will* in overplus;
More than enough am I that vex thee still,
To thy sweet will making addition thus.

In fact, a close examination of Sonnet CXXXV, the 'Will' sonnet, reveals that two of the three lines ending in *Will*, contain exactly 33 characters. Thus, the eleventh line reads:

So thou, being rich in *Will*, add to thy *Will*

The final line also ends in the word *Will*, but this consists of only 32 characters. However, there is a really important teaching point hidden in this line. When we turn to the sense of the line, we see a rather clever play on the numerology, for it runs:

Think all but one, and me in that one *Will*.

If you think *33 all but one*, then you are thinking 32, which is what the line gives you. Shakespeare often permits the sense in his lines to run over and mingle with his encodings.

The last example has been selected to show how the numerology may at times become involved with the sense within the verse or line. A sophisticated example of this may be seen in two lines from a poem by Abraham Cowley. These lines actually deal openly with numerology, for they reflect upon the Pythagorean notion that numbers proceed from the unity of One, which has neither beginning nor ending. Cowley's metaphor refers to Pythagorean doctrine, which insists on the rather obvious truth that all numbers flow from this monad, or One, just as branches grow in their myriads from the trunk of a single tree. Cowley writes:

Before the Branchy head of Numbers Tree
Sprung from the Trunk of One.[15]

If you count the number of words in the first line, you will find they total 7. In fact, this count of seven — a most mysterious and powerful number in Pythagorean terms — is obtained here only at the expense of English grammar.

Cowley appears to have made a grammatical error in these lines. As the word *Numbers* was evidently meant to be possessive, it should properly have been written as *Number's* (that is, *Number's Tree*), thus:

Before the Branchy head of Number's Tree

This apostrophized 's is the traditional abbreviation for the old possessive, *Number his* (or, *Number his Tree*). Properly speaking, in a numerological count, **Number's** should count as two words. In view of this, if Cowley *had* introduced the correct possessive, **Number's**, then he would technically have been inviting a count of eight for the line. However, this latter (8) does not have the same Pythagorean resonance or significance as the proto-magical seven.[16] Thus, Cowley seems to have been prepared to write ungrammatical English in order to point a septenary moral.

Of course, it is clear that Cowley was not deficient in the English language: whatever he was up to when he wrote this line, he was doing it intentionally. In fact, by means of this slight dislocation of English, Cowley was encoding a truth, which is that the mystic Seven proceeds from the monadic One. So far, then, Cowley's encoding is simplicity itself, even if it demands a slip in grammar. However, Cowley was intent on introducing a far more subtle encoding in the two lines: this proves to be an encoding that enables us to claim the verse for inclusion in Shakespeare's own *Secret booke*.

If you count the letters in the first of the two lines of verse, you will find that they total 33.

Before the Branchy head of Numbers Tree

Now, the presence of this number leaves us swimming in an entirely different stream of hermeneutics. If you re-read the above two lines, bearing in mind that Cowley is writing about more than merely Pythagorean numbers, but also in reference to Christ, then the meaning of the lines changes. Christ had become human: he had descended into the multiplicity of being represented by the 33 — a suitable numerology because he remained incarnate on the earth for 33 years. However, he had descended into this multiplicity of 33 from the One, which is the God-head. When this second reading is construed from the lines, then the words take on a different significance: Christology mingles with Pythagoreanism, and the single Tree of Christ's descent merges hermeneutically with the Tree, or wood, on which Christ died, at the end of his 33 year term. It is hermeneutics of this quality, which, as it were, invites the imaginative involvement of the reader, that enables us to place Cowley's two lines on the margins of Shakespeare's *Secret booke*.

Strangely, we may note a similar play with the apostrophe 's in the pen of Shakespeare. Consider the line from Biron's speech in the opening of *Love's Labour's Lost*:

These earthly godfathers of heaven's lights

The line above is from a modern edition of Shakespeare's play.[17] The line below is from the *First Folio* of 1623:

These earthly Godfathers of heavens lights

Now, this is a most interesting difference, brought about by a mere apostrophe 's. If Shakespeare had written the words **heaven's**, then the wonderful speech which opens with this line would have consisted of 33 words.

These earthly Godfathers of heavens lights,
That give a name to every fixed starre,
Have no more profit of their shining nights,
Then those that walk, and wot not what they are.[18]

It would be foolish to condemn Shakespeare for lack of grammar, yet it is worth asking why the Bard should have marred a rather obvious encoding? The entire speech of 22 lines, spoken by Biron, touches upon certain esoteric notions, in that their meanings require second-reading. As a matter of fact, the 33rd line down in this second column of the first page of the play (see figure 2) is the esoteric nub of the speech, concerning Biron's urge to things *hid and barr'd* and *to know the thing I am forbid to know*:

Light seeeking light, doth light of light beguile:

Although it might seem improbable, I am quoting accurately the misspelling of the word **seeeking**. Was Shakespeare intent on drawing attention to the line, and thus to the fact that it was linked with the idea of 33? In this case, the 33 is derived not from a letter count or a word count, but from the position of the line in a column. The philosophical implications within this speech concerning 'light of light' are far-reaching, and, in invoking forbidden knowledge, certainly touch upon esotericism. However, the full implications are beyond our present remit: it is sufficient to note that what may be taken as an error (albeit an intentional error) can be worked into an encoding. The error points to a *vertical* encoding with 33 as in the column-length number (in figure 2, I have marked the line, for ease of reference). It has also an *horizontal* encoding of 33, once one counts horizonally from the rather obvious error:

eking light, doth light of light beguile:

Fortunately, not all 33 encodings are as sophisticated as the last two examples. Even so, in the hands of such a master as Shakespeare, this particular encoding may be used with both a wit and ingenuity that are surprising.

As we shall see in the following chapters, many leading esoteric writers — alchemists, occultists and Rosicrucians — have contributed to the Bard's *Secret booke*. Among the more outstanding English literary figures, who made use of this intriguing 33 code, were the turbulent Ben Jonson, of *The Alchemist* fame, and the more sedately classical Edmund Spenser, whose poem, *The Faerie Queene,* is the finest esoteric work of that period. Less a poet, and more an adventurer-courtier, Sir Walter Raleigh also indulged in this encoding. Later, we shall glance at relevant encoded passages or images from each of these remarkable individuals.

Contemporaneous with the Bard was the youthful Johann Valentin Andreae, supposed author of *The Chymical Wedding* — a Rosicrucian work replete (as we shall find) with sophisticated examples of this encoding. The Rosicrucian-minded encoders were the most influential esotericists of the period. These include the remarkable Jacob Boehme, whose codes were later adapted by such learned followers as Dionysius Freher and William Law. Among the earliest arcanists was the polymath Elizabethan, Dr. John Dee, the German alchemists, Heinrich Khunrath and Michael Maier, and the English esotericist, Robert Fludd. I reproduce engraved portraits of these four luminaries. Their personal images prove to be of immediate interest because each portrait displays, with varying degrees of opacity, the 33 encodings, and thus reveals an affiliation to the fraternity. In historical terms, we may be sure that in all four cases the arcane number 33 was not encoded in an empty display of learning: rather, it was encoded within the portrait image to indicate a supposed, or real con-nection with the Rosicrucians.[19]

D.² Dee avoucheth his Stone is brought by Angelicall Ministry.

The portrait of John Dee (above, left) is from Meric Casaubon's work, which studies Dee's commitment to contacting the spiritual world, by way of disincarnate spirits, in search of higher knowledge, *A True & Faithful Relation of What passed for many Yeers Between Dr. John Dee . . . and Some Spirits. . . .* (1659).[20] The portrait of Heinrich Khunrath (above, right – see

TRES SCHOLA, TRES COESAR TITVLOS DE:
DIT; HÆC MIHI RESTANT,
POSSE BENE IN CHRISTO VIVERE, POSSE MORI.
MICHAEL MAIERVS COMES IMPERIALIS CON:
SISTORII etc. PHILOSOPH: ET MEDICINARVM
DOCTOR.P. C. C. NOBIL: EXEMPTVS FOR-OLIM
MEDICVS CÆS etc.

also figure 3, where it is reproduced in a larger format) is from his most remarkable work. *Amphitheatrum sapientiae aeternae* (1602) purports to be a study of alchemy, but is in fact a survey of the relationship that Man holds to the Macrocosm.[21] It was, as Khunrath admitted on this very title page, a text that would be of value to scarcely one person in a thousand.[22] Needless to say, this incomparable esoteric work bore on its title-page (and within the book itself) the stamp of the 33 encoding.[23]

The portrait of Michael Maier (above, left) is from his *Atalanta fugiens* (1618). This work was openly designed to be accessible to the three-fold nature of the human being, for Maier arranged the text and accompanying music so that the work might be read, sung and struggled with intellectually. The 33 encoding is more obvious than in any of the other three examples given here.[24] The portrait of Robert Fludd (previous page, bottom right), engraved by Matthieu Merian, is from his *Philosophia Sacra* of 1626, with its Christian and philosophical themes. As one might expect from a man as learned and sophisticated as Fludd, the 33 encoding in this plate is fairly complex.[25]

Details of how we may decode the encoding of this number 33 in each portrait, are set out in the relevant footnotes on pages 215–17. However, the four portraits are merely representative of a huge body of arcane imagery that exhibits this particular esoteric numerology. The fact is that the 33 is itself almost ubiquitous in the arcane art and literature of the sixteenth and seventeenth centuries. In many cases, if the significance of the 33 is missed, then so is the real content of the passage or image in which it plays its part. A good example may be seen in the first poem of merit to have been written in the American colonies.

Between 1621 and 1631, the scholar George Sandys had worked as the treasurer of the Virginia colony, during which time he had completed his translation of Ovid's *Metamorphoses*, published in 1626. Book 15 deals with Ovid's vision of how the expiring soul of the murdered Julius Caesar was received by the goddess Venus, and translated to heaven.

For reasons that are not at first apparent, Sandys departed radically from the original text. Ovid had not actually specified how many times Caesar had been knifed by the collaborators, but Sandys, in a marginal note, insisted there had been 33 wounds in his body:

> Now Caesars soule, expiring through three and thirty wounds, is received by ascending Venus; and in her odorous bosome contracting a deity, mounts up in a blasing starre to heaven.

In specifying that the body of Caesar had received 33 wounds, Sandys was linking the apotheosis of Caesar with a number that was, in ecclesiastical symbolism at least, more usually reserved for Christ. Sandys had no intention of likening Caesar to Christ – he was merely intent on demonstrating, numerologically, that the apotheosis took place in that interface between the material and spiritual realms. So far as I can determine, no scholarly appraisal of this translation has noted the real significance of this introduction of the Christian 33 into the Ovidian text: this suggests that what Sandys had in mind has not yet been fully appreciated.

This 33 is, then, the number of numbers. It is a number that helps lift an image, a text or a verse onto a higher level of meaning, investing it with an arcane and, at times, Christological significance. It is the link with Christ that helps explain why the Rosicrucians should have chosen this 33 as their signature encoding. Later, we shall discover that the 33 is associated with even more than Christ, but for the moment it is sufficient that we see how the 33 is involved with a highly charged spirituality.

Whilst the medieval concern for the symbolism of the 33 flowered in non-religious art during the sixteenth-century Renaissance in England, its lifetime in this country proved to be relatively short. As we shall see, the heyday of the 33 code was the seventeenth century, and the encoding was still in use in the following century, with the followers of Jacob Boehme. The last important exponent of the encoding in England was the English mystic-poet, William Blake. So sophisticated was Blake in his use of this form of symbolism, that he combined words and images in a way that earlier exponents of the code had never dared to do.

Over is a page from Blake's own hand-written and self-printed poem, *Jerusalem*, completed between 1804 and 1820.[26] Each of the three concurrent images within the picture are involved with varieties of spiritual transition. First, the print depicts an eclipse – the cancelling out of the solar light by the Moon: an eclipse such as was believed to have happened on the Hill of Golgotha, when our Lord was crucified. Second, it depicts an entrance into another space, into cosmic space. The trilithons, based on those that Blake saw in Stonehenge, symbolize great antiquity, strength and durability: this trilithon is a thing of the earth, in contrast to the eclipse, which is an event in the cosmos. Third, it depicts a dislocation in time: as the poem tells us, the three figures represent Bacon, Newton and Locke. Only Newton and Locke were contemporaries. Francis Bacon had died before either were born.[27] Thus, whilst none was alive at the time the illustration was made, they could never have been alive

contemporaneously: this implies that the triple image includes a clever dislocation in time. Given this triad of elements, and given that the theme of the picture is linked with the interface between worlds, we should not be surprised to find that Blake has evoked the 33 encoding. If you count the number of lines on the page, you will discover that they total 32. However, the space between lines 16 and 17 incorporates this image, and is integral to the text itself.

The triadic nature of the imagery almost invites this association with the number 33. There are three personages, three giant stones, and, for an eclipse to occur, there must be three cosmic bodies in a straight line – the Earth, the Moon and the Sun. Numerologically, the threes themselves suggest 33, if not 333. Thus, the picture, with its triple theme, placed at the very centre of the 32 lines, is intended by Blake to represent the completing line of the 33 encoding. Text and pictures can rarely have been so well integrated.

In the hands of a Master, the encoding of the 33 became a matter of hiding something, of obscuring (save from the mind of a specialist) that there is a code at all. Some Masters of encoding were even prepared to distort their symbols in order to carry the cipher into their works. In literature, the primal entrance is the title, which is why the 33 encoding appears so frequently on the title-page. One such encoding reveals how Robert Fludd was prepared to distort a lesser symbol to achieve the greater symbol of the 33 encoding. Fludd is historically important for a number of reasons, but, for us, one reason is that he was probably the first English arcanist to write openly about Rosicrucianism.[28]

The title-page of this book, *De Naturae Simia* is dominated by a tondo-like design which, in its simplest aspect, resembles an eye (page 28). This consists of eleven segments in an outer concentric, with the inner concentric a sort of pupil, within which sits a monkey, holding a stick. Surprisingly, we find only one reference to the give-away 33 in the titling. This is contained in the long italic reference to the printer, in the penultimate line:

Ære Iohan-Theodori de Brÿ Typis Hieronÿ-

The break of *Hieronÿ-mi* is forced and unnecessary – there was sufficient room on the line to add the hyphenated two letters. The break is clearly intended to permit the line to distinguish itself with the requisite 33 letters: to do this, one must count the ligatured Æ as a single letter.

In fact, the really interesting encoding of the 33 is that found within the eye itself. This has involved an error that any practised esotericist is likely to have seen at a glance: it is an error intended to encourage one to search for a secret symbolism or an encoding. The relevant section is at 11:00 o'clock on the face of the eye. This relates to the art of geomancy, which is an art of constructing divinatory figures from simple numerology. For a detail of this plate, see figure 4. The shield-like device in this section represents the standard form by which sixteen geomantic figures are located. Some say that the pattern of figures is located by chance, others insist that the pattern is imposed by the geomantic spirits. Either way, the

diagram is itself an interface with a world beyond. Its mundane purpose is to provide an answer to a question put to the geomancer. I enlarge this shield below, the better to reveal the error.

Each geomantic figure must, by definition, consist of four levels, each level being distinguished by a single point or by a double. If for example we examine the central register of this figure, we see two such regular figures, that combine pairs and singles:

```
  *   *                    *   *
    *                      *   *
    *                        *
  *   *                    *   *
```

In the geomantic tradition, these figures are called *Conjunctio* and *Albus*, respectively.

Now, after contemplating these two geomantic figures, we recognize that the first figure, in the top left of the shield, cannot be accurate. This consists of only three registers, as though it were a five, marked upon the face of a dice. Given this simple error, it is reasonable to assume that the five is intended to point to something hidden within the shield. This hidden thing is the 33 encoding.

If we count the number of points within the six geomanic figures, including those in this incomplete figure, we find that they total 33. If the first figure had not been compounded with an error, then the 33 count would not have been possible. Fludd is being sophisticated, for the top half of his title-page contains a literary encoding of the 33, whilst his lower contains a graphic encoding of the same number.

Many of the arcane plates in Fludd's books contain references to the sacred 33. In every case, the 33 is clearly separated from the other elements in the design, and increments the meaning of the symbolism of the design as a whole. An excellent example is the engraving overleaf, from a book of 1624.[29]

This illustration shows Fludd's vision of the harmony of the celestial Spheres. In the engraving, he speculates on how the cosmos might be a mighty musical instrument, with its single string being tuned on a peg by a hand emerging from heaven. At the bottom, the string is fixed over a bridge at the bottom of the finger board, in a position that corresponds to the Earth.

The series of curved Latin designations on either side of the instrument reveal the various harmonics derived from the different ratios on the single sounding board of the instrument. What is of immediate interest to us are the letters of the English alphabet, the non-curved Latin words, and the planetary symbols, all of which mark the finger-board of the mono-

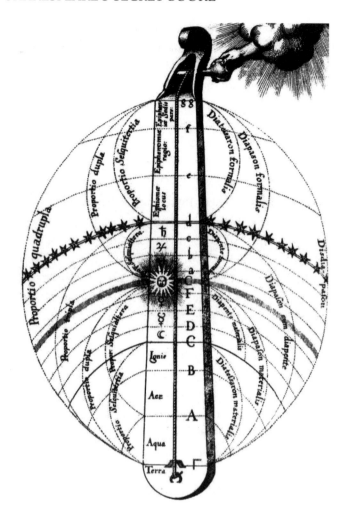

chord instrument. If you count these words, letters and symbols, you will find that there are 33. This total must have been intended by Fludd, for the marker at the top consists of a lower-case **g** which has, for no immediately apparent reason, been repeated. The hermeneutic or numerological significance of this **gg** may be seen in the Greek letter g, or gamma, Γ, at the bottom of the string. This is the only Greek letter in the series, and its introduction serves no purpose, other than to invite us to reflect upon the double **gg** at the top of the instrument. Had this **gg** not been doubled, then the 33 would not have been preserved upon the instrument.[30]

Anomalies are often a clue to the existence of the 33 code, whether in geomantic diagrams, or portrayals of the Music of the Spheres. The anomalies linked with Shakespeare the person, and Shakespeare's own poetry are legion. Both the memorial and grave to Shakespeare in Holy Trinity Church, Stratford-upon-Avon, are replete with 33 encodings and anomalies. We shall examine some of the encodings shortly. These two fascinating inscriptions – the one vertical on the memorial, on which we see the famous image of the Bard, the other a horizontal lapidary, set in the chancel floor – contain the greatest mysteries concerning Shakespeare, each displaying a variety of anomalies. Thus, in an anonymous and perceptive re-assessment of Shakespeare in terms of Mystery lore, an interesting point is made about the Bard's monument in the church.[31] This *anonyme* points out that there is a puzzle – an anomaly – pertaining to the two cupids that sit on top of the monument.

> One is resting upon an inverted torch, and has his eyes *closed* – signifying death. *The other* rests upon a *spade, and has his eyes distinctly open.* What this signified, we were at an immediate loss to understand. To associate Love with the office of sexton, is hardly classical, particularly when we consider how faithful the other Cupid is to the ancient symbolism! If these two Cupids signify *Life and Death*, in what way are we to understand the *spade that one holds in his hands?* The spade is there to dig with, that is plain! And we ask, to dig *what?*[32]

I should explain that this description is valid only for the modern version of Shakespeare's memorial in Holy Trinity Church. The engraving of the so-called 'original Stratford monument', given by Nicholas Rowe in his *Life of Shakespeare* (1709), certainly displays two cupids, but no such symbolism.[33]

It is, indeed, tempting to read the two modern Cupids in terms of the Mystery lore, as one representing Genius, the other Eros. The *anonyme* had dismissed this notion, even though he had alerted the reader to its possible application by quoting from Lord Lytton's excruciating 'Rosicrucian' novel, *Zanoni:*

> From the Sarcophagus and the urn I awake the Genius of the extinguished Torch, and so closely does its shape resemble Eros, that at moments I scarcely know which of ye dictate to me, O Love! O Death![34]

One suspects that this symbolism related to digging is of much the same hidden meaning as the word **DIGG**, which appears on the nearby curse-stone, in the chancel floor, and which is traditionally believed to mark the proper resting place of Shakespeare. The curse-stone begs one not to *digg the dust encloased* beneath the lapidary. Are we being advised not to dig out

mouldered remains, or not to dig out hidden secrets? The spade of the alert cupid has much the same hermeneutic force, for it too suggests that there is, in connection with either Shakespeare or his tomb, some mystery into which one should dig.

In the following pages, I shall ignore the warning on the curse-stone, and run with the alert, sexton-like cupid. I shall dig into secrets, some few of which have not been revealed since the days when Shakespeare wrote.

Chapter 2

Shakespeare's Curse Stone

Omnibus artis huius amatoribus notum facio, quod Philosophi veritatem, &
mendacium, uno sub dicto complectantur: veritatem videlicet ipsorum liberis,
& discipulis: mendacium vero stupidis, rerum imperitis, & insipientibus, qui
mendacium ad veritatem referunt ...

To all lovers of this art, I make known the fact that the Alchemists are
accustomed to using words, which offer truth and lies. The truth they offer to
their children and disciples. The lies they offer to the ignorant, the foolish and
the unworthy, who take the lies for truth.

[Anonymous, *Gloria Mundi, Alias, Paradysi Tabula* (1677) in *Musaeum*
Hermeticum Reformatum (1678), p. 235.]

The skull that peers through empty sockets from Shakespeare's memorial,
into the chancel of Holy Trinity Church in Stratford-upon-Avon, is jawless:
was this symbolism *intended* by the sculptor, Gerard Johnson? Did Johnson feel it necessary to emphasize that the skull was dumb to talk of the
secrets hidden in the memorial, and in the grave below?

Shakespeare's memorial (overleaf) on the north wall of the chancel of
Holy Trinity Church, is said to have been sculpted by Johnson about 1623.
This was the same year that the first Folio of the Bard's works was pub-
lished.[1]

Below the socle, upon which the jawless skull sits, is a shield bearing a
spear, 'the point steeled, proper' — an heraldic pun on the poet's name.
The spear is a reminder that John Shakespeare — or perhaps the poet
himself — had twice tried to persuade the College of Arms to grant a coat of
arms in the last years of the sixteenth century.[2] The grant was confirmed
in 1599, but not without the help of inside influence.[3] What is of great
importance behind this act of social climbing is that it was only after the
family had applied for a coat of arms that the name Shakespeare was
officially adopted by them, and the variants such as Shagsper or Shaxper
were adapted to a form similar to that we now use. It is merely an irony
that in 1599, when one of the first plays was published with William

Shakespeare named as author in this modernized orthography, the work later turned out not be from the pen of the Bard at all.[4]

The name Shakespeare seems to have been established by 1600. Within 10 days of the arrival of James I in London as King of England, in 1603, Shakespeare's Company of players were granted a licence to perform at the Globe Theatre, and in suitable buildings in the provinces. In this licence,[5] now preserved in the Public Record Office, he is named in the now-familiar guise as Shakespeare.

These footnotes to history reveal one reason why — even today, after the publication of thousands of books on his life and works — Shakespeare is still such a mystery. Almost every issue or question pertaining to Shakespeare, towards which we turn our attention, is soon transformed from the simple to the complex: virtually any pathway we follow in pursuit of Shakespearean truth rapidly transforms into a labyrinth that would delight a minotaur.

Few who study this ornate memorial, and gaze upon the bald-headed image of Shakespeare, with his quill and paper at the ready, are aware that this is not the original, erected circa 1623.[6] An engraving used by Rowe (below), illustrates the most important differences between the ancient and the modern.[7]

There is an astonishing difference between the monument in this engraving and what we now see on the north wall of the chancel of the church. In the former, Shakespeare is not portrayed as a literary figure, but is shown resting both hands upon what is probably a woolsack. The two cupids dangle their legs and symbols of spade and hour glass over the edge of the architrave. Even the enfolding niche that frames this portrayal of Shakespeare is of a different form.

We note that, alongside his drawing of the memorial, Rowe has expatiated on the funerary inscription below the effigy. He has also reproduced a version (inaccurate, as it happens) of the famous curse-stone, which lies in the chancel floor, below and near the monument. Rowe believes that this curse-stone actually constitutes an epitaph.

Comparison of a similar image by Dugdale (above) with the modern version encouraged the scholar, Edward D. Johnson, to look again into the early history of Shakespeare's life. The result was an amazing revelation of the little that is actually known about the Bard. Through his insistent probing, Johnson virtually destroyed the academic-seeming *Life of Shakespeare*, by Sidney Lee, which until that time had been regarded as a reliable work.[8]

As Johnson contemplated the Dugdale image, alongside that in the church, he found himself nonplussed. How was it possible that an image portraying a thin-faced man with a drooping moustache and ragged beard, resting his hands on a woolsack, should become so thoroughly transformed? How had this become the portrayal of a well-groomed man with a pen and paper, which we now identify with the William Shakespeare of literature.[9] Johnson believed that the modern version of the monument was the result of a conscious attempt to pervert history: he concluded that the Shakespeare monument had been faked.

Johnson's theory may appear far-fetched, for it does seem to fly in the face of established belief. However, the more one investigates his claims, in the light of the known facts concerning Shakespeare's life, the more acceptable his theory becomes.

The simple truth is that there is virtually no record that the man of Stratford, whose name was variously spelled Shagsper, Shaksper, and Shaxsper, was the same as the person whose name was later spelled as Shakespeare in the Folio of plays published in 1623. On examination, the memorials, monuments, houses and documents, which are now the centre of a vast industry in Stratford-upon-Avon, disappear, as though the residue of a baseless fabric of myth. For example, there is no evidence that Shakespeare was born in 'Shakespeare's birth house' in Henley Street.[10]

What, then, is known about the Bard's monument, in Holy Trinity Church?

Shortly after November 1748, following a resolution made by a Stratford committee, 'the original Monument and Bust through length of years and other accidents having become much impaired and decayed', was substantially repaired and 'beautified'.[11] This operation was made possible by finance supplied by a special repair fund established by a company of players led by the actor John Ward, the grandfather of the famous actress Mrs. Siddons. During this restoration, the bust seems to have been removed from its pedestal, for a plaster cast was made. Afterwards, the bust was repainted by John Hall. During this stage of the proceedings, the nose was damaged, and the indications are that the restorer made the upper lip too long, and perhaps even changed the moustache.

To judge from drawings and engravings of the 1623 version, this beautification involved other adjustments. These included the placing of the symbolic quill and paper in the hands of the great Bard, and changing altogether the symbolism of the two cupids. In the early engraving of the memorial (see page 35) the two cupids hold a spade and an hourglass — two well-established emblems of mortality.

Did the original effigy resemble Shakespeare in life? Gerard Johnson is said to have carved it from a death-mask — but there are many legends about Shakespeare, and few are to be taken seriously. Henry Condell, Shakespeare's friend and partner in the same company of players, had confirmed that the bust of the deceased poet *was* a good likeness. However, we cannot be sure if this likeness survived the changes of 1748. A comparison between the early prints and the modern version suggests that the modern image does not in the least resemble that seen by Condell. Certainly, the bust does not resemble the mask-like face of the so-called Droeshout portrait,[12] which appeared in the 1623 Folio of plays, and which the Bard's friend, Ben Jonson, claimed *was* a good likeness.

The epitaph, picked out in gold below the memorial bust, is in Latin and English, and of unknown authorship (below). I shall look more closely at the secret symbolism of this epitaph later. Meanwhile, I should observe that its English contains several puzzles, if not arcane mysteries, the majority of which need not detain us here.[13]

However, there is one mystery that is of immediate interest, in the second and third lines of the English:

READ IF THOV CANST, WHOM ENVIOUS DEATH HATH PLAST,
WITH IN THIS MONUMENT SHAKSPEARE...

If thou canst? Does this mean, *if we can read Shakespeare* or does it mean, if we can read the secret of the inscription — or is there some other sense in this injunction to read? In fact, I doubt that this has much to do with our literacy: it is more likely an intimation that there is some hidden meaning in the monument – a meaning which will be a challenge to our ability to read purposely obscured truths. In the period that Shakespeare wrote it was commonplace to construct a text of truth combined with 'lies':

> The truth they offer to their children and disciples. The lies they offer to the ignorant, the foolish and the unworthy, who take the lies for truth.[14]

In this memorial epitaph, Shakespeare is not only figured in a coloured bust, but is also mentioned by name, if only as Shakspeare. However, the name is not mentioned overtly in the four-line inscription set in the actual tomb, below the monument. This slab is the famous curse-stone – a lapidary inscription cut on what is generally believed to be the actual gravestone of the Bard. For all its fame, it is tradition alone that insists this slab is the one laid over the grave of the famous playwright. Could the monumental epitaph refer to *this* crude text? Does the epitaph actually challenge one to make an attempt to read and decode the mysterious curse?

Even though the indications are that the so-called curse-stone has been 'beautified', or at least restored, since Shakespeare's day, I reproduce a photograph of this, below.[15]

The words cut into the slab, begging the reader not to disturb the bones, must be familiar to millions of visitors to the church. Indeed, it may be the most famous epitaph in the whole of England.

GOOD FREND FOR IESUS SAKE FOREBEARE
TO DIGG THE DUST ENCLOASED HEARE.
BLESE BE Y/E MAN Y/T SPARES THES STONES
AND CURST BE HE Y/T MOVES MY BONES.

The curse-stone may be quaint by modern standards, yet it is thoroughly Jacobean. There was no 'standard' English at that time: the spelling of FREND (i.e., FRIEND) is acceptable for the period, whilst the ligatures of TH in THE, and TE in BLESTE were used widely in epitaphs of the period. The single-letter form Y/E (that is, THE) and the abbreviation Y/T (THAT) are, as we have already seen, based on the use of the Anglo-Saxon letter *Thorn* [þ = th] which had the sound-value *th*. It is a letter-form which is still used and misunderstood in such familiar joke-like archaisms as, *ye olde tea shoppe*.

The curse-stone has attracted the attention of many scholars, some of whom have attempted to make sense of its curious structure. The American author, Washington Irving, after visiting Stratford himself, in 1815, recorded with only fair accuracy the inscription, and emphasized how effective the curse had been:

> The inscription on the tombstone has not been without its effect. It has prevented the removal of his remains from the bosom of his native place to Westminster Abbey, which was at one time contemplated. A few years since also, as some labourers were digging to make an adjoining vault, the earth caved in, so as to leave a vacant space almost like an arch, through which one might have reached into his grave. No one, however, presumed to meddle with his remains, so awfully guarded by a malediction.[16]

However, an old sexton — who kept watch over the collapsed wall for two days to keep back marauders — was not deterred. He *did* look inside the tomb. He could see nothing — 'neither coffin nor bones; nothing but dust'. Yet, as Irving sighed, 'it was something, I thought, to have seen the dust of Shakespeare'.[17]

How different was this breach of an empty grave to a similar accident, in 1849, with the burial shaft of Shakespeare's boisterous friend Ben Jonson. This drinking-companion and brother playwright (who may even have attended Shakespeare's funeral) seems to fare better than our national hero, for he had been buried among the illustrious poets of Westminster Abbey, in 1637. Some years later, while the gravediggers were preparing a space in the Abbey for the body of Sir Robert Wilson, they accidentally disturbed the contiguous grave of Jonson, and his remains were dramatically revealed. His two leg-bones were 'fixed bolt upright in the sand' (confirming the legend that Jonson had insisted on being buried in a standing position). A moment later, his skull 'came rolling down among the sand ... to the bottom of the newly-made grave. There was still hair upon it, and it was of a red colour'.[18] Jonson seems to have been a clowning dramatist to the last. At least, the disturbance showed that the remains were still *in situ* – which seems not to have been the case with Shakespeare's curse-stoned tomb.

Jonson was famous as the author of *The Alchemist*, which is not about alchemy but about con-men, 'cozeners at large'.[19] He was in the same encoding and double-meaning business as Shakespeare, but played the game with a touch more humour. As by now we may be inclined to imagine, the first edition of the play, printed in 1616, displays a title-page distinguished by a count of 33 words, and the hilarious acknowledgement that, *The Author B. I.* – a delightful play on the notion of Ego.[20]

THE ALCHEMIST.

A Comœdie.

Acted in the yeere 1610. By the
Kings MAIESTIES
Seruants.

The Author B. I.

LVCRET.

———petere inde coronam,
Ynde prius nulli velarint tempora Musæ.

LONDON,
Printed by WILLIAM STANSBY

M. DC. XVI.

Is it true that there was no body in the Bard's tomb? As a matter of fact, those scholars who studied the remains of Shakespeare most thoroughly seem to have been very doubtful about this. In 1883, C. M. Ingleby, while recording several attempts to persuade the authorities to explore the grave and exhume the body, remained convinced that the curse would not have been effective as a deterrent.

> I should almost be disposed to say, that no superstition, or fear of Shakespeare's curse, nor any official precaution and vigilance, could have been a match for that combination of curiosity, cupidity, and relic-worship, which has so often prompted and carried out the exhumation of a great man's bones.[21]

However, even though convinced the body was no longer in the grave, Ingleby sighed (almost echoing the thoughts of Washington Irving), 'What would one not give to look upon Shakespeare's dead face!' Ingleby, who had access to documentation that appears not to have survived, added a further statement, with quite extraordinary implications:

> I wish I could add that these two were the only occasions when either grave or gravestone were meddled with. I am informed, on the authority of a Free and Accepted Mason, that a Brother Mason of his has explored the grave which purports to be Shakespeare's, and that he found nothing in it but dust.[22]

If we are to treat Ingleby's claims on their face value, then, it would seem that, just as almost all the original manuscripts of William Shakespeare have disappeared from the world, so have his mortal remains. In fact, Ingleby's extraordinary story probably hides a secret. It is quite possible that the inquisitive Freemason believed — as once many Freemasons believed — that the real author of Shakespeare was Francis Bacon. If this were the case, then he was convinced that any body beneath the curse-stone would be that of Francis Bacon, Lord Verulam, and not the Bard. This might appear to be a curious belief. After all, it is well known that the body of Francis Bacon was buried in St. Michael's Church, in St. Albans. However, this widely held belief proves to be based on an insecure foundation. Records indicate that, on the occasion of the interment of the last Lord Verulam in St. Michael's, a fruitless search *was* made for the remains of the more famous Francis Bacon:

...a partition wall was pulled down, and the search extended into the part of the vault immediately under the monument, but no such remains were found ... Can it be possible that ... not only Bacon's skull, but that his whole remains have been removed surreptitiously from the place where they were once laid?[23]

That Bacon's remains should have disappeared is perhaps more remarkable than that those of Shakespeare should have been lost. The burial of Lord Verulam had been consistent with the terms of his will, which specified his place of burial, and the interment was arranged and overseen by his faithful servant. However, records suggest that Bacon's remains *were* disturbed — they may have been removed — shortly after their interment in St. Michael's Church. The seventeenth-century historian, Thomas Fuller, recorded that 'Bacon's scull (the relique of civil veneraton)', was pulled from the tomb by a certain Dr. King, and made the object of scorn and contempt. Fuller was quick to hang a moral on his tale, however, for, 'he who then derided the dead, has since become the laughing-stock of the living'.[24]

Were Ingleby's suspicions well founded? Had Shakespeare's body disappeared? Indeed, had there never been a body beneath the curse-stone at all?

A year or so earlier, the American, J. Parker Norris, had been less cynical than Ingleby. He seems to have had no doubt that the remains of the Bard were still in the tomb, and had gone so far as to propose exhumation in order to obtain a photograph of Shakespeare's skull. The purpose of this desecration was that it 'would help us to make a better portrait of him'.[25] Parker Norris was a Mason, and had written his article on the proposed exhumation for another Mason, who will emerge in a very different, and somewhat arcane context later. Norris was writing for the *American Bibliopolist*, which was then under the editorship of the brilliant Charles Southeran, an influential Mason who was, at that very moment, helping Madame Blavatsky write her occult best-seller, *Isis Unveiled*, which was to be published in 1877.

The Masonic interest in Shakespeare was intense — possibly because many of the brotherhood recognized — like Blavatsky — that there were many doubts about the true identity of the Bard.[26] In the last decades of the nineteenth-century, some scholars were beginning to suspect that Francis Bacon might have been involved with authorship of the Shakespearean literature. Others — in particular Masonic scholars — were beginning to suspect that Bacon had not only been a Mason, but had probably introduced Masonry to England.[27] Possibly because of this, the Masonic bodies began to embrace Shakespeare within their mythology. For example, on 23 April 1877 (the year following the publication of Norris' plea to have the body of Shakespeare exhumed), the Provincial Grand Master of the Worcester Masons, Lord Leigh, officiated at the laying of the foundation stone of the original Shakespeare Memorial Theatre.[28]

Ingleby must have read Norris' article with quiet amusement. He had investigated the stories relating to the skulls of several famous men — including those of the Italian artist, Raphael, the English dictator, Oliver Cromwell, and the Swedish savant-mystic, Emanuel Swedenborg. Armed with some knowledge of the dark secrets he had learned through this extensive research, his work on the Shakespeare grave had convinced him that there were hidden factors at work in this case. These were suggestive of a conspiracy theory:

> There may yet be some among us who have a personal interest in preventing such an exploration, and in thus maintaining the general belief, that Shakespeare's relics still rest in the mould in which they were buried.

He is not specific. Did he *really* believe that there was some conspiracy theory connected with the body? We cannot tell, but it is worth recording that when he wrote his book on Shakespeare's bones, the controversy about the authorship of the plays, and the real identity of Shakespeare, was already in full swing, in both England and North America.

Few who read the doggerel on the curse-stone realize that it is not the original verse. Indeed, few who gaze down upon it are aware that the stone into which the epitaph was cut is not the original stone. In 1737, the antiquary, George Vertue, at the end of a tour with the Earl of Oxford, made a rough drawing of the monument, and of the graves of Shakespeare and Anne Hathaway, along with a not very careful copy of the curse inscription.[29] If this Vertue sketch is to be taken seriously, then there must have been a third variant of the stone, with words cut in lower case, intermingled with a few in upper-case, and several variant spellings to those presently on the stone. The sketch that Vertue made of the monument was also significantly different from that *in situ* today — for example, Vertue's sketch does not show the monument surmounted by a skull.

It is far from clear when the original curse-stone was moved. The historian, Halliwell-Phillipps, found good reason to believe that the stone now visible was put there in the nineteenth-century. He proposed that, as an alternative to exhuming the body of Shakespeare (a sacrilege that was being actively considered, even as he wrote), it would be better to lift the ancient curse-stone, 'however decayed', beneath the modern one, and restore it. He felt that exhumation of the body would reveal little of value:

> It must be recollected that we are almost destitute of information as to the extent to which the series of graves in the chancel have been tampered with during the 267 years which have now elapsed, it being only by the merest accident that we know for certain that one of the Shakespearian tombs was disturbed in the last century for the interment of a stranger.[30]

Such doubts as to whose body lies beneath the stone serve only to increase the mystery of the curse itself. The curse-stone has always been something of a mystery, and was intended to be so. Its versification, epigraphic structure and intention are themselves mysteries: to my knowledge, there is nothing quite like this encoded Shakespeare curse-stone in any other English church.

It is curious that this uniquely-formed doggerel epitaph, dedicated to the most important poet England has ever produced, should not mention his name. Inevitably, this alone has fuelled contention that the body of the Bard is not buried below. Even so, the mute inscription, with its capitals SAKE and HEARE, seems, as it were, to be mumbling an alliterative rhyme for the name Shakespeare — a rhyme almost as barbarous as many of the variant spellings of the Bard's name during his lifetime.

It is highly likely that the earliest curse-epitaph recorded in the church, prior to 1748, bore a similar inscription to that now in place. However, it is also likely that this was written in such a way as to suggest that it hid a coded message. The reason for this is that records suggest the original consisted of quite ungrammatical combinations of upper and lower case letters. An example of the first two lines of this 'encoded' inscription is:

Good Frend for Iesus SAKE forbeare
To diGG T-E Dust Enclo-Ased HERe.

This fact has led several Shakespearean students to treat the original inscription as though it were written to accommodate a biliteral cipher. This in itself is not surprising, as many such bilateral ciphers or encoding techniques were widely used in the Elizabethan and Jacobean periods. In particular, certain students have examined the curse in the light of the biliteral cipher published by Francis Bacon in 1624.[31] Bacon seems to have been adroit at writing texts which incorporated, or encoded, hidden messages: indeed, in his work, *The Advancement of Science*, he discussed such a code in great detail, showing how it might be used to insert secret messages into an ordinary-seeming text. In dealing with such secret writing, he observes:

> ... the examiner [that is, the reader] falling upon the *exterior Letter*, and finding it probable [as a reading], shall suspect nothing of the *interior Letter*.[32]

Thus, in three concise lines, we have a perfect definition of esoteric art. In fact, the versification and form of the original curse-epitaph to Shakespeare was so improbable, so lacking in linguistic or orthographic grace, that it has *not* remained 'voide of suspition', as Bacon required of his own method of encoding. Indeed, on the contrary, it has alerted examiners to the fact that it contains a code. In view of this, it is surprising that, to date, no one has succeeded in applying Bacon's method to the inscription in a sufficiently consistent or logical way to reveal its *interior Letter* with any satisfaction.

A clue to the working of this cipher had been published by Francis Bacon himself, in 1624.[33] In this work, Bacon had set down a biliteral cipher, which he called a *Biliterarie Alphabet*. In this, consecutive groups of 5 letters, made up from the first two letters of the alphabet (a and b), were treated as codes, with corresponding alphabetic equivalents.

The entire *Biliterarie Alphabet* is given below:[34]

Exemplum Alphabeti Biliterarij.

A aaaaa . B aaaab . C aaaba . D aaabb . E aabaa . F aabab .
G aabba . H aabbb . I abaaa . K abaab . L ababa . M ababb .
N abbaa . O abbab . P abbba . Q abbbb . R baaaa . S baaab .
T baaba . V baabb . W babaa . X babab . Y babba . Z babbb

Bacon showed that, with the aid of this cipher, it was possible to construct a series of sentences that would appear to make sense, yet which would, at the same time, hide a subsidiary message. For example, the line

We are presently writing about a code.

Could be enciphered as a binary system of upper and lower case letters as follows:

We arE prEsentlY wRiting aBouT a cOde.

In order to discover what this encoded message means, we would have to break the sentence into 5-letter groups, as follows:

WearE prEse ntlYw Ritin gaBou TacOd e.

From the biliteral transcription of these 5-letter groups, proposed by Bacon, we would obtain:

baaab aabaa aaaba baaaa aabaa baaba (e)

The final single letter (and indeed, all non 5-letter groups) does not fit into the Baconian method, and is, therefore, discarded in the encoding and decoding. In the cipher key provided by Bacon, these six groups correspond as follows:

baaab aabaa aaaba baaaa aabaa baaba (e)

S   E   C   R   E   T

Thus the encrypted line, formulated above, contains the hidden message, SECRET.

As we have seen, certain records show that, in spite of the curse, Shakespeare's grave has been disturbed at least once. Dr. Ingleby recorded that, in the year 1796, the supposed grave of Shakespeare was accidentally broken into, in the course of digging a vault in its immediate proximity. Furthermore, not much more than fifty years earlier than Ingleby wrote (i.e., circa 1830), the curse-slab over the grave was also removed. Because this had sunk below the level of the raised pavement, it was lifted, the surface was levelled and *a fresh stone* laid over the old bed.

Ingleby was of the opinion that the curse on the stone was replaced – 'the four lines appear upon the new stone in exactly the same literal form as they did upon the old one'. I have reason to believe that Ingleby was wrong, for the original encoding has survived. It is evident that the inscription *was* changed, and I shall deal with the implications of this shortly.

Such accounts as these at least encouraged me to search for a copy of the inscription cut upon the original curse-stone. After some time, I located a record that offered, in a single source, *two* identical versions of the curse cut on the stone. One version was in a printed illustration, the other set in an adjacent typography. These were dated 1795, but the curse-epitaph had clearly been copied in 1792 or the following year.[35] Almost certainly, they showed the original epitaph prior to 1748, when the 'modern' version of the stone was set in the pavement.[36]

The acquatint of the 1795 epitaph (below) was by the author Samuel Ireland, and serves as an indication that he had troubled to visit Stratford Church in person, probably in 1792.[37]

Ireland actually confirmed such a visit, for in this same book, when discussing the doorway to the west of the Shakespeare wall monument (visible in the plate above), he mentioned that it 'opens to the charnel house, which contains the greatest assemblage of human bones I ever saw'. Ireland *saw* for himself the memorial and the epitaph, which he observed was in the following 'uncouth manner, in small and capital letters'. However, against these certainties of a personal inspection, we should balance the fact that the curse-stone inscription in this aquatint is wrongly orientated: it actually lies on a north-east axis. Further, it is wrongly placed – it is not directly below the wall monument, but is located more towards the centre of the chancel.

There is no reason, however, to question the accuracy of the text recorded by Ireland in the aquatint.[38]

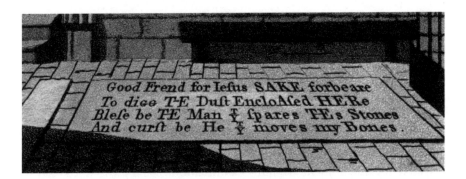

As if this print were not enough, on the page opposite the aquatint, Ireland gave an identical version of the curse in a typographic form.

" Good Frend for Iefus SAKE forbeare

" To diGG T-E Duft EncloAfed HERe

" Blefe be TE Man Ɣ fpares TEs Stones

" And curft be He Ɣ moves my Bones."

It is quite possible that an earlier version of the epitaph may surface as our knowledge of Shakespeare expands. For the moment, however, I think that it is reasonable to accept the earliest reliable version of the curse-stone is that given by Ireland.[39] I can see no reason for doubting the accuracy of Ireland's transcription: the version recorded by Vertue was given mainly in lower-case letters, and evidently was not copied with any care.

We note, of course, that this earlier version of the curse-stone combines upper- and lower-case letters, whilst that now in situ consists only of upper-case. What can we make of this epitaph, which is so obviously written in some kind of biliteral code? I think that it was crabbed and awkward simply because it combines an original use of the Baconian biliteral code, inserted meaningfully into the lines of the text. After much research, I have concluded that the code is designed to encrypt the name of the person buried beneath the stone.

Furthermore, it seems also to have contained a reference to a second encoding, which was also linked with both Shakespeare and Bacon. I shall examine this second encoding in the following chapter, for it is of importance to the development of Rosicrucianism. Meanwhile, we might consider merely the bilateral encoding of the Baconian bilateral itself.

Is it possible, by means of a study of this early version of the epitaph, to determine a logical process by which the name of the person buried beneath the stone may be revealed? I think that the answer is yes. In support of this opinion, I will set down the logical process by which I deduced, by way of the biliteral inscription on the curse-stone, the name of the great playwright.

First, I decided that, in terms of the Baconian code, to which these uncouth 'small and capital letters' relate, the bottom two lines should be rejected, for the moment, from my examination. The top two lines refer to the *Dust* below, and thus form an epitaph proper. The bottom two lines constitute both a blessing and a curse. I would argue that the sense alone is intended to direct us to the first two lines only, wherein the Baconian system of 5-letter divisions help identify the person, whose *Dust* is buried below.[40]

As I have already intimated, the name hidden in these two lines is not revealed by a straightforward application of the Baconian cipher. The code, when decrypted, reveals itself to be a little more sophisticated than a simple bilateral system. However, it does employ the *method* of Bacon, which requires that the lines be broken down, initially, into groups of five letters. One of the logical steps I have taken is to discount the ligature of ÆE. As a ligature, it works quite well in suggesting a letter H, yet it seems to me that the purpose behind it is to discount this compressed letter, in order to ensure that it is not incorporated into the 5-letter groups.

This procedure leaves, in the first line, a hanging four-letter group **eare**. In fact, this hang-over should offer us a clue as to what we are about to receive: **eare** is the last four letters of the word Shakespeare, authenticated in the grant of arms, so prominent on the monument that towers above the curse-stone. The five-letter groups give the following divisions:

GoodF rendf orIes usSAK Eforb eare
TodiG GTEDu stEnc loAse dHERe.

In the Baconian method, these are ciphered as:

Baaab aaaaa aabaa aabbb baaaa [eare]

Baaab bbbba aabaa aabaa abbba

In the Baconian code, these ciphers are the equivalent of the following letters:

S   A   E   H   R

S   E   E   P

(The second 5-letter group, **bbbba**, has no meaningful corresponding reading within the Baconian code, and must therefore be discounted.) One observes immediately that not only do both lines begin with the sought-after initial S, but each of these letters are found in the name Shakespeare.

To grasp the encoding fully, we must follow the instructions contained in the code itself. From the first line, we must take the fourth 5-letter group, **usSAK**, which in the Baconian key represents the letter H. The line of text begs us to 'forbeare' — which is an encoded linguistic form of a command, directing us to 'carry to the fore'. Follow this instruction, and carry forward (to the group before 'forebeare') this letter H. The verse does not tell us precisely *where* to carry it, but, in view of the clue offered by the hanging word **eare**, we may be tempted to insert it into SAK at the point S H AK, to make the first letters of the name Shakespeare. In this way, we arrive at:

S H AK

To this, we may add the letter E following the new construct, from the word SAKE of the epitaph, to give

S H AKE

Now consider the first 5-letter group on the next line, **TodiG**. The two words behind this 5-letter construct remind us that a spear has a point with which one may dig. The Baconian cipher for **TodiG** (or 'to dig') is **baaab**, which is the equivalent of S. Following the instructions of the first line, carry this forward also. As you do so, bear in mind that the text itself may be interpreted as an instruction to 'enclose an S (EncloAs)'.

By now, it is all too evident where this must be placed or enclosed: before (fore) the **eare**, to give.

S H AK E S

Take the final 5-letter group, which is **dHERe** (rhyming in the verse with *forbeare*, and once again, the fourth in the line). In the Baconian cipher **dHERe** is **abbba**, which is the equivalent of **P**. Carry this word forward, in sequence, to the first line. By a most simple logic, combining the meaning implicit in the verse with the Baconian code, we have arrived at the following groups:

S H AK E S P

Since these letters have been brought forward, and enclosed in this section of the line-ending, it is possible to complete the name by running on the part-word into the lower-case finial of the line, **eare**, that has played no part in the encoding.

S H AK E S P + eare

By this logic, which seems to be inbuilt into the secondary meaning within the verse, we arrive at the name of the great poet:

SHAKESPEARE

If we take this encoding seriously, then we see that the curse-stone *did* contain the name of the great man, despite what many people have believed.[41]

The coincidence of the survival of an epitaph for Shakespeare, encoded in a cipher favoured by Francis Bacon, leads us to inquire into the connection between these two great personalities in English literature.

There may be no doubt whatsoever that Bacon knew Shakespeare personally. The historian W.G. Thorpe has shown conclusively that in 1594 Bacon was Master of the Revels at Gray's Inn, London – a salaried post he held from 1588 to 1614. During 1594, and on several occasions afterwards, he employed the Lord Chamberlain's Company of Players (to which Shakespeare was attached, sometimes as player, sometimes as investor) to perform at least one play in the hall of the society.[42] Thorpe has also been able to show, perhaps with less conviction, that the two great men were entangled in their financial affairs.

Bacon and his brother, Anthony, ran the Srivenery's Company (a public scriptoria for copying manuscripts, and for providing translation, enciphering and decoding services). It had been located at Gray's Inn, but later moved to Twickenham Park. Eventually, the Park was gifted (perhaps through subtle extortion) by the Earl of Essex to Bacon.[43]

Although Francis Bacon's income was high, he seems always to have been short of money – perhaps because he was a spendthrift. His self-induced perpetual penury meant that he was greedy for 'copy', and did not always trouble himself about the author's consent before publishing. It is extremely likely that Shakespeare paid for several of his own manuscripts to be copied there – perhaps even the 'true and originall copies' from which Heminge and Condell compiled the First Folio of 1523.[44]

Thorpe contends that Francis Bacon, as Master of the Revels, asked Shakespeare for loans, 'when on his good will depended the retention of the Inn pageant work, for which other theatre companies were eager'. Dare Shakespeare refuse the loans and risk the loss of his established position? The Bacon-controlled Scrivenery was:

> the place where the priceless manuscripts of the plays would be kept under the control of Lord Bacon, at all events up to 1608.[45]

Save perhaps for a few pages, most of the original Shakespearean manuscripts have vanished, yet copies must have existed until 1623. In that year, they were used in the printing of the first Folio of the Bard's works. The editors of this Folio – both friends and fellow actors of Shakespeare himself – had commented on the fine quality of these scripts. It is very likely that the manuscripts had been prepared in the scriptoria, or Scrivenery, controlled by Bacon.

One of the duties of the copyists working in this scriptoria was to decode ciphers, and it is highly likely that they also ciphered documents for certain customers. It may even have been during this period of transcription that Bacon amended the texts, or inserted the codes and ciphers which are undoubtedly in the First Folio, but the important question (of what happened to these manuscripts) has never been answered.

It has long been recognized by scholars that the number 33 was adopted by Francis Bacon as one of his codes because the numerical value of the word *Bacon* was itself 33:[46]

B A C O N

2 1 3 14 13 = 33

As so many esotericists have claimed that Shakespeare, the literary personage, was none other than Francis Bacon, we should not be surprised to find that many of the works published on Bacon display the 33 encoding. Even as late as 1679, when *Baconiana* was published, this 33 encoding is found on the title page: there are precisely 33 words in the upper register of the page.[47]

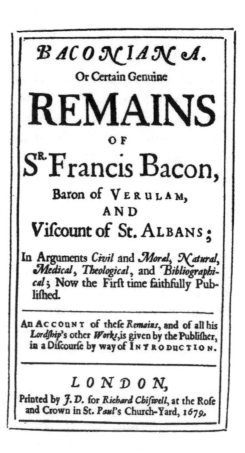

It is in the introduction to this work that we find an explicit reference to Bacon's bilateral cipher, as well as to the fact that Bacon introduced numerologies into his texts, requiring us to distinguish between roman and italic letter forms.

As anyone conversant with this sort of encoding might anticipate, this paragraph, which deals with the encoding systems of Bacon, actually employs that system itself. The first two lines of the paragraph contain 33 letters. Further, the six words in italic within this paragraph contain a total of 33 letters.[48]

> The faireſt, and moſt correƈt Edition of this Book in *Latine*, is that in Folio, prin- ted at *London*, *Anno* 1623. And who- foever would underſtand the Lord *Bacon's* Cypher (*y*), let him confult that accurate Edition. For . in fome other Editions which I have perufed, the form of the Let- ters of the Alphabet, in which much of the Myſterie confiſteth, is not obferved : But the *Roman* and *Italic* ſhapes of them are confounded. *(y) In l. 6. c. 1.*

As I have noted, this same 33 has been held sacred by writers and authors because of its connection with the life-time of Christ — a con- nection that was rendered even more sacred by extensive use in art and literature. The number 33 was held to be an encoding of such Christo- logical importance that it figured in the greatest secular Christian poem of the late Middle Ages. This number was held to be of such importance by Dante that he ensured his *Purgatorio* and *Paradiso* in the *Divina Commedia* each consisted of precisely 33 cantos. In the final tremulous line of Dante's *Divina Commedia*, we are required to count all the characters to obtain this same number.[49]

l'amor che move il sole e l'altre stelle.[50]

The love that moves the Sun and the other stars.

It is hardly surprising that the 33 should have been widely adopted into encodings during the Elizabethan and Jacobean periods, which exhibited such a deep interest in hidden symbolism. Thirty-three letters figure in the opening line of Edmund Spenser's poem, *The Faerie Queene*, a line that terminates in the relevant word, *maske*:

Lo! I, the man whose Muse whylome did maske, ...

As we have already seen, to emphasize and enhance the magic of the number, Spenser also insisted that Book III, Canto III (that is, 3 + 3 = 33) of this same poem should also open with a line of 33 letters:

Most sacred fyre, that burnest mightily ...

Even the title-page of this work, published in 1611, contains a count of 33 words (figure 5).[51]

Here we have merely three examples of the 33 at work, but there are many more pertinent examples in *The Faerie Queene*. It is no secret that this poet is now recognized by academics as an exponent of Elizabethan numerology at its best.[52]

One can offer numerous examples of the 33 encoding in the plays attributed to Shakespeare, and, a little later, we shall consider some of these. Meanwhile, because we have seen the peculiar relevance of the 33 to funerary art, in so far as the number deals, among other things, with exits and entrances, it is worth glancing at Kent's memorial to Shakespeare, in Westminster Abbey.

The inscription, incised on the marble sheet, to which Shakespeare is pointing on this memorial (above) has been treated as a code by several commentators in the past.[53] However, so far as I have been able to determine, none of these commentators have discovered the relatively simple method by which the encoding of 33 was preserved.

The memorial was not introduced into Westminster Abbey until 1740. It was sculpted by William Kent, who also carved the nearby tomb to Isaac Newton.[54] As our interest lies solely in the encoded inscription, I reproduce an enlarged detail of this, opposite.

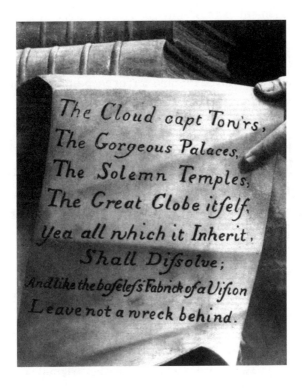

There is a good reason for believing that the inscription on the paper contains a code. For example, the last word of the first line is represented in incorrect English, for the abbreviation of the word *Towres* (as represented by Shakespeare himself) should be *Towr's,* not *Tow'rs.* The abbreviation could serve only one purpose, which is to suggest that the elision was required to meet a letter-count. Furthermore, the inscription as a whole, which gives the impression of being copied from *The Tempest,* Act IV:1, is copied very badly indeed. Below, I give the relevant section from this play, for ease of comparison.[55]

And like the bafeleſſe fabricke of this viſion
The Clowd-capt Towres, the gorgeous Pallaces ,
The ſolemne Temples, the great Globe it ſelfe,
Yea, all which it inherit, ſhall diſſolue,
And like this infubſtantiall Pageant faded
Leaue not a racke behinde :

The first line of this quotation has been wrongly located on the memorial inscription. In this latter, it has been transferred to the equivalent of the fifth line, whilst the original fifth line has been dropped altogether. It is difficult to accept that a sculptor could have made such a substantial error in quoting what is, in effect, a well-known passage: we find it reasonable to assume that he was involved in some sort of encoding. The equivalent text, then, for the lapidary inscription is:

The Clowd-capt Towres, the gorgeous Pallaces ,
The folemne Temples, the great Globe it felfe,
Yea, all which it inherit, fhall diffolue,
And like the bafeleffe fabricke of this vifion
Leaue not a racke behinde :

The word count of this adjusted quotation from the original text still contains 35 words, as does the sculptural inscription. However, there are two subtle suggestions that emerge from the comparison of these two versions. In the sculptural version *it self* (in the fourth line) is represented as one word. In the sculptural version, Shakespeare's *Cloud capt* is represented as two words, whereas in the original it may be read numerologically as being only one word, in that it is hyphenated as *Clowd-capt*. Now, it is precisely these two anomalies that offer clues to the hidden numerology. A new count of the inscription text, made whilst bearing in mind the 'single' words, *itself* and *Clowd-capt,* gives a total of 33 words.

There is one other encoding clue built into the inscription. The incised lapidary does not copy precisely the original 1623 typographical setting, for it breaks lines. By so doing, it constructs fully eight lines from a nominal five. Only one of these breaks is indented.

Yea all which it Inherit,
    Shall Dissolve;

Since anomalies generally serve as indicators of encodings, we may assume that this indentation is intended to offer a further clue, and perhaps invited a letter-count. A count of this broken line reveals that it consists of 33 characters.

In Shakespeare's plays, the 33 is often used in a most sophisticated way in order (as some Baconian supporters argue) to point arcanely to Francis Bacon. This encoding may well have nothing to do with the Christian significance behind the number, or even with the Rosicrucian number, with which the encoding is rightly associated. A good example – if only because it is introduced in a spirit of good humour – of this Baconian encoding may be studied in the 1623 *Folio* printing of *Loves Labours lost*. Act V of this play begins with a play on words, in both Latin and English. The first full page of text in Act V is numbered 136.

136 *Lowes*

Curat. A moſt ſingular and choiſt Epithat,
Draw out his Table-booke.
Peda. He draweth out the thred of his verboſitie, fi-
ner then the ſtaple of his argument. I abhor ſuch pha-
naticall phantaſims, ſuch inſociable and poynt deuiſe
companions, ſuch rackers of ortagriphie, as to ſpeake
dout fine, when he ſhould ſay doubt; det, when he ſhold
pronounce debt; d e b t, not det:he clepeth a Calf, Cauſe:
halfe, haufe:neighbour *vocatur* nebour; neigh abreuiated
ne: this is abhominable, which he would call abhomi-
nable:it inſinuateth me of infamie : *ne inteligis domine*, to
make franticke, lunaticke ?
Cura. Laus deo, bene intelligo.
Peda. Bome boon for boon preſcian, a little ſcratcht, 'twil
ſerue.

Enter Bragart, Boy.

Curat. Vides ne quis venit ?
Peda. Video, & gaudio.
Brag. Chirra.
Peda. Quare Chirra, not Sirra ?
Brag. Men of peace well inceuntred.
Ped. Moſt millitarie ſir ſalutation.
Boy. They haue beene at a great feaſt of Languages, and ſtolne the ſcraps.
Clow. O they haue liu'd long on the almes-basket of words. I maruell thy M.hath not eaten thee for a word, for thou art not ſo long by the head as honorificabilitu-dinitatibus : Thou art eaſier ſwallowed then a flapdra-gon.
Page. Peace, the peale begins.
Brag. Mounſier, are you not lettred ?
Page. Yes, yes, he teaches boyes the Horne-booke : What is Ab ſpeld backward with the horn on his head ?
Peda. Ba, *puericia* with a horne added.
Pag. Ba moſt feely Sheepe, with a horne : you heare his learning.

Line 33, in the first column of this page, contains a joke, made within a given context of *horn-books*, by which alphabets were taught in schools. Over, I give an enlarged version of the text from line 31 to 36 inclusive:

Brag. Mounſier, are you not lettred?
Page. Yes, yes, he teaches boyes the Horne-booke:
What is Ab ſpeld backward with the horn on his head?
Peda. Ba, *puericia* with a horne added.

We need these four lines to see how the 33rd line (which contains the little joke, and which is the third line down in the excerpt above) is itself introduced by a speech of 33 characters — a speech inflated to that number of letters purely by the orthography:

Yes, yes, he teaches boyes the Horne-booke:

Evidently, the puerile joke is that Ab spelled backwards is BA. With a horn on its head, BA becomes a sheep. However, it proves to be a little more than puerile, as the Latin for horn was *cornus*, and in medieval legalese had become *cornu*, so the joke may be taken as being a reference to BACORNUS or BACORNU — an encoded reference to Bacon, the lawyer. For the *hoi polloi* in the audience that did not get this joke, there was the residual humour of the cuckoldry associated with the derived word *cornuto*, which meant to tip with a horn, and to cuckold.[56]

It is evidently a part of this clever encoding that the relevant speech, which contains the joke (as quoted above), consists of exactly 33 words.[57]

A simple yet effective example of this 33 encoding, which is unequivocally linked with the Sun, may be seen in a design for the magical square of the Sun, from a seventeenth-century book on talismanic magic and sigils. Such magical squares were designed for painting or engraving, or otherwise fixing, upon pieces of metal, with the notion that the square itself would both attract and exude the influence of the planet associated with it. For example, the square of the Sun would usually be incised or painted on the solar metal, gold, and would be expected to attract and exude all the creative and life-enhancing properties of the Sun.

Opposite, is the obverse and reverse of a design for a circular talismanic lamen of the Sun.[58] The reverse is marked SOL (Sun), and, in the centre of the image of the ten-rayed sun, is the late medieval sigil for the Sun, which is an encircled dot: ⊙.

The encircled magical square of the Sun is given on the obverse. This magic square consists of 36 small squares, with the sequence of numbers from 1 to 36 so arranged that, whichever direction vertically or horizontally a single line is added up, the sum is always 111 (the magical number

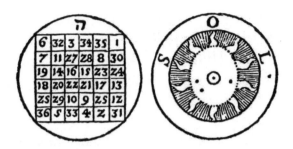

of the Sun). Now, because Christ is traditionally linked with the Sun, surrounded by the twelve disciples of the zodiacal images, the number 33 is regarded as being also a number of the Sun. This notion is expressed in the magical square, in which the number 33 (on the bottom line) has been located in the 33rd square (counting left to right, downwards, in the familiar manner of reading).

It is from such talismanic theory that the number 666 is represented as being the number of the demon, *Sorath*, one of the adversaries of the Sun. This is the solar number 111, repeated six times, when the horizontal sequences, or the vertical sequences, are added together.[59]

We have examined with sufficient care the well-known inscription on the Shakespearean curse-stone, in the chancel of Holy Trinity Church, to recognize that it is tinged with an esoteric numerology. By means of the application of Bacon's bilateral encoding system, we derived from the first two lines of this inscription the name Shakespeare. We ignored the last pair of lines, on the grounds that they related to the blessing and curse which is almost uniquely associated with this memorial stone. Now we must be prepared to look at this so-called curse-stone once again, in the light of the 33 encoding.

> " Good Frend for Iefus SAKE forbeare
> " To diGG T-E Duft EncloAfed HERe
> " Blefe be ↑E Man ☿ fpares ↑Es Stones
> " And curft be He ☿ moves my Bones."

If we count the capital letters in this inscription, we find that they number 35. This is the case if we regard the ligatured letters T-E as reading THE. In such a case, they would count as 3 letters, thus:

G	F	I	SAKE					=	7
T	GG	THE	D	E	A	HER		=	12
B	THE	M	TY	THE	S			=	11
A	H	TY	B					=	5

$$35$$

However, if we examine the double **GG** of the word **diGG**, in the curse inscription, we observe that these are quite unlike the other capitals, in that they line to the lower-case x-height. If we assume that this distinction has been introduced as part of the encoding, then we may reject the **GG** from our count, and deduct 2 from the 35 so far obtained. This, of course, gives us 33.

It is perhaps one thing to study the 33 encoding in memorials associated with Shakespeare, but quite another to expect to find these used with hermeneutic meanings in his plays. However, I have already shown that Shakespeare did at times resort to the 33 encoding in certain passages, where the hermeneutics were both relevant and important. For example, he resorted to this sacred solar number in the most famous soliloquy in English literature, which should appear in its printed form in 33 lines (opposite).[60]

Furthermore, besides ensuring that the soliloquy consists of 33 lines, Shakespeare (or his editor) has arranged for the first line of the speech to consist of 33 characters:

Ham. To be, or not to be, that is the Question:

As if this were not enough, in the final line, where the soliloquy is brought to an abrupt end by the appearance of Ophelia, we also find exactly 33 characters:

And loose the name of Action. Soft you now,

Thus, the 33rd line is itself distinguished by 33 letters.

As though to underline the importance of this number, the final line of the soliloquy, in which Hamlet greets Ophelia, is followed by one of precisely the same number of characters:

The faire Ophelia? Nimph, in thy Orizons
Be all my sinnes remembred.

As we have seen, this hidden numerology was printed in the First Folio of 1623. Even so, its numerological significance has been missed by most

Enter Hamlet.

Ham. To be, or not to be, that is the Queſtion:
Whether 'tis Nobler in the minde to ſuffer
The Slings and Arrowes of outragious Fortune,
Or to take Armes againſt a Sea of troubles,
And by oppoſing end them: to dye, to ſleepe
No more; and by a ſleepe, to ſay we end
The Heart-ake, and the thouſand Naturall ſhockes
That Fleſh is heyre too? 'Tis a conſummation
Deuoutly to be wiſh'd. To dye to ſleepe,
To ſleepe, perchance to Dreame; I, there's the rub,
For in that ſleepe of death, what dreames may come,
When we haue ſhuffiel'd off this mortall coile,
Muſt giue vs pawſe. There's the reſpect
That makes Calamity of ſo long life:
For who would beare the Whips and Scornes of time,
The Oppreſſors wrong, the poore mans Contumely,
The pangs of diſpriz'd Loue, the Lawes delay,
The inſolence of Office, and the Spurnes
That patient merit of the vnworthy takes,
When he himſelfe might his *Quietus* make
With a bare Bodkin? Who would theſe Fardles beare
To grunt and ſweat vnder a weary life,
But that the dread of ſomething after death,
The vndiſcouered Countrey, from whoſe Borne
No Traueller returnes, Puzels the will,
And makes vs rather beare thoſe illes we haue,
Then flye to others that we know not of.
Thus Conſcience does make Cowards of vs all,
And thus the Natiue hew of Reſolution
Is ſicklied o're, with the pale caſt of Thought,
And enterprizes of great pith and moment,
With this regard their Currants turne away,
And looſe the name of Action. Soft you now,

scholars and editors, in consequence of which some of Shakespeare's subtle meanings, set out in this soliloquy, have been lost, even in careful editions of the play. The speech is one of the first soliloquies in literature to reveal the insecurities felt by the new Ego in the face of the mysteries of life and death: it is fitting that it should have been represented within a lattice-work of 33 encodings.

Beyond this cunningly wrought numerology within the speech, there is one other thing worthy of note, and relevant to our pursuit of the idea of the Ego, in connection with the 33 encoding. This speech has been most cleverly worded to ensure that the speaker, Hamlet, avoids use of the personal pronoun **I** — that uniquely descriptive word that designates the Ego. In view of this, it is reasonable to ask what symbolism Shakespeare intended, when he so magnificently orchestrated the 33 encoding in this soliloquy.

The notion that Shakespeare did not write the plays attributed to his name had been circulating shortly after his death. Some scholars, who read both Shakespeare and Bacon with care, could not help observing the many parallels that existed in their writings.[61]

Bacon had been one of the greatest scholars of his period, with a fine grasp of the classics and a wide familiarity with the literature of the period, in both Italian and French — whilst Shakespeare, in comparison, had been relatively uneducated. Thomas Fuller, writing very close to the period when Shakespeare was alive, admitted that the actor-playwright, whose name in Latin was *Hasti-vibrans*, was not well educated — 'Indeed, his learning was very little'.[62] Such observations offered good reasons for speculation in the eighteenth- and nineteenth-centuries, but everything changed dramatically when scholars began to observe that both Shakespearean and Baconian literature were riddled with codes.

Chapter 3

Some Rosicrucian Works

*It would be a useless labor to enter here upon a defence of symbolic writing,
when nothing is more certain than that men of genius in all ages, seemingly by
a constraint of nature, have fallen into it. That the Sacred Scriptures are full
of it must be confessed by all who are not in a condition to read as literal truth
the history of Robinson Crusoe and of Gulliver's Travels...*

[Ethan Allen Hitchcock, *Remarks upon Alchemy and the Alchemists*
(1857), p. vi.]

A glance at the photographic portrait of Ethan Allen Hitchcock (below)
would leave one in no doubt that he was an American general; beyond
that, his face, charged with superior wisdom, is impenetrable.

There is little or no sign in his eyes that Major-General Hitchcock was a
personal friend of Abraham Lincoln, a militant Christian, a student of
Dante, Shakespeare, Spenser and Swedenborg, or that, immediately on his
retirement from the military, he dedicated himself to the study of

alchemical literature. There is no sign in his face that he was the most advanced thinker, in nineteenth century America, on the true nature of alchemy, that he is now regarded as having anticipated the alchemical interpretations of Carl Gustav Jung, and that he was one of the first modern scholars to recognize the true purpose behind the study of alchemy as self-regeneration.[1]

Outside the attention of a hand-full of scholars, Hitchcock is now scarcely remembered in the ordinary way of things. Nonetheless, the truth is that when we think of the alchemists as being involved in the pursuit of something other than the search for earthly gold, we are seeing the world through the eyes of this remarkable man. Carl Gustav Jung, whom Hitchcock influenced, was foolishly prone to imposing his own highly personal interpretation on alchemical texts, and thereby both mutilating and misunderstanding them. In contrast, Hitchcock had the humility and grace to permit the alchemists to speak for themselves, in their own language, which happens to be a tongue that few of the modern age can truly understand.[2]

As a scholar of Shakespeare, Hitchcock cannot fail to have grasped the deeper symbolism in his reference in that most magical of all plays, *The Tempest*. In discussing those men who 'live principally in the sensuous world', an iridescent thought from *The Tempest* came to his mind. These sensuality-bound men (Hitchcock tells us) can never forgive those who take the hint from the melting of a piece of ice, and think it possible that

> The cloud-capped towers, the gorgeous palaces,
> The solemn temples, the great globe itself,
> Yes, all which it inherit, shall dissolve . . .[3]

The deeper meaning behind this poetic description of the dissolution of things must have been in Hitchcock's mind even as he turned to *The Tempest* to copy out these words. The deeper meaning is found not only in the play, which makes of this speech a misplaced valediction. As we have seen already, it is also in a lapidary version on the memorial to the Bard in Westminster Abbey.[4] However, on that late valediction of the Abbey lapidary, the words had been tampered with, to ensure that they were encoded with the secret and sacred 33.

The words, and the long speech from which the three lines are derived, are perfect for a tomb-like memorial, which, almost by definition, stands between the two worlds. The eternal truth is that what has vanished is not quite lost, as the poetry insists. Here, Shakespeare was lamenting only the illusion, what *seems*. What seems dissolved is only what has vanished from human sight, and lives, even now, behind a veil. This is the imperishable reality 'prepared from the foundation of the world', which Hitchcock recognized, as he contemplated the three lines of Shakespeare, or the entire speech from which the three were taken.

Yet, by studying these things, we recognize that Hitchcock had copied down one of Shakespeare's numerological secrets. The third line of the quotation consists of 33 letters.

Yea, all which it inherit, shall dissolve...[5]

Whenever, flicking through this great book on alchemy by the American Major-General, I come across his reference to *The Tempest*, I find myself wondering if he knew about the secret encoding on the memorial in Westminster Abbey. More than once, he had recognized the importance of numbers in alchemy, and in the spiritual search that alchemy represented, but he had never written about the numbers encoded in *The Tempest*. How could a man of such learning, of such wide interest in hidden things, not have known about the Shakespeare codes?

It was left to another American, younger than Hitchcock by 33 years, to discover – or, rather, rediscover – that Shakespeare wrote in codes.[6] The rub was that this American, Ignatius Donnelly, already breathtakingly famous for his book, *Atlantis: The Antediluvian World*, was convinced that the Shakespeare plays had been written by Francis Bacon.[7] He had been persuaded into this view by the writings of the American, Delia Bacon who, in her later life, claimed descent from the famous Francis. Donnelly's study of the Shakespearian codes is full of fun, but more full of errors. In spite of this, the evidence he adduces, that there is as much of Francis Bacon in the plays as Shakespeare, seems utterly unassailable. In spite of this, it was easy, in the nineteenth century, to trip up over the true meaning of the 33. The fact that it was the numerical equivalent of the word Bacon, tended to blind some scholars to the much wider classical and Christological importance of the number.

If the living Shakespeare took delight in introducing the sacred number 33 into various passages in his plays, after his death this same number was also explored by his admirers. The sacred number, which had been adopted first by medieval Christians and later by Rosicrucians, appeared on the Bard's first memorial. In the church of the Holy Trinity, in Stratford-upon-Avon, we may trace examples of this numerology of 33. Indeed, it is not too much to claim that the inscription beneath the famous memorial bust was constructed shortly after Shakespeare's death, as a sort of paeon to that mysterious number.

The encoding of the 33, in this memorial, focuses on the larger upper-case letters and the ligatures within the text. Below, I reproduce a photograph of the inscription, which is followed by a carefully made copy that is probably easier to read.[8]

The two lines of inelegant Latin that head the epitaph are set out in such a way as to hide the 33 code. If you count the number of small caps in the top line (discounting the large caps) you will see that they total 33 characters.

VDICIO YLIUM GENIO OCRATEM ARTE ARONEM

If you count the small caps in the lower line of Latin (again discounting the large caps, and counting the ligatured Æ of MÆRET as two characters, then once again you will find they total 33 letters.

ERRA TEGIT POPULUS MAERET LYMPUS HABET

Each of the remaining lines in English (and the final dating in Latin) may also be resolved into 33 letters.

The curious ligature TH of THOU is evidently intended to represent two letters. If we count it as such, then the first line of English is made up of 33 characters.

STAY PASSENGER WHY GOEST [TH]OU BY SO FAST

At first glance, the second line of English seems made up of 39 characters. However, if you discount the three conjoined TH ligatures of THOU, HATH and DEATH, and, of course, the non-lining capital of DEATH, you may count 33 characters in the line.

READ IF [TH]OU CANST WHOM ENVIOUS EA[TH] HA[TH] PLAST

The third line of English consists of 33 characters. To arrive at this number, you must count the three elided TH (of WITH, THIS and WITH) as single letters. Furthermore, the elided NT of MONUMENT must be read as a single letter.

WI[TH] IN [TH]IS MONUME[NT] SHAKSPEARE: WI[TH] WHOME

The numerology of the fourth line is more subtle than the others. To establish that it contains 33 characters, one must first distinguish the subtle ligatures in the five pairs of letters, which are either dipthongs, or have communal serifs.

Q[VI]CK NAT[VR]E DIDE [WH]OSE NA[ME] DO[TH] DECK [Ys] TOMBE

The juncture of serifs in the VI of QVICK,
The juncture of serifs in VR of NATVRE
The juncture of serifs in WH in WHOSE.
The dipthong of ME in NAME.
The dipthong of TH in DOTH.
The abbreviation Y, which is based on the seventeenth-century version of the Anglo-Saxon runic letter, *thorn* [þ = th]. With the superscript S it means THIS. In each case, these junctures must be regarded as an abbreviation and counted as one letter.

When these amendments are taken into account, the line consists of 33 characters.

FAR MORE [TH]EN COST SIEH ALL YT HE HA[TH] WRITT

The fifth line of English is even less obvious. To reveal a secret count of 33, one must examine the unique structure of the word THEN, which ligatures the first three letters, the H being resolved from T and E: this word is intended to be counted as 3 characters, as though it read, TEN – curiously, this word finished on the tenth character count. The ligatured TH of HATH is to be read as one character. The abbreviated YT is a seventeenth-century version of the Anglo-Saxon runic letter, *thorn* [þ = th]. With the superscript T it is intended to be read as THAT: here, it must be read as two characters. Counted in such a way, there are 33 letters in the whole line.

On a casual inspection, the sixth line does not appear to be encoded with 33 characters. It contains no ligatures, and on a first count appears to have 36 letters. However, the encoded 33 is revealed when one reads it in connection with the Latin subscript, which, when the ligatures are read as one character, consists of 30 letters. Since the English and Latin together total 66 characters, they may be construed as encoding between them 2 sets of 33.[9]

LEAVES LIVING ART BUT PAGE TO SERVE HIS WITT
OBIIT AÑO D[OI] 1616
[AE]TATIS 53 DIE 23 A[PI]

As though to confirm the omnipresence of this 33 encoding, there is another reminder of the number in this complex epitaph. If you add together all the dipthongs, large capitals and abbreviations in the entire script, you will find that there are 33 in all. There are 13 dipthongs, 15 large capitals, and 5 abbreviations.[10]

In passing, I should observe that the representation in this memorial of the year of life in which he died (given accurately as 53) seems on close examination to resemble a 33. This is quite clear on the memorial itself (below), but is not quite so clear in the engraved reproduction, given above.

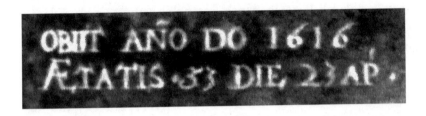

I think that it is undeniable that the mystery of our being required to read (IF THOU CANST, indeed) the monument, must somehow lie in the secret of this number 33. The analysis above indicates that there can be no doubt whatsoever that the person who constructed this epitaph knew about the secret code. Already, even within the context of Shakespeare alone, the number 33 is beginning to take on the character of an early seventeenth-century mystery.

Of course, the work that went into this brilliantly executed tapestry of encodings was really stupendous, yet it has remained unobserved for almost five hundred years. This page of Shakespeare's *Secret booke* has remained unread until these modern times.

Among all the literary references in early Rosicrucian works, the most mysterious are those to *Liber M*, The Book of M. This *Liber M* is mentioned in the *Fama* of the Rosicrucians, and it may just be identical to that about which Raymond of Sabunda and Thomas Aquinas wrote.[11] As we have seen, this was sometimes claimed to be the *Liber Mundi*, or *Book of Nature*, and sometimes the *Book of Memory*. Since it was most certainly a book that people had forgotten how to read properly, it is possible that the word Memory (*Memoria*) had some relevance to its title.

Many modern scholars accept the former meaning. They seem to be convinced that the M stands for *Mundi*, and that the word represents the secret work of the Rosicrucians, as investigators of the material realm. However, this is really a matter of speculation, rather than of established fact. We have seen enough of the way secret meanings are hidden in Rosicrucian codes to expect more of a single initial. It is reasonable to ask if *Liber M* has some other meaning than that usually ascribed to it. Does the M really stand for *Mundi*? Is it really the *Earth* that the Rosicrucians were studying? Or were they pursuing some other Mysterium?

An engraving of 1682, derived from an impeccably Rosicrucian source, seems to offer a sermon on the mystery of the letter M. This forms the frontispiece to an arcane work, *Mysterium Magnum*, of the Rosicrucian-shoemaker, Jacob Boehme, which was published by his disciple, Gich-tel.[12] The plate (below) contrasts the realm of light with the realm of darkness.

On one side is Christ, and on the other the personification of Darkness, which in terms of Rosicrucian symbolism, is Ignorance. The face of Darkness is being unveiled, so that he may gaze on the face of Christ. Symbolically, Christ is being brought into the light of day, for the benefit of darkened mankind. It is a Rosicrucian who does the unveiling. The affiliation of the latter is confirmed by the encircled cross around his neck, and the heart-handled key in his belt. However, far more revealing is the solar halo, at the centre of which is a seeing eye, hovering over his head. This device – symbol of the Ego – points to an individual who is blessed with higher vision.

Those who now find themselves gripped by the compulsion to count symbols in images, will no doubt have already seen something of great interest in this Rosicrucian engraving. When we count the number of letters, and add to these the number of zodiacal sigils on the globe, we find that there are 33 in all.

MYSTERIUM MAGNUM		=	15
essias	oses	=	10
M	M	=	2
♍ ♎ ♏ ♐ ♑ ♒		=	6 = 33

The engraving is dominated by the letter M. The title of the work includes four words beginning with M — *Mysterium Magnum, Messias* and *Moses*. From a processional cross, in the hand of Christ, hangs a banner within which a letter M is displayed in a radiant circle. On the other side, over the head of the personification of Darkness, emerges a trumpet, from which hangs another banner. On this is blazoned another M, within a device of flames.

I think we may take it that these two M letters are not intended merely as a repetition of the title *Mysterium Magnum*. In my opinion the letter M is itself an encoding, linked with the secret word of the Rosicrucians, generally supposed to be *Mundus* (the *World*). For the Rosicrucians, the created world was twofold, as it is made from the inter-working of light and darkness. This is perhaps symbolized in the distribution of stars on the celestial globe. The first three divisions of the globe are in the light: these contain 33 stars, in all. The lowest of the divisions is in total darkness: this contains only 5 stars.

Part of the imagery in this fascinating plate is certainly derived from the very earliest of Rosicrucian symbols. For example, on the first day of his journey to the *Chymical Wedding*, Christian Rosencreutz is given a gold piece 'for Remembrance', and for expenses on the way.[13] On the obverse of the coin is an image of the rising Sun. On the reverse are the three letters, D.L.S. These three letters have been interpreted in several ways, but it seems likely that they stand for *Deus Lux Solis*. I elect to choose this Latin version because it is a phrase of 12 letters, and is thus zodiacal and solar-centred, like the numbered circles around Christ in the above figure. The Latin translates as 'God, the Light of the Sun': further, the numerology suggests that God is invisible at the centre of the twelve zodiacal signs, which represent the totality of the stellar realm.

The importance of this abbreviated Latin is that, when considered in relation to the 'key-cipher', the standard numerical equivalents of the European alphabet, it incorporates letters that total 33:

D   L   S
4 + 11 + 18 = 33

The two M-bearing flags are of similar interest. They seem to be confirmed by the sigils for Virgo and Scorpio, below the key in the belt of the Rosicrucian. Both these sigils recall the form of the letter M:

♍   ♏

The first of these sigils, the symbol of the feminine side of dual Nature, reminds us that Virgo is linked with the Virgin Mary: indeed, one explanation for its form is that the ♍ is itself a combination of the initial letters M and V of the words, *Maria Virgo*.[14]

I have never felt happy with the idea that the secret word of the Rosicrucians was *Mundi*. To be truly esoteric, the sound would have to begin not with MU, but with MA — the Sanskrit-derived sound of the Feminine. Could it be that the two M-flags in Boehme's intriguing plate hint at something that unites, or even makes use of the two worlds of Light and Dark?

Is it possible that the secret word of the Rosicrucians, hinted at in such titles as *Liber M*, does not point to *Mundi*, but to some other word beginning with M? Is it also possible that this secret word is linked with the number 33, which we have seen extends well beyond the relative parochialism of Shakespeare or Bacon, into the early Rosicrucian movement as a whole? Is there a word beginning with M, and encoding in its structure the number 33, which would be relevant to the Rosicrucian teaching? Try as I will, I can think of only one such word. This is *Magica*, the feminine nominative Latin word meaning 'magic'. The numerological basis for the word in terms of the encoding system known as the Bacon code is:

M   A   G   I   C   A
12   1   7   9   3   1 = 33

Is it the word *Magica* that it hinted at in the numerous references to M in the Rosicrucian image, above? Is it magic, which has the power to unveil Darkness? *Magica* is the key that enables man to pass from Light to Darkness and back again, with impunity and safety — it is the key of the magician Prospero.

The word *Magica*, and its masculine and neuter equivalents, do appear in important Rosicrucian texts. For example it appears as *Magicum* on the title of Heinrich Khunrath's *Ampitheatrum* of 1602 (above), which seems to have been in circulation in manuscript form as early as 1598.[15]

We observe from the detail above that the word M of MAGICUM begins the third group of 33 letters in the title. To make the correct

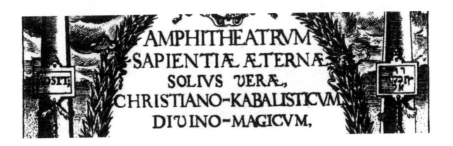

count, one must regard the ligatured Æ as one letter, and ignore the italic *V* of VERAE.

Like the *Mysterium Magnum* engraving itself, this title-page also emphasizes the duality of light and darkness that was a recurrent theme of the Rosicrucians. The obelisk to the left is founded in 'that which is below', while the one to the right is founded in that which, although represented by solid earth, is, 'as it were superior'.

Perhaps it is not surprising that the last line of the descriptive subtitle (*E MILLIBUS VIX UNI*) indicates that the text – like so much arcane Rosicrucian material – is intended for scarcely one in a thousand!

I have another reason, beyond studying this example of the 33-letter coding in the title, for introducing this extraordinary book as an important Rosicrucian work. One distinctive plate in this work has been called 'The Cosmic Rose', and with very good reason.[16] This plate illustrates an exquisite use of numerologies to express hermeneutic truths.

The engraving shows a circle bounded by the ten petals of a rose (the *Ros* of the word, Rosicrucian). Half the petals are in light, and half in darkness. The outer petals are inscribed with the Ten Commandments (in Hebrew). An inner concentric of ten clouds is interspersed with the ten names of the Hebraic Cabbalistic Sephiroth, emblazoned in the branches of the sacred Tree.

In the centre is a blazing circle, which contains ten of the Divine Names of God, and incorporates the image of a burning phoenix. This is the Bird of Resurrection, which is sometimes called the *Hermes Bird*, and sometimes the *Azoth*. The notion of resurrection is well expressed in the tradition that the bird lives for a period of 500 years before immolating itself, and being self-reborn from its own ashes. This is a popular myth of Reincarnation, and there was a time in the history of mankind when the period of 500 years did accord fairly accurately with the periodicity between lifetimes.[17] This wondrous bird had many names, but it is the name *Azoth* that attracts us here. The conjunction of A and Z, at the beginning of this word *Azoth*, suggests a parallel to the *alpha* and *omega*, of which we have seen much of late. Like the *alpha* and *omega*, the A and the Z measure an entire alphabet, and may be regarded as measures of Time itself.

In fact, this mysterious word seems to be a play on the *beginning* and *end*, in the major languages of the West that deal in esoteric verities. The A is communally the first letter of the Greek, Roman and Hebrew alphabets. The Z is the last letter of the Roman alphabet: the Ω (an equivalent of the Roman O) is the last letter of the Greek alphabet, and the TH, or *tau* [ת], is the last letter of the Hebrew.

Furthermore, the Hebraic terminal plural, **oth**, suggests the idea that this measure of time recurs many times. It is a perfect construct to use of the secret Resurrectional Bird, the secret *Bird of Hermes*.

The petal-surrounded plate is to be understood in terms of the old notion that God is here and everywhere — He is, so to speak, a circle whose centre is at the periphery. The periphery is to be seen as continually contracting inwards to the centre, and then expanding outwards to the periphery.

What is of profound importance for our own study is that this philosophical idea is superbly represented in terms of the 33-code, which is central to Rosicrucian symbolism.

Between the petals of the rose and the clouds is the New Commandment, in Latin.

DILIGES DOMINUM DEUM TUUM EX TOTO CORDE TUO
ET EX TOTA ANIMA TUA ET EX OMNIBUS VIRIBUS
TUIS ET EX OMNI MENTE TUA ET PROXIMUM TUUM
SICUT TEIPSUM

(Thou shalt love the Lord thy God, with all thy heart, and with all
thy Soul, and with all thy strength, and with all thy Mind, and thy
Neighbour as thy Self.)

So accustomed have we become to finding spiritual ideas expressed in
terms of 33 that we might be disappointed by the numerology of this New
Commandment. The Latin text consists of 28 words. Fortunately, we shall
not be disappointed for long: the significance of this number will become
clear, shortly.

Inside the clouds we see the heart of the rose, a five-pointed flaming star
(below).

At the centre of the Cosmic Rose is an image of the risen Christ,
hovering in His Resurrectional form above a flaming phoenix. Christ is
surrounded by a pentad of words, which read, in clockwise direction:

Verè filius DEI ERAT IPSE
(In truth he was Himself the Son of God).

This pentad of words is reinforced with a corresponding pentad of Hebrew letters within the flames. These spell out the name of Jesus, as *Jeshua*:

I   E   SH   U   A

This word, both Christ-like and human, represents the central point of incarnation into matter – the clothing of spirit in the five-fold materiality of the physical world.[18] This is the mystic centre of descent into matter.

The numerological symbolism of the Cosmic Rose now becomes clear. The outer periphery (expressed in the New Commandment of 28 words) descends like dew into the centre, where it merges hermeneutically with the 5 words of the incarnate Christ. By means of this descent, the two make a total of 33 words.[19] It is in this – or in some related Christian Mystery of the descent of spirit into matter – that the true Rosicrucian secrets may be found. It is the same with the meaning of Khunrath's title. The *Amphitheatre* of the title is the great circle of spirit, while the *Sole True Wisdom* is Christ, who descended from outer realms of the spiritual realm, and contracted into matter, to redeem the world.[20] Those symbolists who claim that the number 33 relates to Christ are not far from the truth. As Khunrath's extraordinary plate intimates, the number 33 represents the earthly Christ – the Christ who has united himself with the Earth, until the end of time.

The central fire of the flaming circle around the figure of Christ suggests that the flames are already leaping back to the periphery whence they came. On a more esoteric level, the three-fold tongues, which punctuate the clouds beyond, are not flames, but the celestial water – the mystical dew of the Rosicrucians. This is the *ros* (Latin for 'dew'), which returns to the *ros* (also Latin for 'Rose') at the outer periphery of this magic circle of being.

Between the clouds and the petals are the 22 letters of the Hebrew alphabet, the language of holy writ. It is this number which explains the curious structure of the innermost phrase:

Verè filius DEI ERAT IPSE

A casual examination of the phrase reveals that the initials of the last three words spell out DEI, the Latin meaning, 'of God'.

Verè filius **DEI ERAT IPSE**

This would mean that the phrase *filius DEI* was intended to encapsulate, as one of its hidden meanings, the notion of the 'Son of God', and all the promise this phrase contains.[21] However, while there may be no doubt that this is one of the levels of arcane meaning in the phrase, there is a much more profound one, more deeply hidden.

The phrase *Verè* filius DEI ERAT IPSE consists of 11 capital letters (the initial *V* of *Vere* is an italic and is not counted). When the **22** letters at the periphery meet with the **11** at the centre, they combine to make the magical **33**. This 33 is the pulse of incarnation and excarnation, the in-breathing and out-breathing, of the Cosmos, and of Man. This is the true secret of the flaming rose, which so dominated the symbolism of the seventeenth-century.

The examples of the 33 encoding in Rosicrucian and related alchemical documents are virtually endless. In many cases, the encoding is intended to point to the Ego, with its direct associations to Christ. Even those documents that seem to have originated in the pre-Christian era, were later subjected to amendments to introduce concepts pertaining to the newly-developed Ego, Christology and numerical encodings. At other times – especially in Rosicrucian contexts – the encoding was used to point to the importance of Light, both in a literal solar sense and also in a metaphorical sense. A delightful example of this may be seen in a detail from a formal portrait of the English esotericist, Robert Fludd (below, left).[22]

As may be seen from the enlarged detail (previous page) the contrast of light and dark is found in the pleats of Fludd's ruff. Three of these pleats are in darkness, whilst 33 are in the light. In view of this portrait numerology, we may scarcely be surprised that Fludd's monument, in the Church of the Holy Cross, Bearsted (below), is also replete with the 33-letter coding.

This code may be seen not only in the Latin epitaph, but also in certain details of the statuary. For example, the first line of the lapidary (after the introductory SACRUM MEMORIÆ) runs:

CLARISS DOCTISSQz VIRI ROBERTI FLUDD

This is very neatly encoded, for the count must include the two letters of abbreviated Q[UE], the presence of which is hinted at in the lower case z, to reveal the 33 letters.

CLARISS DOCTISSQ[UE] VIRI ROBERTI FLUDD

Almost with a touch of funereal humour, the second line also gives 33 letters when the similar abbreviation is counted, though (as is often the case with monumental encodings) the dipthong Æ must be counted as one letter:

ALIAS DE FLUCTIBUS UTRIUSQz MEDICINÆ

On the statuary itself, there are 32 visible buttons. There are two sets of 7, on each upper arm, two sets of 5 on the sleeves, and 8 on the front of the doublet. To these last, however, we must add an additional one that must, of necessity, invisibly complete the buttoning, beneath the ruff. The book in which Fludd is writing also hides the number 33, for beneath his left hand (which turns the page) are two sets of 3 pages, unaccountably separated. The 3 and 3 are clearly intended to suggest the sacred 33.

The alchemical document known as the *Tabula Smaragdina*, or *Emerald Tablet*, which seems to have formed the basis of much hermetic philosophy and discussion, is supposed to have seven levels of meaning attached to it, each opened by one of seven separate keys.[23] This may not have been a seminal alchemical text, but it has been treated as such by many later historians. It actually opens with a reference to what can only be the *Monad*, the *One only thing*. On one level, the *One thing* (which is 'the thing of One') in the *Tabula* is Man. Within the hermeneutics of this literature, Man is one of the names given to the manifestation of the *Ego*. Thus, in this alchemical stream of thought, the *Ego* is this *One thing*, and is itself the Mysterium.

Of this *One only thing*, the *Tabula* says:

The Father of that one only thing is Man. Its Mother is the Moon. The Wind carries it in his bosom, and its nurse is the Spirituous Earth.

On the principal that, on one level of this septenary of interpretations, the *one only thing* is the Ego, we might care to take a look at what later alchemists of the Renaissance period made of this symbolism. The seventeenth-century alchemist, Michael Maier, had obviously been struck by the wisdom of the *Tabula Smaragdina*, for he introduced texts from it into his alchemical work, *Atalanta fugiens*.[24] Maier emphasized the One, rightly linked with the Ego, by treating of it in Emblem One of this book.

This work is itself curious, in that it represents the first attempt to present esoteric knowledge on three levels, corresponding to three levels in the being of Man. In his preface to the work, Maier writes of the structure of his book,

> We have joined optics to music, and the sense to intellect — that is, rarities of the sight and hearing and alchemical emblems that are proper to this science.

With each Emblem there is an arcanely wrought engraving (the Emblem), an Epigram, or verse in Latin verse, and a fugue, or *Fuga*, intended to be sung to music provided within the text.

The first engraving in the series of 50 (below), depicts the *One* in the form of a foetus, hidden in the womb of the North Wind, *Boreas*.

The exhortation in the epigram is that one should encourage this embryo to be born beneath the influence of good stars (*bono sydere sed genitus*). If we are correct in identifying this *One Thing* with the Ego, then we may read this exhortation as an instruction to ensure that only influences of good quality surround the birth and growth of the Ego: the true moulding force of the Ego is by means of morality.

Given the context of this alchemical work, and given Maier's evident interest in the Rosicrucian movement, we might be inclined to inquire whether this first attempt to deal with the Ego, in Maier's 'triple' book, is in any way linked with the number 33? With this question in mind, let us first consider the double- page spread of the first edition of this work. This opens with the music for the *Fuga*, which contains the Latin text set to verse, and, below, a translation into German of the Latin Epigram. On the opposite page (see also figure 6) is the Emblem or engraved picture, and the *Epigramma*, or Latin verse, relating to what Maier calls *The Secret of Nature*.

If we count the number of lines on both pages (above), combining the notes for voices (set alongside the musical notation) with the Latin and German texts, we shall find that there are 33 lines altogether.[25]

If, with the same purpose of revealing further examples of the 33 encoding, we attempt to analyse the first line of the *Epigramma*, we must first be prepared to discount the large intended capital E, which drops over two lines, and disqualifies itself for such a count. We must, in the spirit of this encoding, count the dipthong Æ as a single letter. Given those logical restrictions, we find that the first line has a count of 33 letters (figure 6).

[E] Mbryo ventosâ BOREÆ qui clauditur alvo,

We may feel inclined to submit the entire right-hand page, which contains the engraving (*Emblema*) and the *Epigramma*, to a similar letter-count. As we might expect, if we count the number of capital letters (rejecting the two numerals and the one dipthong, which is not a single letter) within the headings and text, we find that the page contains 33 such capitals.

EMBLEMA I. De secretiis Natura.   9
Portavit eum ventus in ventre suo.   1

EPIGRAMMA I.	9		
EMbryo ventosâ BOREÆ qui clauditur alvo,	6		
Vivus in hanc lucem si semel ortus erit;	1		
Unus in Heroum cunctos superare labores	2		
Arte, manu, forti corpore, mente, potest.	1		
Ne tibi sit Cæso, nec abortus inutilis ille,	2		
Non Agrippa, bono sydere sed genitus.	2	=	33

Such texts and numerologies are so insistent in this use of the 33 encoding that we are, finally, compelled to accept that it carries several accretions of meaning. The 33 is the number of Christ and of the Ego, for sure, but it is also an adopted signal that the text in which it occurs is either Rosicrucian or seriously hermetic. Already, the reader will have observed that the proper use and recognition of the 33 generally demands a creative leap. The expert in this numerology rarely sets down a naked and explicit 33: rather he hints at certain rules by which the passage or the letters must be adjusted slightly (and usually in accordance with specific rules) in order for the hidden numerology to announce itself. This alone is a sign of Rosicrucian belief, for it was widely held by the adepts or Philosophers that all seeing and all understanding demanded creative activity, of which true thinking was the highest activity.

Chapter 4

The Sacred *Monas* of John Dee

*Nondum nostrae MONADIS esse exhausta Mysteria, facilè liquebit. Si
secretiora quedam ARTIS SANCTAE Vasa (omnino Cabalistica illa quidem)
Solis Initiatis Revelanda; ex iusdem MONADIS officina cautè desumpta,
Vestrae Serenitatis Regiae, nunc exhibuerim spectanda.*[1]

*It will easily be made clear that the Mysteries of our Monas are not yet
exhausted, if I now reveal to the sight of your Royal Serenity certain greater
mysteries selected warily from the vessels of the sacred art in the laboratories
of the Monas – these are indeed entirely cabalistic and such as may be
revealed only to Initiates.*

[Address by John Dee to the Roman Emperor, Maximilian II, King of
Hungary and Bohemia, at the beginning of Theorem XXII in his *Monas
Hieroglyphica*, (1564), p. 22.][2]

Carved on the interior walls of the magnificent cathedral of Santiago de
Compostela, which has served for many centuries as a focus for pilgrim-
age, is a lapidary bearing a number of hermetic symbols. This must have
had considerable importance to the cathedral builders, for the same
design is repeated on the same interior walls.

The original lapidary I photographed is difficult to read (opposite). The five symbols are partly obscured by a double candle-holder, and the lapidary surface badly stained by wax, so it may be as well for us to contemplate this symbolism in a drawing, from which these deficiencies have been removed (below).

The device consists of an equal-armed Cross, within the four spaces of which are arranged four other symbols. To the left of the top register, is a crescent moon. To the right, is a radiant sun. Within a Christian context, these recall the sun and moon that the artists of the medieval period so frequently portrayed above the Cross at Golgotha — perhaps in reference to the eclipse which was believed to have occurred at the time of the Crucifixion.

In the bottom register, hanging from a short rope, which is attached to the arm of the Cross, is a capital A that represents the first letter of the Greek alphabet, the *alpha*.[3] Alongside, also hanging from an armature, is the last letter of the Greek alphabet, the *omega*. Reduced to their bare essentials, the five symbols make up the following figure:

This may be reduced to the following five-fold schema:

MOON	SUN
CROSS	
ALPHA	OMEGA

The construction of the cathedral of Santiago de Compostela was extended over a period of centuries, stretching from the eleventh to the eighteenth century. However, there is no reason to doubt that the grouping of the five symbols we are discussing here belongs to the earliest phase of construction up to 1128, when the nave was completed. Even if these carvings were added later, at the time when the magnificent Portico de la Gloria was added, they would still date back to the twelfth century.[4]

The symbol brings together, into the four protective spaces of the Cross, two important strains of Christian thought that are relevant to our own inquiry.

The symbols on the top register, the sun and moon, are relics of the early Christian symbolism designed to reveal that the deed of Christ was of a cosmic dimension. The notion that there had been an eclipse at the moment of Christ's death seems not to have been founded in any cosmological reality: even so, it did have a certain symbolic significance. As the art historian, Gertrud Schiller, points out, the main function of such cosmological symbolism was to show that Christ's victory embraced the world as a whole.[5]

Symbols of the sun and moon, or of personifications of these cosmic bodies, linked with the Crucifixion, have been traced to artwork of the third century, and are embodied in thousands of Christian works of art. Arcanists have offered a wide range of explanations for this lunar-solar symbolism, one of the more interesting relating to the destiny of the Earth itself. When linked with the notion (imaginative or otherwise) of an eclipse, we recognize that *two becomes three*: without the earth an eclipse could not take place. In an eclipse, solar or lunar, the three cosmic bodies of sun, moon and earth form, however briefly, a relationship described three-dimensionally by a straight line.

Within the Crucifixion imagery, the location of the Cross must be linked directly with this cosmic image of the earth: it thus proclaims the esoteric truth that Christ died to renew the waning vitality of the Earth itself, and that His death and resurrection were somehow linked with the future of the sun and moon. The details of such esoteric speculation need not detain us here: it is sufficient that we see how an apparently simple arrangement of symbols may point to the deepest levels of esoteric lore. This upper register of the Cross was clearly intended to reflect upon the cosmic relation that Christ held to the earth, in His role as a spiritual Saviour in cosmic space.

The lower register of the Cross, with its two pendant Greek letters, points to the role of Christ in the stream of time. This symbolism is even older than that of the sun and moon, for it is derived mainly from the biblical *Revelation*, which surely dates to the first century of our era. In effect, the *alpha* and the *omega*, within Christian symbolism, refer to the words of Christ, set out in *Revelation*. Here, Christ discusses the two words to reveal his own role, in the sequence of time, or duration:

I am Alpha and Omega, the beginning and the end, the first and the Last.[6]

The words are pregnant with many meanings, for Christ was proclaiming himself the whole of the Word. This Word was conveniently symbolized by all the letters of the alphabet between the first (alpha) and the last (omega). Christ, it is maintained, encompassed all written and spoken words, and proclaimed himself the Lord of Time itself, the master of the beginning and ending of time. To some extent, this association with duration or time is carried over from an earlier reference to the *alpha* and *omega* in the first chapter of *Revelation*.

I am Alpha and Omega, the beginning and the ending, saith the Lord, which is, and which was, and which is to come, the Almighty.[7]

These, the words of God Almighty, help to cement the explicit relationship between God and Christ, as set out in the latter reference in *Revelation*, to the two Greek letters.

However we feel inclined to explain these symbols within Santiago de Compostela, we may have no doubt that their ancient forms, though originally designed for pagan use, were thoroughly Christianized by the twelfth century. Further, we may not doubt that they express certain ideas relating to cosmological truths and to the nature of Time itself.

The five symbols, of the one Cross, the sun and moon, and the two letters of the Greek alphabet, form a composite whole. The upper half of the Cross is associated with the higher realms of the cosmos, with what we may call the eternal or spiritual realm. The lower half is associated with the overt symbolism of human thought — that is with words, and with what may be expressed through words. Words may be uttered only in duration or time, which means that, on the level of speculation with which we are involved, the two letters of the Greek alphabet mystically portray the sequence of time — the mystic beginning and the ending within which all humans dwell.

Thus, the Cross expresses the truth that Christ arose from cosmic and eternal realms, and governed over the lower time-bound world.

Give the majestic esotericism behind these five symbols, thus combined, we should not be surprised that one of the most learned men of the sixteenth century should have constructed a proclamation of arcane truths from precisely these five symbols. In 1564, John Dee published his *Monas Hieroglyphica*, which consisted of 24 theorems constructed around a sigil, or symbol, devised by Dee and called by him the *Monas*.

The *Monas* consisted of a union of four symbols — the cross, the sun, the moon, and the *omega*. On the face of it, this treatment seems to ignore the primal letter, the *alpha*. However, in the analyticial text of this work, Dee introduced the fifth symbol, the *alpha,* which he ingeniously derived from the structure of his Monas. Not surprisingly, Dee's *Monas Hieroglyphica* offers a link between the ancient multi-layered symbolism of medieval Christology, and the esoteric lore that was to be developed in the sixteenth and seventeenth centuries.

I personally find it almost impossible to think of John Dee in isolation. His spirit — if not his life and work — was certainly bound up with that of his French contemporary, Michel Nostradamus. Dee, the confidant of Queen Elizabeth, was younger than the French prophet, who was the confidant of the French Queen, Catherine de' Medici, by twenty-four years. If only from the point of view of the development of esoteric history, both these men were immensely influential in their own time, and their reputations as scholars and astrologers have persisted to this day. There is no indication that they ever met, yet they did have one remarkable secret in common. They each had an identical zodiacal degree operative in their horoscopes. The Mercury of Dee's chart was in precisely the same degree as the Jupiter in Nostradamus' chart: both were in 11 degrees of Cancer.[8]

It is possible that only someone proficient in astrology will immediately grasp the significance of such a relationship. It is not generally recognized, in modern times, how insistently destiny manifests through such communalities as zodiacal degrees. The one thing these two remarkable men had in common seems to reflect the imaginative nature of Cancer, for both were deeply interested in sophisticated encodings and in the prediction of

the future. We shall turn to one or two of the many codes established by
Nostradamus in due course. Meanwhile, we shall examine one
particularly sophisticated encoding that John Dee constructed around a
sigil, or symbol, which he called the *Monas*. In following the implications
behind Dee's *Monas*, we are led into one of the most closely guarded
secrets of history.

Educated in mathematics at Cambridge, John Dee was a polymath,
with a deep interest in astrology, cartography and symbolism. Destiny
brought him close to Queen Elizabeth, whom he taught and advised on
esoteric matters, and, by virtue of his interest in cartography, advised
her on various questions relating to the dominions and far-flung
possessions of England. Dee was a highly unconventional figure, who
gained for himself a somewhat dubious reputation as a magician. He
established, for his own use, a complex spiritual machinery, designed to
grant him intelligent access to what he called angels, but which might
have been spirits of a rather different designation (below).[9] We have
already noted the connection between the portrait of Dee and the 33
encoding (see page 22).

D'. Dee *avoucheth his Stone is brought by Angelicall Ministry.*

Dee balanced his academic interest in a wide range of subjects with the
imperatives of his private search for esoteric knowledge: he wrote a
number of works, some merely academic, but others deeply imbued with
a mystical approach to knowledge. Our present interest lies only in his
achievements as an arcanist, set out in his *Monas Hieroglyphica* of 1564.
This is an esoteric work which, quite typically of such works, deals with a
variety of arcane subjects, ranging from mathematics and philosophy to

Christology. The text purports to be an analysis of what Dee called the *Monas* – a hieroglyphic figure of his own invention. To remind readers of the structure of this figure, I reproduce it once more, from the text of the *Monas.*[10]

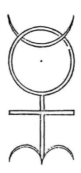

Viewed in its most simple aspect, the sigil consists of a union and adaptation of four sigils that were well known to all sixteenth-century astrologers, and which are still used in modern astrology. We may trace in it the encircled dot ☉ that stands for the Sun, the crescent ☾ that represents the Moon, a form that resembles the sigil for Aries ♈, and a four-armed cross +, which Dee associated mainly with the four elements – each armature representing one of the traditional elements of Fire, Air, Earth and Water.

Dee's analysis of this sigil is set out in 24 theorems. These start with propositions indicating how the central dot in the figure is the basis of the figure as a whole, and leading on to abstract semi-geometric speculations on the nature of time and space. As one might imagine of a man with such a deep interest in esoteric matters, it is not an easy book to understand – especially as Dee incorporated many encoded references into its text. Some modern scholars are of the opinion that the *Monas Hieroglyphica* is a book on alchemy, but this is certainly not the case. In a sense, the work is fed and enlivened more by Dee's astrological interest than by the alchemy that was undoubtedly one of his interests. If we are to take his claims about this *Monas* seriously, then we must accept that Dee believed that its relationships of graphic forms contained all esoteric knowledge. Among the more recondite material with which Dee dealt in this book, is the nature of the Ego, which, as we have seen, entered an interesting phase of development during Dee's own lifetime.

The *Monas Hieroglyphica* is one of the most tantalizing esoteric works to have come from sixteenth-century England. The work consists of a series of analyses of various symbols, or sigillic constructs, which Dee had devised to express spiritual verities. Among these verities are reflections on the nature of Man and the Cosmos. It emerges from the work that, in the eyes of Dee at least, the spiritual nature of Man is symbolized in the *Monas*. The *Monas* (sometimes, *monad*) is the *One*, the *Ego*, and it is quite possible to see this book as the earliest treatise on the Ego. This may explain why some modern scholars have confused the *Monas Hieroglyphica* as being an alchemical work.

We do not look to the Latin language (in which the *Monas Hieroglyphica* was written) but to the Greek for an understanding of the word *Monas*. The word actually means 'solitary', and was used in a substantive sense as meaning 'a unit', 'a single one'. The more we contemplate Dee's remarkable book, the more we realize that it is a treatise on consciousness, and that the *Monas* of which he writes is the Ego — that solitary entity in the human soul, which looks out from the centre into the periphery of the myriad things, the created world. It is surely no accident that the first diagram in the book is one that portrays how everything in the created realm began with a point, which is symbolic of the true *Monas*.

THEOREMA II.

A T nec fine Recta, Circulus; nec fine Puncto, Recta artificiofe fieri poteft. Puncti proinde, Monadisque ratione, Res, & effe cœperût primò: Et quæ peripheria funt affectæ, (quantæcûque fuerint) Centralis Puncti ._____ ⊖
nullo modo carere poffunt Minifterio.

But the circle cannot be artificially produced without either the straight line or the point. It follows that things first came into being from the point and from a Monad. And (it follows further) that those things linked with the periphery — no matter how large these might be — cannot exist without the help of the central point.

Dee's theorem seems to rest upon the notion that the *Monas* is central to all things: as the related diagram records, from the point proceeds the line, and the line moved upon the point produces the circle. This analogy may be extended into life, for all created things begin as a point, whether as an idea, piercing from the spiritual levels into the realm of matter, or as an organism, born into the material world from the embryonic seed.

Below, is a page from Dee's work, in which the geometric construct of the *Monas*, with each of its forms proceeding from a point (five points in all, for the *Monas* itself has five letters), is writ large. Here, Dee has marked it with letters of the alphabet, to help with the exposition in his text.

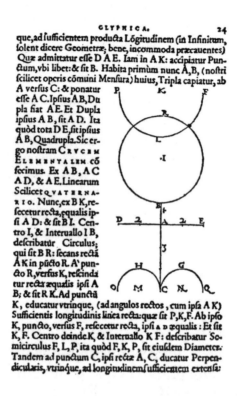

One thing about this *Monas* diagram, which concerns us here, is that it was intended to depict the Ego in the human being. The Ego itself may be sexless, but it manifests through the differentiated masculine and feminine. In Dee's diagram, the masculine is represented as the Sun sigil, whilst the feminine is represented by the crescent of the Moon. In such a way, the Ego is portrayed as a meeting of the two sexual impulses.

The circle contains a dot — this alerts us to the fact that the unit represents the *solar* force in Man — which is to say, that part of the male human being directly in contact with the solar Christ.

The half-circle, which Dee himself links (among other things) with the Moon, represents what we might call spiritual antennae, reaching up into the higher realm: this symbolizes the feminine aspect of the original, archetypal Man. The central dot by which this crescent has been formed may be invisible here, yet its presence is determined by Theorem 2 in Dee's sequence. The two curved armatures seem to be reaching upwards, in search of spiritual sustenance and contact with what the alchemists called the Soul of the World, the *Anima Mundi*.

Dee offered several graphic analyses of the structure of his *Monas*, of which the following is probably the most simple.

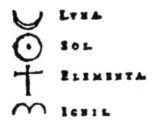

As we have seen already, the two uppermost symbols represent the solar and lunar (male and female) aspects. The two lower symbols, which are the cross and a form similar to the inverted Greek *omega* (ω) represent the Elements and Fire (IGNIS) respectively.[11] The Fire element is not at first apparent in this link that Dee has drawn with the *omega*, but we later learn that this **ω** is for Dee the equivalent of the zodiacal sigil for Aries, which is drawn ♈.

Secret schools are precisely that: they are secret. This is perhaps one reason why it has proved so difficult for scholars to prove that there is a connection between John Dee and early Rosicrucianism – a movement that was intensely secret in its activities and in its teachings. However, one real advantage of esoteric schools is that they generally leave some vestigial sign of their passing through civilization, to revitalize it. There may be no surviving documentation that enables us to draw a connection between Dee and the Rosicrucian school that was, already in his day, laying down the foundations for their work in the following century. However, the undeniable fact is that the *Monas* sigil has found its way into a huge number of Rosicrucian works of the seventeenth and eighteenth centuries – to a point, indeed, where it seems to be the secret sign used communally by Rosicrucians who have ventured to reveal themselves openly.[12]

The *Monas* symbol is unique, if only because it represents mankind and includes a diagram of the Ego. This interpretation is readily visible to those trained in esoteric matters. However, we may seek the *Monas* symbol itself in vain for any reference to that give-away number 33. Even when divested of its alphabetical notations (below) the *Monas* does not give up its numerological secret easily.

There is no way that one may deconstruct the *Monas* in order to reveal that it hangs upon a substructure of this numerology. In spite of this, Dee's references to the all-important 33 in his book on the *Monas* are not so well hidden that we cannot see them for ourselves. If you examine the lines of Latin text on the full page reproduced on page 94, and in figures 7 and 8, you will find that there are exactly 33 lines on the page. Furthermore, every one of the pages in Dee's *Monas Hieroglyphica* is designed to contain precisely 33 lines.[13] Dee has gone to great lengths to preserve this 33: as you will see in figure 8, the page is broken by a large image of the *Monas* itself, numbered and alphabeticized for analysis.[14] A count of these numbers and letters reveal that there are 21 altogether — exactly the number of lines occupied by the diagram. Dee is ensuring that both the lines of the text, and the numeration of the *Monas,* conforms to the overall number 33.

In the introductory Latin quotation, which heads the present chapter, I have given another example of this encoding, for Dee's Latin sentence, written for the attention of the Roman Emperor, Maximilian II, consists of 33 words.

As though to promulgate this 33 theme, Dee has ensured that the first line of the first theorem in his book (opposite page, top) should consist of 33 letters (one must, of course, in the manner of these encodings, discount the indented capital **P**, which stretched over the four lines.)

A further example from Dee's book is given in figure 7, which represents page 23 from the *Monas*. This not only reveals something of the nature of the languages in which this remarkable book has been written, but offers further examples of the 33 encoding.

Theorema I.

Er Lineam rectum, Circulúmque, Prima, Sim-
pliciffimáque fuit Rerum, tum, non exiftentiū,
tum in Naturæ latentium Inuolucris, in Lucem Productio, reprefentatioque.

On this page 23, we see, intermingled with the Latin, both Hebrew and
Greek. Here, Dee is in the final stages of dealing with the magical nature of
the two letters, *alpha* and *omega* (α and ω), which we ourselves glanced at
earlier, on page 87. Dee has been attempting to reinvest these two letters
with their original mystagogic meanings. To this end, he issues propositions which, in effect, take him to the very limits of sixteenth-century
esoteric knowledge. He recognizes, in the lower two arcs of the *Monas*
symbol, the form of an inverted ω, the *omega*. Since the higher part of the
Monas is touching, or is immersed in the spiritual realm (as is required of
the solar-lunar Ego), this lower form, the *omega*, must be immersed in
time. Seemingly to emphasise the importance of this conclusion, he
centres the text on the page in a manner that proves to be almost a graphic
praise of archetypal Time:

ω, autem, O M N I V M eft HORARVM H o M o.
Πόρισμα.

However, the ω is a man of all hours.
Corollary.

Not only has Dee centred this strange and almost inexplicable conclusion,
to emphasize its importance within the theorem: he has also ensured that,
taken with the Greek sub-heading, the phrase encapsulates precisely 33
letters. However, what is of prime importance in this delicate hermeneutic
is that we are being invited by Dee to note a reversal of time — of the
universal time-span. The phrase opens with the *omega* (the future), and
closes with the *alpha* (the past). In this Latin sentence, Dee is reversing the
flow of time. Because we in the West generally read from left to right, we
have learned to anticipate futurity to the right. The direction → indicates
the flow of time. By opening his 33-word lines with the final *omega*, and
ending it with the *alpha*, Dee is inviting us to consider a reversal in the
temporal sequence.

Then, with extraordinary graphic cunning, Dee proceeds to reverse this reversed temporal sequence from **ω** to **a**. He carefully reverses the direction of time by his choice of words in the Latin text. He opens this Latin with the **a** of **autem**, and ends with the **O** of **HOMO**. To see why this is a reversal, we must bear in mind that the final Greek letter **ω** represents one of the **O** sounds in the European alphabet.

This operation with time only makes sense within the framework of Theorem XXII, of which these hermeneutics play an important role. Dee recognizes that he is on perilous ground in making this kind of knowledge available in his book. It is knowledge of a kind, he insists, that may be revealed only to initiates – *Solis Initiatis Revelanda,* as he puts it.

Here, we cannot plumb the depths of this knowledge of how the flow of time can change, or under what circumstances, for such considerations play little or no part in our present studies. However, it is interesting to observe that the Christ, who is so often depicted between the *alpha* and the *omega*, may be visualized here, pinned, as it were, on the vertical of the Cross that is central to this *Monas* symbol. The Cross stands vertically upright in the midst of the *omega* of time, with its special emphasis on futurity. The Ego, which is so intimately linked with Christ, hovers above the Cross, as though it were the halo of Christ himself. From a Christological standpoint, Dee is suggesting that the deed of Christ could somehow reverse time, or (perhaps) the depredations of time.

Before examining a translation of Dee's colophonic valediction, below, it is worth observing that a count reveals that there are 33 words in this passage.[15] This count naturally includes the Greek delta.

AMEN, DICIT
LITERA QVARTA,
Δ:

Cui, DEVs, *Voluntatem Ha-*
bilitatemque dedit, Diuinum
hoc Mysterium, æternis Sic con-
signare Literarum Monimen-
tis: Laboresq́, hosce Suos, pla-
cidissimè absoluere, Ianua-
rij 25: die eiusdem 13,
Inchoatos:

An. 1564. Antverpiæ.

The above passage translates,

AMEN, SAYS

THE FOURTH LETTER,

Δ:

> To whom GOD gave the Will and the Ability to thus record this Divine
> Mysterium in a Monument of Letters: and to absolve most peacefully
> these, his labours, on 25 January, [Labours] that he had begun on the
> 13th day of that month.

The 'fourth letter' is the *delta* of the Greek alphabet, usually written Δ, as in
the typography above: Dee often used this Greek equivalent of the letter **D**
to stand for his own name. Thus, in this context, it is Dee himself, the
Fourth Letter or *Letera Quarta*, who says *Amen* to the preceding labour, set
out in the *Monas Hieroglyphica*. Although the Δ may be equated with a
symbol for the Trinity, Dee at times refers to it as 'the triple fourth letter',
by which he probably means the *Tetractys*. This was the name of God, in
four Hebrew letters, arranged on four levels within a triangular form
(below). The numerology of this *Tetractys* was 72 – the most sacred of all
numbers.[16]

With his symbol-seeking mind, Dee reads into the letter-form proposed by
his own name all manner of hermeneutics. Being an esotericist, Dee sees
or intuits connections between all things.

Even the two dates that Dee offers in this section, and which most
scholars have taken as reference to the period on which he worked on the
Monas Hieroglyphica, have a hidden meaning that we may eventually come
to appreciate.

Hermeneutically, these dates in the Latin colophon refer to Dee's own
birth chart. On 25 January 1564, there was a conjunction of Saturn and
Jupiter. What was of direct importance to Dee is that, on this day, Saturn
was in 29 degrees of Cancer. It thus happened to be exactly upon the Sun
in his own birth chart.[17] It is evident that he was linking his own

undertaking, as author of the *Monas Hieroglyphica* with certain supportive cosmic factors.[18]

It is well beyond our scope to examine fully this seminal work by John Dee. However, something of the connection that the *Monas* itself holds with the Ego may be found on the very last page of the work, which concludes with what can only be called a colophonic farewell from Dee. This includes an arcane device, derived from the *Monas Hieroglyphica*, which plays upon the nature of the Ego.

Before we examine these two important elements, we should observe that the entire final page on which this colophonic valediction and the device are found, contains 33 words. This is the count of those words that are written wholly in capital letters. We must exclude those words cut directly on the wood, within the encircled motto of the device.[19]

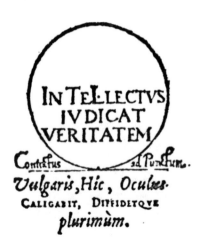

The three Latin words within the circle translate, *The Intellect judges Truth*. The three Latin words along the horizontal tangent to the circle translate, *Contracted to a point*. Below this horizontal, the six Latin words translate, *Here the eye of the vulgar will be blind and most distrustful*.

The first thing that strikes us about this colophonic device is that it resembles the form of the capital Greek *omega*: Ω. Whilst Dee has marked the tangential point with a *punctus*, indicating where the centre of the circle has itself contracted to a point, the capital letter contains a space. It is perhaps this notion, that the point transforms into a space, which Dee regards as being a truth hidden from the eyes of the vulgar. The fact is that the form he has represented above is closed (like the eyes of the vulgar). In contrast, the form of the *omega* has a small aperture, suggesting that the eye is open. These are the eyes of the knowledgeable man.

Either way, this graphic proposition serves as a most remarkable philosophical mechanism, touching upon the nature of point, line, circle and space. This aside, the Ω is a highly satisfactory device on which to end this book on graphic philosophy, for, as we have seen, the *omega* is the last letter of the Greek alphabet, which, in terms of Christian symbolism, marks the end of things.

On a much deeper level, the above device may be seen as representing a sophisticated play upon the secret underlying the *Monas Hieroglyphica* and its relation to the Ego. In the diagram, the circle retains its central point (which may be seen after the letter L). The centre and the circle combine to portray a seeing eye, with the circle the ball of that organ, and the point its pupil. It is this seeing eye with which Dee contrasts the vulgar eye (*Vulgaris Oculus*), which can see nothing, because it is blind and distrustful of higher truths. The point-centre is then conceived, within the device as having contracted to a point, bringing with it the circumference of the circle. This circumference is now reduced, or flattened, to a tangential diameter line, at the centre of which we may see the contracted point, extended on either side in space, to form a tangent. The device is a union of the three-fold diagram, of point, line and radius-circle that we earlier noted as being represented in the second theorem.

Thus, so far as Dee is concerned, we find in his beginning, or *alpha*, this same triad, which is his end, or *omega*.

The seeing eye represents the intellect which can judge the truth of things. It is, in a word, the Ego, which sees through the frame of the human body, and in so seeing embraces the entire world.

Arguably England's greatest poet, John Milton, was born within a few weeks of the death of John Dee, England's greatest esotericist.[20] Few knew more about the circle-bounded Ego, and the relationship this held to the Godhead than John Milton, and few knew more about the darkness of the outer world and the light that sparkles within the inner. It is therefore doubly pleasant to find the poet echoing the concept that had been so

deeply embraced by Dee, when he placed in the mouth of Adam, in
Paradise Lost, the words,

> Well hast thou taught the way that might direct
> Our knowledge, and the scale of Nature set
> From centre to circumference, whereon
> In contemplation of created things
> By steps we may ascend to God.

As we are presently interested in Elizabethan encodings, as much as in the
impact of the new Ego on the world, it will be as well for us to concentrate
on Theorem 22 in Dee's *Monas Hieroglyphica*. It was in this theorem,
expressed largely in esoteric terms, that Dee made his arcane position
clear, and came closest to dealing with the human Ego. Here, as we have
seen, Dee made it explicit that some of the things he had to say may only
be revealed to initiates and understood by initiates. To develop his thesis,
he re-constituted certain elements within the sigil, in order to reveal
aspects of their inherent forms as two letters of the Greek alphabet, *alpha*
and *omega*. The two new forms he derived he likened at one point to
alchemical vessels, at another point to fruit. To this transmuted alphabetical duad, Dee adds a third in the form of the *crux*, or cross, which is
central to the structure of the *Monas* sigil itself.

Of course, the extent to which the reconstituted *alpha* and *omega* (above)
resemble fruit is open to question: however, within the context we are
studying, it is sufficient that Dee claims this resemblance. Dee does not
attempt to justify the cross as a fruit, save by way of an arcane reference.
The cross, like the *alpha* and *omega* symbols, was 'most sweet and health-
giving' (*suavissimos & saluberrimos*). We should recall that it was the
sacrifice upon the Cross that redeemed the damage caused when Adam
and Eve ate the fruit in that other garden, in Eden. To help establish an
unexpected arcane connection between the fruit and the cross, Dee
explains that the *alpha* reconstruction makes use of a radius line — a
straight line which is analogous to the line in the cross. This straight line is
the tail-like appendage that appears to the left of the first symbol above
(the *alpha*): it is actually a tangent line. Thus, Dee makes some effort to

link graphically the curvilinear fruit of the *alpha* with the rectilinear fruit that is the cross.

In fact, the link, drawn here by Dee, between the fruit and the cross, is well established in Christian art. One is reminded of a number of prints and paintings in which the crucified Christ is depicted between a pair of fruit-growing trees, one of which is the Tree of Death, linked with Eve, the other a Tree of Life, linked with Mary. In a woodcut of *c.* 1470, now in the Museo Civico, Pavia, we see an image dominated by a crucified Christ, with numerous related symbols.[21] To the right, Eve grasps a human skull as she reaches for the fruit on the tree alongside her: this is the fruit of death. The artist has left no doubt of this, for the fruit on the tree are in the form of skulls. To the left, Mary holds up to her tree an image of her Son on the Cross: this is also the tree of death, but it is now redeemed by the Cross. It is interesting that Dee should announce a mythological and alchemical background to this ternary, rather than the Christian theme, which proves to be the most obvious.

Dee equates the *alpha* and *omega* with the fruit of the mythological gardens of the Hesperides. The fruit of the Hesperidean garden was nothing less than the secret treasure of the ancients, which the hero Hercules stole, after killing the dragon.[22] The myth was one of the constants of Elizabethan and Jacobean poetry. In his riotous play, *The Alchemist*, Ben Jonson included it in his long (and surprisingly learned) list of mythological associations with the sacred Stone, or *Lapis*, of the alchemists.

> I have a piece of Jason's fleece, too,
> Which was no other, than a book of alchemy...
> Such was Pythagoras' thigh, Pandora's tub;
> And, all that fable of Medea's charms...
> The dragon's teeth, mercury sublimate,
> That keeps the whiteness, hardness, and the biting;
> And they are gathered, into Jason's helm,
> (Th' alembic) and then sowed in Mars his field,
> Both this, th'Hesperian garden, Cadmus' story,
> Jove's shower, the boon of Midas, Argus' eyes,
> Boccace his Demogorgon, thousands more,
> All abstract riddles of our stone...[23]

In Dee's text, the triad of *alpha, omega* and *crux* are evidently likened to the three celebrated nymphs called The Hesperides (overleaf).[24] These

beautiful women were the guardians of the golden apples (the sweet-smelling fruit, of Dee) which Juno had given to Jupiter on the day of their marriage. The garden of the Hesperides abounded in delicious fruit, but the invaluable golden apples in particular were guarded by a fierce dragon, which had no need of sleep. Dee appears to be drawing over his three symbols a cloak of mythology which helps emphasize their great value and rarity.

With the above background, we should now be in a position to examine Dee's handling of Theorem 22, wherein he represented these three amended forms of *alpha, omega* and *crux*. In doing this, we shall recapitulate some of the insights gathered above, but within the context of Dee's own esoteric arguments. The first graphic operation or amendment Dee made was to disassemble the various parts of the *Monas*. His aim in doing so was to build from certain elements within the *Monas* two Greek letters – the *alpha* and the *omega*. The diagram below reveals this disconnection and reassembling, with two approximations to the two Greek letters joined by a dotted line, to the right.

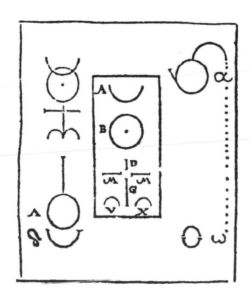

Before we attempt to understand this curious diagram, it is worth observing that Dee has ensured that it contains precisely 33 graphic and
alphabetical components.[25]

From the lunar crescent and the solar disk, Dee constructs what he calls
a certain artfully-made vessel (*Vas quoddam Artificiale*). To this diagram he
adds a short straight line that, he argues, represents their common radius
(*Semidiametro*):

The diagram might give the impression that it resembles a vessel, such as
one of the glass retorts one might find on the shelf of a medieval chymist:
however, I have never seen such a vessel, and cannot possibly imagine
what its use would be.[26] Having made the point that it is a vessel, or *vas*,
Dee remarks that it resembles the first letter of the Greek alphabet
(*Alphabeti Greci Prima*). However, in truth, any such resemblance is slight.
Dee then returns to the idea that it is a vase, or retort, implying furthermore that it is a glass one. The fact that this device does not resemble any
known alchemical retort should cause us pause for thought. If Dee had
really wanted to create from the Sun and Moon sigils an alchemical *vas*, or
retort, then he could have done so with much greater simplicity. For
example, a simple combination of the sigils would have given a form that
had no need for the invisible radius.

The form above certainly resembles far more closely the Greek *alpha* than
does the triple-design retort given by Dee. From this consideration, we are
led to the realization that Dee was not interested in making a retort that
resembled an *alpha*. He was more interested in creating a triple form that
had some connection with the *alpha*, yet preserved three elements, rather
than the two proper to the *alpha*. As in Christian symbolism, the *alpha*
marked the beginning of things, it is reasonable to assume that Dee
wanted his *Monas*-derived image to relate hermeneutically to the Trinity.
The circle would represent God: the letter C would represent Christ,

whilst the straight line that was supposedly invisible, yet which had been a radius of the circle, represented the Holy Spirit.

This proposal is not so far fetched as it may at first seem. Dee insists that his design is mystic (*Mysticum*). Further, he writes of it in a mysterious way: it is worth reproducing this short text in its original form, if only to show how elusive Dee's meanings can be. The main problem with offering a translation of the *Monas Hieroglyphica*, even in part, is that it is not possible to do this usefully without recourse to extensive commentary, in the form of notes. I have restricted the notes below to only the most essential. The bracketed letters in the translation refer to a key in the end-notes.

> Hoc tamen erit confiderandum, *a*, fui Muneris ob-
> eundi captare Occafionem, ex Secretifsimo breuifsimoque
> Spiraculi ᴀʀᴛɪꜰɪᴄɪᴏ : Et (·םרס נטית שש שמיד תהלה
> (·גומנ לעמט אהר *litroVinium* ןא] Tyronibus Oᴘᴇʀɪs
> expeditiffimum eliciet Primordiale Specimen : Interim dū
> Sᴠʙᴛɪʟɪᴏʀᴀ Præparandi, artificiofior illis innotefcat
> Via.

However, it will be worth bearing in mind that the *alpha* is waiting for an occasion to reveal its gifts by means of a most secret and rapid art of skilful inspiration [1]. { ... [2] ... } And to the aspirants in this work [3] the *alpha* will bring forth the original afflatus [4], until a more subtle method of preparation, by a more skilful route, becomes known to the aspirants.[27]

The general view of most commentators is that the theme of this enigmatic passage is alchemical. However, it is not, and there is no indication from the translations into other European languages, which I have examined, that any commentator has actually understood the passage sufficiently to translate it. If we do read it within a context of the Holy Trinity, then we may begin to understand the afflatus to which Dee has referred. The *alpha* – especially in its upper-case form, as A, with its distinctive triangular apex – was at that time linked with the primordial and eternal Trinity, and it is the Holy Spirit that is traditionally associated with inspiration. The text seems to aver that the original inspiration will continue to work through the *alpha*, or Trinity, until a more skilful means of inspiration becomes known. We seem here to be bordering on the religious issues that split Christendom in the sixteenth century, for they touch upon the role that the religious life holds in relationship to God. It was the Ego – or, more precisely, changes in the Ego – that were to help question and even destroy the traditional hierarchical mediations and ministrations of a priesthood, then held to be necessary to enable communication between humanity and God.

In contrast to the *alpha* figure, which is said by Dee to be made of glass, the figure constructed from the two lunar crescents at the foot of the *Monas* is, however, an earthenware vessel, seemingly an alchemical *cupanum*, with an arched top.

Of this, Dee writes:

> Lastly, the small vessel (*Vasculum*), which, as you see, has been marked ω, is most full of mysteries (*Mysteriorum Plenissimum*). It differs from the last letter of the Greek alphabet (restored now to its original mystagogic meaning) only by an obvious and slight changing of its parts, whilst both forms remain as two half-circles.

Dee leaves it to our own imagination to grasp that the *alpha* is reassembled from the images of Sun and Moon, whilst the *omega* is reassembled from the image of Fire – that is, from the fire associated with the sign Aries. In Christological terms, the beginning of things was linked with the Creation of the Sun and Moon, whilst the End of things is prophetically linked with destructive Fire. After further discussion (not to say mystification), Dee asks of his readers, in a mix of Greek and Latin:

Τῆς ἱϼᾶς Τέχνης, Quisiam non poteſt ſuboderari , ſuauiſsimos & ſaluberrimos Fructus:vel ex iſtarum(dico) duarum tantùm literarum enaſcentes Myſterio?

> From this holy Art, who can not detect the scent of the most sweet and healthy fruit that sprout from the mystery of those two letters alone?

Almost in passing, I should observe that in commencing this passage with three Greek words, and with an unnecessary capital Q, Dee has ensured that his line contains 33 lower-case letters. Similarly, the third and final line, when divested of the half-word carried over from the previous line, consists of 33 letters.

As we have seen, Dee is associating these two letters, derived from the *Monas*, with the treasured golden apples of the Hesperides. He is also hinting that the real fruit of both letters is the cross, which is central to the *Monas* figure, and which, besides being the cross of the four Elements, is also the Cross of Christ. The cross of the *Monas* grew upwards from the two curvatures of the lower symbol that represented the Fire sign, Aries. At the top, the Sun and Moon were supported by that same Cross. As was clear from the diagram above (page 104), the *alpha* and the *omega* are to be conceived as being separated by the Cross. Dee will return to this important point, shortly.

More openly, Dee tells us that by examining this fruit carefully — even with the aid of a magnifying glass — we shall see that the straight line drawn on the *alpha* is (besides being the invisible radius line) also one of the lines from the cross. The arcane implications are considerable, for Dee is now openly, rather than by implication, linking one of the standard symbols associated with Christ (the *alpha*) with the Cross upon which Christ died in preparation for Resurrection. In a word, the invisible (radius) line on the alpha-vase has become visible in the armature of the Cross. In this way, Dee has lifted the *Monas* from a consideration of a more or less pagan symbolism, linked with the planets, the zodiac and the Elements, to one that is suddenly intensely Christian.

Dee's question — as to who could not now detect the scent of the sweet and holy fruit behind the mystery of these two letters — has taken on a Christological meaning. We are now dealing with the *alpha* and *omega* of the Christ who died as a fruit upon the Cross to redeem the fruit that brought about the Fall of mankind. Dee's question may be rhetorical, for at this point he introduces a most intriguing diagram. In this, the two forms of the *alpha* and *omega* appear, alongside the cross, in a number of more or less Christological designations that reflect their symbolic nature. This, as we shall discover, does indeed offer fruits on the holy art.

As we contemplate these three derived figures, one thing emerges almost directly. The *alpha* was constructed around three different elements. The *omega* was constructed from only two, yet this *omega* itself represented in its shape a third element, which is the circle. Both the *alpha* and the *omega* contain a circle. Whether we see this as a reference to God or to the Ego depends very much upon one's point of view. Either way, there is a progression in time, for the *alpha* refers to what was, whilst the *omega* refers to what will be.

Evidently, the potential for meditative exploration of these symbols that Dee created is quite enormous. At this stage, however, I would like to move on to contemplate them in a different context, remaining within Theorem 22.

The text of the *Monas* is replete with secondary and tertiary meanings: for this reason, it is not surprising that scholars cannot agree about the precise meaning of certain passages. Dee himself tends to brush aside mere scholarship, making the point that the text can only be understood by one initiated into the Mysteries. That does indeed appear to be the case, for it is only with the aid of speculations rooted in a knowledge of the Mystery lore that one can make sense of the text. This seems to be especially true of Theorem 23 of his book, the text of which consists of the intermingling of Latin, Hebrew and Greek, designed to evoke the ideas of other authors than Dee himself. It is this theorem that contains what must surely be the most esoteric diagram to have been produced in England during the sixteenth century. Even though this diagram is likely to remain opaque without some sort of explanatory commentary, I reproduce it below.[28]

⊙ɑʊ	Exiſtens ante Elementa.	Adam Mortalis Maſculus & Fœmina.	Mortifi-cans	Adumbra-tus.	Natus in Stabulo.
✝	Elemētaris œconomia.	Elemētalis Genealogie Conſum-matio.	Crux.	Crux.	Holocau-ſtum in Cruce
ʒ	Exiſtens poſt Elementa.	ADAM IMMOR-TALIS.	Viuificans.	Manifeſtiſ-ſimus.	Rex Regum Vbique.
Conceptus Singularita-fluentia.	Potentiæ Semen.	Creatio Hyles.	Matrimo-nium Ter-reſtre.	Principium·	⊙ɑ
Paſſus & Se-pultus.	יהוה Virtus Denaria.	Deputatio Elemētalis.	Crucis Martyrii.	Medium.	✝
Reſurgens, propria vir-tute.	Gloriæ Triüphus.	Transfor-matio.	Matrimo-nium Diuinum.	Finis,	ʒ

The diagram is intended to be read as a single rectangle of twelve vertical sections, three registers high, opening with the three *Monas*-derived sigils and ending with the same sigils, in the manner of one of the then-popular *scalae*. The format of the book precludes such a long diagram: the diagram has been cut, and the three registers are presented as though they were six. However, if we contemplate the figure in the form that it appears on the page, we cannot help but observe that Dee has divided the figure not merely in order that he can fit it on the page, but also to incorporate a hermeneutic system. We note, for example, that the upper block, as printed, contains exactly 33 words. In this count, we must ignore the three opening sigils, because these are archetypes, and therefore not words.

If we count the words in the lower registers (that is, from the block, beginning **Conceptus**...) we find it contains only 30 words. It is this number that alerts us to the fact that Dee is requiring us to count the end blocks of three sigils *as now being the equivalent of words*, for us to arrive at the desired 33. This is, of course, an intrinsic part of the hermeneutics. The final blocks of sigils are no longer to be regarded as archetypes: they have become words, descended and materialized onto the material plane. Thus, whilst the numerology points to the Christian or Rosicrucian stream of arcane thought, the entire diagram is designed to point to the notion of the descent, from the Archetypal realm into the material realm, of the Word. As we shall discover, this notion is confirmed by the Christological theme set out within the blocks themselves. It is also confirmed numerologically in the fact that there are 36 blocks within the design, but, since three of these pertain to the archetype, only 33 are involved with the actual reading on the material plane. The whole numerology of this simple-seeming woodcut is steeped in the Christian number 33. Another example of this numerology may be seen in the letter count of the topmost lines of the five divisions:

Existens   Adam   Mortifi-   Adumbra-   Natus in

In particular, the word-hyphenations seem to have been peculiarly arranged purely in order to allow for a count of 33 letters.

If we wish to make an attempt to grasp the meanings within these 33 squares, we must translate some of the Latin words as best we can. The Latin itself is not particularly obscure, but the ideas expressed by the Latin prove to be extremely arcane and elusive. We shall discover that, for our purposes, we need not translate all the blocks: it will be sufficient to translate only half a dozen or so for Dee's hermeneutic plan to be revealed.

Existens ante Elementa — Existent before the Elements. This is partly a play on the form of the *alpha*, which Dee has introduced by deconstructing and reconstructing elements within the *Monas* itself, to make an approximation of this Greek letter. How he effected this reconstruction we shall see, shortly. As we have noted, the *alpha* is the beginning of things. So defined, it must have come before even the Elements, from which matter is supposed to have been made. When, in 1618, the alchemist, Daniel Mylius attempted to portray this pre-Elemental period, he did so by reference to *Genesis* 1:2, representing the Earth that was *inanis et vacua (without form, and void)* and *in Tenebris* (in darkness), within the representation.[29]

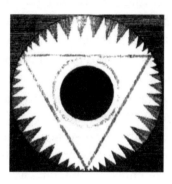

The Earth itself is in darkness, yet it is surrounded by the creative light of the Godhead.

Adam Mortalis Masculus & Fœmina — Adam mortal, Male and Female. This is a reference to the male-female androgyne created by God before the creation of Adam — see *Genesis* 1:27. Technically, Dee is wrong to use the name Adam here, as that name was not used in the Bible in reference to the male-female androgyne. In biblical terms, Adam was a separate creation — see *Genesis* 2:7. Dee mentions this Adam, in the line apportioned to the *omega*.

Mortificans. With some trepidation, I translate this as meaning **capable of death**: However, I suspect that Dee had in mind the idea of something that was **death-dealing**. The word *Mortificans* is clearly intended to contrast with *Vivificans,* on the third level below.

Adumbratus. Enveloped in darkness. Perhaps this is a reference to the stream of humanity that was formed by God from the dust of the ground. See *Genesis* 2:7.

Natus in Stabulo – Born in the stable. This is the first direct indication Dee has given that he is dealing, in this diagram, with Jesus Christ. The reference is to the birth of Jesus told in Luke's gospel: see *Luke*, 2:7.[30] This is Dee's first intimation that he is interested in dilating upon the two different births apportioned to the two Jesus children in the biblical accounts of Luke and Matthew.

The line of development set out in the horizontal lines apportioned to the *alpha* relate to the Jesus, whose birth was described by Luke as taking place in a stable. The line of development apportioned to *omega* relates to the Jesus whose birth was described by Matthew. This was the birth attended by the wise men from the East, who recognized Him as being the Christ, whom they must worship. The child, whose birth is described in *Matthew* 2:1 as taking place in Bethlehem in the days of Herod the king, is held to be the King of Kings. We thus have a humble birth in a stable, of a child worshipped by shepherds. We have also another birth – of a child destined to fulfil the prophecies – a child of the line of Solomon, born in Bethlehem, and worshipped by wise men.

The progression in the tabulation so far is almost cosmological. We have started at a point even before the creation of the Elements. We have reached a point at the beginning of humanity, when the androgyne male and female was created by God, before the creation of Adam. We have noted that this stream of humanity is subject to death and enveloped in darkness. We have reached one of the culminating points in the story of Redemption, for the first sequence of this cosmology ends with the birth of the Jesus of the Luke gospel in the dark and humble stable.

Now we have uncovered the basic hermeneutic pattern that lies hidden in this curious diagram, we need not translate all the 33 squares manifesting below the three archetypes. We have sufficient information to reveal the secret message that Dee has left in this diagram.

To understand fully the threefold structure of this diagram, we must recognize that the top register relates to the Luke Jesus (born in a stable). In contrast, the bottom register relates to the Matthew Jesus (who is born of the Solomonic kingly line) – this latter is the **Rex Regum Ubique** – 'everywhere the King of Kings'. The third register deals with the product, or union of these Jesus children, who is, of course, the Christ. As the various words and phrases in the register make clear, Christ is the consummation of the physical genealogy of Christ (**Elementalis Genealogie Consumatio**); his destiny is the cross (**Crux**). He is to be offered in holocaust on the Cross (**Holocaustum in Cruce**). He is the middle

(**Medium**) because he stands not only horizontally between the beginning (**Principium**) and the end (**Finis**) but also vertically between the two children, who served as the physical tool for his Incarnation. He is raised to martyrdom on the cross (**Crucis Martyrium**) because he was the product of the terrestrial and divine marriage (**Matrimonium Terrestre** and **Matrimonium Divinum** – which was not a marriage between man and woman, but between Jesus and the Christ.

From these 33 divisions, I would like to abstract those elements that point to one of Dee's more remarkable insights. Dee seems to have been aware of one of the esoteric traditions that was known to a number of leading scholars and artists then working in the full flood of the Italian Renaissance. This tradition was concerned with Dee's awareness of an ancient teaching that there were two Jesus children, who, between them, provided a suitable body for the incarnation of the Christ.[31] This incarnation of the Christ into the body of Jesus took place at the Baptism in the Jordan.

In essence, the tradition of the two children rested upon the undeniable fact that the two descriptions of the birth of Jesus, given in the Gospels of Luke and Matthew, clearly pertained not only to different circumstances but also to different times, and thus to different children. Internal evidence, from within the Bible, reveals that the child born in the stable could not have been the same child as was visited by the Magi. It is to this tradition that Dee's curiously structured 33 segments relate. Below, I will make an attempt to relate Dee's own words to the esoteric traditions graphically.

First, we might like to study the imagery relating to the birth in the stable (*Natus in Stabulo*), which Dee has associated with a spiritual marriage with the Earth (*Matrimonium Terrestre*). The imagery attached by Dee to the *alpha* (below) incorporates the sigil for the Sun, and therefore

permits a correspondence to be drawn between the Jesus born in a humble stable, who is none the less portrayed as a radiant solar being.

The woodcut is from a fifteenth-century work by Franciscus de Retza.[32] The child is shown in a stable, lying on the earth, covered in a radiant aureole of light, and attended by the ox and ass. As we have seen, this stable-birth is described in Luke's Gospel.

The martyrdom on the Cross, and the *Holocaustum* described by Dee is the mid-point of Creation, just as it is the middle register of his own diagram. The agony of this moment will shortly give way to the Resurrection, which is the central message of Christianity, and, incidentally, of the destiny of the Ego.[33] As Dee says, this martyrdom on the Cross is midway (*Medium*) between the beginning (the *Principium* of *alpha*) and the end (the *Finis* of *omega*), which is a Glory and Transformation. The shadowy darkness of the *alpha* period (*Adumbratus*), during which Christ seemed dead and buried, will give rise to the greatest manifestation (*Manifestissimus*), which is the Resurrection of the *omega* period.

The *omega* period relates to the birth of the child, whose genealogy is traced to King Solomon, described by Matthew. This is why, within the framework of the story of the two children, the *omega* relates to the future. The Christ, incarnate into this royal line, will become, 'everywhere', the King of Kings (*Rex Regum Ubique*). The drawing, left, depicts the coming of the Magi to the Solomon Jesus, as described in Matthew's Gospel.[34] Mary and Joseph are depicted outside a rather splendid house, over which hovers the eight-rayed star. The Kings, or Magi, are shown in continuous representation — first, following the star, and then worshipping Jesus.

In their account of the blood-line of Jesus, the two biblical accounts of the birth of Jesus agree about one section only. This is in the list of thirteen generations that follow Abraham, and end in David. However, at this Davidic point the two lists diverge radically. Matthew describes a line of descent which stems from Solomon, the son of David. In contrast, Luke describes a line that stems from Nathan, another son of David. In the literature pertaining to the two children, the two are distinguished as the Solomon and Nathan children. If we take these two genealogies seriously (as indeed we must) then we are forced to the uncomfortable conclusion that the two lines of descent relate to two Josephs, both of whom had sons named Jesus. The Luke account does qualify this, by mentioning that Jesus was the son of Joseph only 'as was supposed'. The following comparison is intended to show the radical difference in this blood line in only the last seven generations:

LUKE	MATTHEW
Janna	Achim
Melchi	Eliud
Levi	Eleazar
Mathat	Mathan
Heli	Jacob
Joseph	Joseph
Jesus	Jesus

Dee is referring to this notion of the two children in a truncated form, as he attempts (perhaps not very convincingly) to represent the many near-unintelligible references in the 33 squares as an exegesis of his own

Monas. Some artists of the sixteenth century were not so obscurantist, and a number of studies have been made of paintings that seem to deal with this heretical theme of the two Jesus children.[35] The artists who exhibited a painterly interest in this theme included, in alphabetical order, Fra Angelico, Joos van Cleve, Carlo Crivelli, Filippo Lippi, Leonardo da Vinci, Michelangelo, Marco d'Oggiono, Marten de Vos and Raphael.[36]

Michelangelo, in particular, seems to have made this heresy of the two Jesus children his own special subject, and with extraordinary *sang froid* carried the theme into the heart of the Vatican itself. The astonishing fact is that the story of the two genealogies, with related imagery depicting the two children, is the main theme of what must be the most famous Christian painting of the late Renaissance − the ceiling of the Sistine Chapel, in Rome.

Thus, we find the greatest esotericist of the sixteenth century − John Dee − concerning himself with the two children in an hermeneutically expressed text. He published these findings in 1564 − the year in which the Italian exponent of the theme, Michelangelo, died. Michelangelo's portrayal of the theme of the two children is not disguised, in the sense that Dee's was. Michelangelo tackled the imagery with refreshing candour and inventive symbolism, and he set this against a framework of recognizable iconographic details and numerologies. The astonishing thing is that the real significance of the Sistine Chapel ceiling has not yet dawned upon art historians. Equally, the true significance of John Dee's study of the *Monas* has not yet dawned upon art historians, either.

Chapter 5

The Rosicrucian Code

...I had good reason to be thankful to my Planet, by whose influence it was, that I had now seen certain pieces which no humane Eye else ... had ever had a view of.

[From the 'Fifth Day', in the Ezechiel Foxcroft translation of *The Chymical Wedding* (1690).]

Scholars who have learned to read the *Secret booke* recognize that much of the advanced arcane thought of modern times may be traced to the Rosicrucian fraternities of the sixteenth and seventeenth centuries. The early fraternity worked silently and anonymously at that period to keep alive certain vestiges of esoteric Christianity. This they did in the face of the imminent collapse of an over-bureaucratized and febrile Christian church. At that time, the Christian church was imploding due to both its inner rigidity and outer immorality, and was evidently in deep need of reform.

An early seventeenth-century engraving, itself replete with encodings, reveals something of the new 'school' or teachings of this Christian fraternity (figure 9).[1] Unlike the churches of the Catholics and the Protestant sects, this was not *established*. According to this image, it had been let down into the world on a rope by the hand of God (see over).[2] The fabric of the temple was itself possessed of wheels, that it might move anywhere, at will: it was, so to speak, a free Church, to which only the worthy were welcome. It was not a universal Church, for a drawbridge ensured that only those who were pleasing to God might enter.[3]

To the right, we see a man falling over a cliff. This is a bit of authorial humility, for the winged message marks him out as being *Nostro T. S.* (Our T. S.). This must be Theophilus Schweighardt, who designed the plate, and published it in 1618.

A ream of paper would be required to do justice to the encodings in this engraving, but within the context we have examined, we might reasonably ask questions. For example, what is the curious sigil ▆▆▁▆▆ beneath the banderol naming this temple as the *Collegium Fraternitatis*? Could it be an abbreviation sign for the two capital S forms, in the banderol below,

indicating that these should read as *Spiritus* and *Sanctus*, thus invoking the name of the Third Person, Christ, within the Temple itself? Again, what is the swan that seems to be sliding down the radiant from the six-pointed alchemical star, in the upper right corner of the image? The four directions of space are out of kilter – the east (ORIENS) should not be overhead. The call for symbolism – the need to orientate God himself in the primal point of sunrise to the East, has disrupted the order of things.

To the left we can see a potential convert being saved from the pit of ordinary opinion (*Puteus opinionum*). After being drawn out of his predicament by those inside the College, he will have to walk over the bridge, which is cleverly encoded with the letter M, as its structural foundation. Almost certainly, this is the mysterious Rosicrucian *booke*, the *Liber M*, which emerges from time to time in the literature of the fraternity.

Naturally, in any engraving relating to the early Rosicrucians, one looks for the anticipated encoding of 33. It has been cleverly done, by means of words. There are 27 words, set out in capital letters.[4] There are 2 dates (1604 and 1618), and there are 4 names of God, the *Tetragrammaton* –

three on the shields of the embattled Rosicrucians, and one in the heavens, at the disrupted Eastern point. In all, then, 33.

This was no ordinary *Collegium*, temple, or church, but it does seem to offer the same promise as the ark, stranded on the mountain to the left – a promise of a new beginning. This new temple symbolized the fact that the fraternity were laying down the foundations for a new approach to esotericism. It is evident to us now that they recognized that the full import of their knowledge would emerge only in the late nineteenth century, and flourish in the twentieth. Perhaps this gap of about five hundred years, between their insemination of certain ideas, and the flowering of these same ideas, explains the importance of the phoenix bird among the symbols of the fraternity? According to some accounts, the phoenix lived for a period of 500 years, before dying and reincarnating from its own cremated ashes.[5]

The very natures of the truths which the early Rosicrucians planted (so to speak) in order to ensure growth some five hundred years later, were such that it was not possible to promulgate them openly, without disguise. This is why the literature, symbols and diagrams in the early streams of Rosicrucianism, are so often difficult to understand. Among these near-impenetrable works is the anonymous, *The Chymical Wedding*, translated into English from the German text associated with Johann Valentin Andreae by Ezechiel Foxcroft, in 1690.[6]

Below, I reproduce an engraved portrait of Andreae, which (as we might imagine) incorporates a most interesting encoding.

If we are to appreciate the cunning behind this encoding we must make some attempt to understand the letters in the two cartouches on either side of the bottom register. That to the left (below the lighted candle) relates to Andreae's birth, and may be decoded as:

N	Natus	
MDLX	1560	
XXVI	26	[taken together, that is, 1586]
AUG	Augustus	
XVII	17	

Since *Natus* means 'birth', this cartouche seems to be telling us that Andreae was born on 17 August 1586. Historically speaking, this was the case. The other cartouche, below the hour glass and skull (standard symbols of mortality) may be decoded as:

O	Obit
MDC	1600

Since *Obit* means 'he died', we may be tempted to read into this the fact that Andreae passed away in 1600, aged only 14 — far too early even for him to write such a work of genius. However, this is not historically true: Andreae died in 1654, at the age of 68. It seems possible, therefore, that either someone has missed out or removed the numerals LIV from the cartouche. Be that as it may, the rest of the cartouche was left blank — presumably for reasons of encoding. In other words, this error in the date of his death seems to be bound into the encoding hidden in the engraving.

If we count the number of letters on the engraving (excluding from this count those letter forms that are actually Roman numerals), we obtain the following results:

SUFFICIT	=	8		
IOH VALENTINUS	=	13		
ANDREAE	=	7		
N [NATUS]	=	1		
AUG [AUGUSTUS]	=	3		
O [OBIT]	=	1	=	33

It is entirely fitting that Andreae, who, rightly or wrongly, is associated with the early publication of one of the three great classics of Rosicrucian literature, should be portrayed in a form that incorporates the Rosicrucian encoding.

Andreae's translator, the English scholar, Foxcroft, was certainly a crypto-Rosicrucian himself. He was a Fellow of King's College, Cambridge, and Senior Proctor of the University for almost two years, up to his death in 1674. In arcane circles, he is remembered because of his friendship with Lady Conway of Ragley, where an esoteric centre had been established, peopled by such influential scholars as Henry More, Ralph Cudworth, Valentine Greatrakes and Franz Mercurius van Helmont.

Foxcroft's translation of the *Chymical Wedding* has had a deep influence on the study of modern esoteric thought, even though (as with the original German of which it is a translation) a true understanding of this text demands considerable knowledge of symbolism and of the subtle spiritual allusions in which the text abounds. Aware of the dangers of the open promulgation of esoteric knowledge, Andreae had introduced into his text a number of occult blinds, to ensure that only those especially trained in arcane matters would be able to truly understand the deeper implications of his text. The prevalence of occult blinds explains why this text, which is so widely read and discussed in modern times, has been so little understood.

Before we move on to review something of this fascinating text, it might be as well for us to examine the title-page of the original German edition of 1616. It is of immediate interest to us, mainly because it succeeds in incorporating two sets of the 33 encodings on the one page.

Christiani Rosencreütz.
ANNO 1459.

Arcana publicata vilescunt; & gratiam prophanata amittunt.

Ergo: ne Margaritas obijce porcis, seu Asino substerne rosas.

Straßburg,
In Verlägung / Lazari Zetzners.
Anno M. DC. XVI.

There are two dates on the title-page, one in Arabic numerals, the other in Roman. The topmost marks the year 1459, which some authorities have presumed (without much external evidence) to point to the year of the foundation of the Rosicrucian movement. The Latin date at the bottom of the page is, of course, the date of publication itself – 1616 – expressed in Roman numerals (M.DC.XVI). It is most unusual to have two dates on a title-page, and one wonders if these could have been included to express some sort of codification. In fact, if you add together these two sets of four digits, you find that they total 33:

$$1 + 4 + 5 + 9 = 19$$
$$1 + 6 + 1 + 6 = 14$$
$$= 33$$

In addition to this unique exposition of the code, one finds that the top line of the Latin quotation (itself intended as a response to the Latin inscription, above) contains 33 type characters. In making this count, one must include in the count the distinctive yet unnecessary colon and the grammatically unnecessary comma.

Ergo : ne Margaritas obijce porcis, seu

As a matter of fact, this quotation is itself involved with an esoteric strand of thought that links the Rosicrucian fraternity with the Mystery wisdom of the ancient world. As the encoding might suggest, the first part of the quotation is different from the second. The first part parallels a verse from the Gospel of Saint Matthew, and translates:

Therefore : do not cast pearls before swine.[7]

In contrast, the second part of this injunction is non-biblical:

... or roses before the Ass.

Within the esoteric tradition, this reference to casting roses before an ass involves a very special source. The phrase is derived from an arcane source of the second century A.D. *The Golden Ass*, written by the initiate, Lucius Apuleius.[8] In the work wherein the quotation is found, Lucius was telling the story of his own adventures after he was meta-morphosed into the form of an ass. Below is one of the more popular themes in the work, touching upon the use to which women put the ass in their bedrooms.[9]

As Lucius freely admits, he had not been transformed by accident. In his wish to learn the secret of a witch, he had meddled with her spells and potions. Things did not work out as planned. Instead of learning the secrets of flight, Lucius found himself condemned to dwell in the body of an ass — though still blessed or cursed with human consciousness. To cut a long and intriguing story short, I should record that Lucius finally learned that he could return to his human form if he ate roses, which at length he did, when these were offered to him by a priest of Isis.

What follows in this remarkable text is as near an exposition of the sacred Mysteries as was possible in those days, when all initiates were strictly sworn to silence. Suffice it to say that Lucius, once more a man, was given 'charge of certaine secret things unlawful to be uttered'.[10] Later, he was initiated into the highest Mysteries of the age. The connection between this command to remain silent in relation to the Mysteries, and the Latin quotation on the title-page of the *Chymische Hochzeit* is evident. The symbolism of the rose — the secret of the *Ros* — is that it permits transformation from one level of being to another. With the power of *Ros*, one may ascend from the human to the divine. Just as the descent of Christ to the physical plane is recalled in the number 33, so this progression from the physical to the higher spiritual is recalled in the same number.

As a whole, these two lines of Latin tell us not to throw valuable pearls before the swine, who will merely trample them. At the same time, one is advised not to meddle in initiation of another (especially an ass) for one does not have sufficient knowledge to know what the outcome will be.

Having glanced at the 'entrance' to the book, we are now in a position to examine some of the symbolism within the text of the *Chymical Wedding* itself.

On the fifth day of the events leading to the mysterious wedding, which form the background to this hermeneutic tale, Christian Rosenkreutz gives an account of a curious experience. Early in the morning of that day, he had been conducted to an underground burial chamber in the castle in which he had been lodged. Rising early, before any of his companions or other guests were awake, he required his page to show him around the castle. Rosenkreutz was guided down a number of steps, which led to a great iron door, on which was affixed a text made from copper letters. Copper is the metal of Venus, so we should not be surprised that the mysterious letters incorporated a reference to this pagan goddess, in a single word-form that is entirely without encoding.

The message on the iron door read:

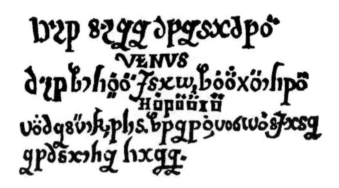

The door being opened, the page led him along a passage that took them to a vault, lighted by (as it seemed) great carbuncles.[11] Thus, almost at the same time as Shakespeare was writing of a chariot of the Sun, lit by a mass of these self-luminant carbuncles, we see that Andreae was writing of a tomb, or initiation chamber, illumined by this same mysterious source.[12]

In the centre of the underground vault stood a sepulchre of strange design, triangular in form.[13] At this point, the page revealed and opened a copper door, set in the pavement of the vault. Together, they descended once again into the darkness, which was dispelled only when the page opened a small chest containing an ever-burning taper. In the chamber, was a bed, hung around by curtains. The page drew one curtain, to reveal Venus herself, lying on the bed.

When, much to Rosenkreutz's surprise, the page pulled back the coverlets, he saw that Venus was stark naked. Her beauty was such that, even when the curtains were drawn once again, he could not dispel the image from his eyes. He did not know whether he had seen a marvellously-wrought effigy or a human body, lying dead.

Behind the bed, Rosenkreutz observed a tablet, on which was another example of an encoded message.

The page declined to reveal its meaning. After encountering this encoding, the pair ascended the lower stairs once more, and returned to the upper chamber.

The true nature of this naked Venus, and of the bed-tomb or marriage bed (*pastos*) on which she lay, has been discussed in a number of modern books. At the same time, the significance of the two sets of encodings which (as it were) bracket this strange experience in the double-levelled tomb, has also been discussed. So thoroughly have certain streams of Rosicrucian endeavour been permeated by these striking images that the tomb has been adapted and adopted into ritual use in certain modern magical rites.[14] In spite of this, there is no real indication that those who evolved these rites really understood the meanings of the encoded inscriptions, or had read correctly the secrets attached to this living-dead Venus.

The German scholar, Richard Kienast, has provided a convincing reading of the two encoded messages. He has shown that each text consists of a simple key-cipher in which a series of strange alphabetic letters correspond to letters in our own European alphabet.[15] When the simple key is applied, both texts reveal a curiously archaizing yet readable German.

The first text transliterates:

Hye lygt begraben
Venus
Dye schoen Fraw, so manchen
Hoen man
Umb glueck, ehr segen, und wolfart
Gebracht hatt.

'Here lies buried Venus, the beautiful woman, who has robbed so many noble men of good fortune, prosperity and well-being.'

The second transliterates:

Van dye Frucht meynes
Baums wyrt vollends
Verschmelzen, werde ych
Aufwachen und eyn
Muter seyn eynes
Konygs.

'When the fruit of my tree finally melts, then will I awake and become the mother of a king.'

Now, as is so often the case with the more sophisticated codes, there is an encoding hidden within this encoding. To appreciate why this secondary encoding (a true occult blind) has been incorporated, we must consider, however briefly, the esoteric significance of these two verses.

Venus, the pagan goddess, who is so frequently linked with voluptuousness and sensuality, is here adopted as an image of the living human body. In esoteric terms, this refers to much more than the meat and bones of the body material: it refers also to those spiritual bodies that maintain this flesh in a state of life, in a state of sensual awareness, and purposive direction. In terms that were once esoteric, but which are now nothing more than weakly semi-occult, these spiritual bodies are the Etheric, the Astral and the Ego.[16] These higher bodies embrace the physical body (the body of flesh and bone) and make use of it as an instrument: they invest it with the capability of a sensuous and purposive enjoyment of life. The first verse refers to the misuse of this Venus, to the perversion of the higher faculties bestowed upon the body by the Etheric, Astral and Ego.

The misuse of these faculties vitiates man, and reduces his well-being. Venus may be beautiful, and her contact desirable, but her presence was intended for other things — for spiritual development and transmutation, rather than to serve as an instrument solely of enjoyment. In truth, the body of Venus was intended to serve as a temple for the indwelling god of the Ego — but this purpose has been forgotten, and in consequence, as we learn from the text, Venus lies catatonic in an underground sarcophagus. Venus has robbed men (and, of course, women) yet she has robbed only with their connivance.

In the second encoding there is mention of the fruit of her tree. We need scarcely ask what this tree of Venus might be. Since the goddess rules the living body, her 'tree' is either the spine or the nervous system, within the body. What the future fruit of this tree may be, we shall see shortly.

The future *melting* (a curious and essentially inexplicable image, by ordinary standards) of this fruit is linked with her awakening and the fulfilment of her destiny. At this moment of awakening, she will become the mother of a king. The words themselves 'tree' [*baum*], 'mother of a king' [*Muter eynes Konygs*], tempt us to place a Christological reading upon the verse. It is possible to misread the words as though they relate to the birth or development of Christ (the King) within the human being. It is precisely to avert such a misreading, that the secondary encoding has been woven with such deftness into this verse. Andreae, or whoever constructed this encoding, was careful to leave a clue, which confirmed that the reference to the king was not intended as a reference to Christ.

The encoding has been second-coded in accordance with the well-established numerology of 33.

In the primary encoding of the passage (below), the letter forms

ȯ̈ and ̈ȯ refer to the letters **m** and **n** respectively.

Thus, the word

öp̌ö̈ p̌b

that appears in the first line, and which transliterates as <u>me</u>y<u>ne</u>s, contains both these encoded letters.

In addition to these triple- and double-accented letters, we find, in the encoding, two letters distinguished by only a single dotted accent, thus:

In the transliteration, this proves to be the equivalent of the letter **o**.

wxö бур fsuɔhɡ öpɟöᵹᵞ
d xuôs uɔɟsɡ uôₛₛpôᵬᵬ
upₛᵬɔhöps̨ᵬpö, uɔpₛᵬpⱥᵹh
xufuuxɔhpö uôᵬpⱥɟö
öuɡps ᵬpⱥö pⱥöpᵬ
ꝁöö·ⱥɡᵬ

If we count all these three o-based letter-forms that appear in the encloding (above), we arrive at the following numerology:

⸫o = 4 [thus, 3 × 4 = 12] = 12

⸬o = 10 [thus, 2 × 10 = 20] = 20

˙o = 2 [thus, 1 × 2 = 2] = 2

The total derived from this secondary encoding is 34 – which is one beyond the requisite Rosicrucian numerology of 33. If we divest the encoding of the **˙o**, we arrive at 32, which is one *less* than the requisite 33. This secondary encoding may seem to be complex, but is in fact astonishingly simple: Andreae has made use of a simple count of dots, or points, which have been so arranged that they intentionally do *not* reveal a connection with 33, yet distinctly reveal the pre- and post-sequential numbers, 32 and 34. Andreae seems intent on showing that there is no way that we may arrive at the Christ-number 33 from this encoding. This was his own way of showing that the passage relating to a Venus that gives birth to a king has nothing to do with Christ.

This king is not the once and future King, who is the Christ, but a symbol of the developed and completed human being – the completed 'Septenary Man'. A number of alchemical images depict this transformed or transmuted king, within the setting of a septenary.

For example, plate 11 in Daniel Mylius, *Philosophia Reformata*, (1622), refers to this king.[17] He is depicted seated on a throne, holding in his left hand the Seal of Solomon, which is, in the next engraving in the sequence, transformed into the six-pointed mystic Star of Alchemy. On either side of the king are two groups of three crowned individuals, who (within our

chosen context) represent the three bodies of the ordinary human being, facing their developed counterparts.

The open numerology of this design is intended to emphasize its Rosicrucian importance. The image contains 7 kings. The central king holds up a Seal of 6 points, with which we are now familiar. This Seal obscures one window, to leave only 9 windows visible. Above the head of the central king, is the number 11, which relates to an earlier sequence of the engraving, but which has no real significance in its present context. These figures add up to reveal the expected total:

$$7 + 6 + 9 + 11 = 33$$

In the alchemical text appended to this image, we learn that it represents the stage of *Rubefaction*, revealing the king resurrected from death. This specialist alchemical term is derived from the Latin meaning, 'making red'.[18] It is the alchemical Red King who crowns his colleagues, and (as the text insists) 'On this occasion, clothes the tender limbs with genuine purple'. This colour purple is another reference to *Rubefaction*. The phrase, *tender limbs*, is one of the images used to denote the physical body itself. The learned esotericist will be tempted to trace in the numerology derived from this secondary encoding, a reference to the nature of the anticipated birth of the new King. In so doing, that esotericist will be tracing ideas that were laid down over five hundred years before they flowered in modern culture.

In the esoteric traditions that came to fruition during the late nineteenth century – mainly through such movements as Theosophy, parts of which were transformed into Anthroposophy – we learn about the future evolution of humanity, which is essentially an evolution that involves the perfection of seven spiritual bodies.

According to this teaching, the spiritual entities that presently serve the living physical organism – the Physical, Etheric and Astral – will themselves be transformed into higher entities. Indeed, in certain highly developed individuals, they are already being so transformed. This higher transformation is symbolized in alchemy by the image of the Red King.

The king (that is, the higher and transformed body) will be born when the fruit of this present 'sleeping' body of Venus melts. Thus, this *melting* describes the emergence, from the incomplete threefold organism of modern man, of the complete septenary Man of the future. In this future *melting* lies the secret of the fifth day experience of Christian Rozenkreutz in the double tomb. The symbolism of the text insists that one tomb is below the other, and is fed by a perpetual light, kept in a dark cupboard. Those who dwell in this lower tomb cannot even see their condition, and are unaware that there is something higher, above them.

In this Rosicrucian teaching about the future destiny of mankind, we find an explanation for the seeming dichotomy behind the arcane tradition. On the one hand, this tradition insists that the human being is threefold (fourfold, if one includes the Ego). On the other hand, this same tradition insists that the fully developed human being will be seven-fold. This is perfectly true, but the fact is that the full development of the three higher bodies will take place only in a distant future. Adam, the archetypal undeveloped Man, was born of red earth, as his name implies.[19] The final archetypal Man will be the redeemed Adam, and will (symbolically at least) be a Red Man entire, in alchemical terms. In this sense, man is both a quaternary and a septenary.

The esoteric teachings pertaining to the future development of mankind have not yet been fully divulged, even by esoteric circles. Even the names of the three spiritual entities that will be developed from the lower spirits have not yet been made available. At present, occult lore tends to make use of Sanskrit terms, derived from the orientalizing process of Theosophy, to denote these higher spiritual bodies. They are called Atman, Buddhi and Manas.[20] As I have said, these three higher bodies will, in a fairly remote future, be developed as a consequence of the transmutation of the three bodies which presently serve as the instrument of the Ego. These are the Physical, Etheric and Astral.

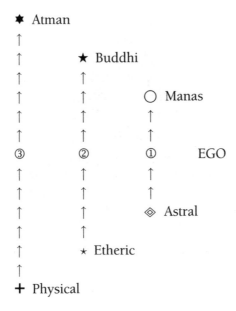

The relationship between the present and future bodies is known, and may best be represented in a simple diagrammatic form (above). The vertical arrows connect the lower faculty to its corresponding higher development: thus, the Physical is connected vertically to the Atman. The three numbers horizontal to the EGO indicate the order of the anticipated transformation: thus, 1 relates to the transformation of the Astral into Manas, whilst 2 relates to the transformation of the Etheric into Buddhi. The six symbols used here for the six spiritual bodies are far from being arbitrary, but they are not in general arcane use.

In some ways, these sophisticated portrayals of the psycho-spiritual nature of mankind are far removed from images of the Microcosm (the androgyne Man) which appear in Rosicrucian diagrams and texts. Even so, we may see in the earlier images and models of the Microcosm certain archetypes which (almost five centuries later) were to be explored by esotericists of the modern period.

In the early seventeenth century, the English esotericist, Robert Fludd, oversaw the production of a number of engravings which would appear, in particular, to have contributed to the modern occult view of things. For example, in one engraving (overleaf) he visualized an upright man standing within the arcs of three large concentrics. These concentrics were centred upon his private parts, the importance of which Fludd emphasized by leaving the organs themselves outside the general frame of the picture.

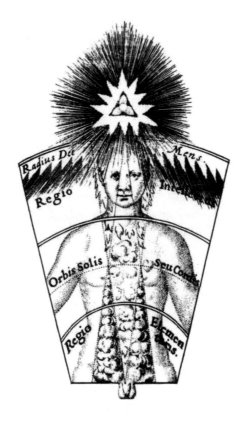

The outermost, or upper concentric arc, corresponded to the area governed by the head, and was thus linked with thinking: Fludd called it the *Regio Intellectus*. The second concentric corresponded to the heart, or thorax region, in the centre of which was inserted an extra concentric arc that portrayed the path of the Sun (*Orbis Solis*) or ecliptic, which was seen also as the equivalent of the heart (*Seu Cordis*). The third concentric arc marks out the stomach area, or what Fludd saw as the corresponding microcosmic realm of the *Regio Elementaris*. This governed the appetitive region of the Elements (that is, of the four Elements, and thus the material realm of Earth). In terms of modern arcane knowledge, we might be more inclined to label the three arcs in terms of *Salt, Mercury* and *Sulphur*, for they certainly represent the forces of thinking, feeling and willing, as portrayed in this diagram.

The duality inherent in these three regions is expressed by Fludd in a novel way. He depicts the duality by means of two narrow interlinking triangles (like a compressed Seal of Solomon) which run vertically through the diagram. In these, Fludd represents the notion that, as we move away from God, to the centre which marks the location of Hell, the light diminishes. The fire of Inferno is a dark fire. Thus, just above the private parts, at the centre of the concentric arcs, the illumined triangle has diminished to a mere point. In contrast, the triangle of darkness, which thrusts upwards from this same level, to a point at the top of the head, starts out in almost complete darkness: it gradates into light (even into flame) as it moves upwards. The contrast between these inter-penetrating isosceles triangles corresponds to the dualities we noted in each of the three principles, as expressed in the microcosmic form.

When we contemplate the radiant triangulation above the head of this microcosmic man, we begin to see how seeds for future development could be laid down by such fraternities as the Rosicrucians. In this case, the trinity portrayed within the twelve-rayed star-burst certainly relates to the Holy Trinity of established religion. The twelve rays may have been the consequence of a direct vision experienced by Fludd, but even if this were not the case, these rays remind us of what Rudolf Steiner wrote concerning the twelve-fold nature of the Ego (see pages 11 and 12). Even so, it demands no great effort to visualize this Trinity as a prototype of the trinity of *Atman, Buddhi* and *Manas*, in which the future evolution of mankind resides.

Almost certainly, the experienced esotericist will be tempted to trace in this arcane tradition, which touches upon the lower ternary, the so-called Paracelsian *Three Principles* of late medieval alchemy. *Salt, Mercury* and *Sulphur* related to the inner Man, in much the same way as the spiritual trinity we have just examined.

In the alchemical and Rosicrucian tradition, Salt (which is no ordinary salt) is usually symbolized by a Greek *theta* (below). Salt represents the human thought process, the power of human thinking, which (in alchemical terms) is regarded as being a life-denying process, linked with death.

In this context, the *theta* is the capital letter of the Greek word *Thanatos*, meaning, 'Death'. The white of the Salt is said to reflect the grey-white of the human brain, and the white light of the stars, which is reflected in the brain. Salt is alchemically inert, unless it is tempered by the imaginative power of Mercury. Within the context of what we know about the brain, as a centre of consciousness, the traditional alchemical link with death may seem to be a dubious one. However, when we consider the nature of consciousness, this dubious element evaporates. The sigil clearly marks a division in the head-process, but this does not point to schizophrenia – but rather, to something of profound importance which is often missed. The consciousness centre, which, for want of a better word, we may call the brain – is divided in the medieval symbol for Salt. This division is there because the early arcanists recognized that there is an important division in consciousness. When we sleep, we live in an entirely different world from the one we inhabit when awake. The division in the sigil points to this fundamental dichotomy in existence. During sleep, our higher spiritual parts (the astral and the Ego) are divorced from the physical and etheric bodies. The two higher spiritual entities are diluted into the spiritual world, into the secret surrounding cosmos. The physical body, with its life-preserving Etheric, remains on the bed, asleep. We might even read the horizontal division of the sigil as a reference to this idea of spiritual division implicit in sleep:

The sigil recalls that, on the fifth day, *two* tombs were found by Rosen-kreutz, one above the other, with the body of Venus asleep or dead in the lower one. This mystery of sleep (for sleep *is* a mystery) is expressed in the *Thanatos* sigil: in some respects, sleep resembles death, though it is a death from which one may easily return and reincarnate.

The brain itself is not a dead place, even though certain forms of thinking are involved in dying processes. A human brain entirely devoid of the soul life furnished by the cultural impetus of Mercury, or no longer infused with a tinge of the passion of Sulphur, would be a most terrible thing. The impulse of the brain is to dry things, to desiccate them. Were the imagery of the brain not refreshed by periodic dips into the pictorial realm of the greater spiritual world, in that activity we call sleep, then the brain would harden and become destructive of all that is joyful and creative. When we contemplate the ancient symbol for Salt, we must bear in mind this polarity of the brain, and its tendency to self-desiccate and destroy life.

When the brain is disturbed by excessive passions, then we weep salt tears. In one of his references to Salt, Shakespeare, consciously or unconsciously, touches upon the division of the brain, emphasizing not the death element, but rather the imaginative element, which is nightly renewed by imagination, or the fall of alchemical Dew. The 'salt flood' to which Capulet refers, in Shakespeare's *Romeo and Juliet,* has a double meaning, one of which links with the alchemical image.[21] This salt flood is, on one level, the sea. But Juliet is crying, and Capulet develops the conceit that Juliet weeps like the air which drizzles dew (*Ros*) at sunset. Her tears also are a flood from the Salt of her imagination.[22] In weeping, she counterfeits in her one little body a ship, a sea, a wind, with the ebb and flow of her watery tears, on the flood of which the ship or bark of her little body sails. Her body is tempest-tossed, but the storms that toss it arise from her own mind or imagination. We see then, in this Shakespearean passage, that Salt refers to the salt of the seas as well as to the salt of her imaginative faculty, locked within her brain. In the esoteric tradition, salt tears are an outer sign of frustration in the process of thinking: it is a frustration that will (in the words of Capulet) 'overset thy tempest-tossed body'.

The death-element in Salt is even more deftly handled by Shakespeare, who uses the image of salt as one of the lynch-pins in the tragedy of Hamlet's death. Salt figures in the overtly esoteric words of Laertes, when he encounters his sister Ophelia, driven mad by grief:

> Oh heate drie up my Braines, teares seven times salt,
> Burne out the Sence and Vertue of mine eye.[23]

Whether the groundlings would have seen the esotericism in these two lines is a moot question, yet esoteric they are. Laertes is inviting the heat of the sulphurous realm to rise up and touch his brain, and by this touch turn his own mind mad. Further, he invites the salt of his brain to increase sevenfold and, by this increase, become a liquid so potent that it also acts as a burning sulphur – the very opposite of its own innate nature.[24] This potent salt will have the power to burn out the true *Vertue* (a word we may scarcely translate into modern English) from his eyes. In other words, Laertes is inviting the destruction of his own constitution by madness that he may not witness the madness of his sister, Ophelia. The full force of this Shakespearean imagey may be understood only when the nature of Sulphur is understood.

Sulphur usually incorporates into its symbol a triangle, with the apex upwards.

🜍

In this form, it is clearly linked with the element of Fire, which is represented as a triangle: △. Sulphur relates to those inner fires in the human being that are experienced through the sexual drive. Esoterically, this is the centre of the human will — the least developed and the least controlled of the *Three Principles*. Sulphur strives upwards, as though seeking to invade the thinking process of the human being, towards which it is so inimical and alien. In terms of the Shakespearean imagery we have just examined, we see that the successful invasion by Sulphur of the realm of Salt would result in madness, in a microcosm being overthrown.

Sulphur is the ruler of the domain of passions, and it is fitting that Shakespeare should introduce the word into a tumultuous, guilt-driven speech by Othello, shortly after the killing of his wife, Desdemona. It is fitting that his imagery should be charged with demonic power, for the realm of passions, whilst centred in the Microcosm at the sexual parts, is, within the Macrocosm, centred in Hell, where jealousy is itself a currency. Othello, recognizing his error, begs the demons to thrash him to Hell, away from the sight of Desdemona:

> Whip me, ye Divels,
> From the possession of this Heavenly sight:
> Blow me about in windes, roast me in Sulphure,
> Wash me in steepe-down gulfes of Liquid fire.[25]

For the Elizabethans, part of the dramatic irony in the speech lay in the fact that Othello, through being consumed by guilt, was *already* roasting in sulphurous Hell, in their eyes. His words reveal how he is basting in the microcosmic fiery passions that arise from uncontrolled sexuality of the Sulphur urge.

The sigil for Sulphur is partly deceptive, for it does not immediately demonstrate the duality readily visible in the other two sigils. However, there is a duality, for the pure still flame of the triangle is said to have a counterpart in an invisible *dark fire*, which is traditionally represented as a black triangle: ▲. This sigillization seems to imply that the triangle of light was so intense that it cancelled out the dark fire, thus removing from the sigil all sense of duality. An earlier form of this dark triangle of Sulphur is given below.

This sigil seems designed to express the notion of duality in the quality of Fire: beneath the triangle of light fire, are three lines, which may be taken as the outer lines of the dark burning.

Mercury is almost always represented as a vestigial drawing of the caduceus, or wand of power, of the pagan god.

Originally, this sigil seems to have consisted of a winged wand, around which were entwined two serpents. It is this duality which permits Mercury, the ruler of human soul-life and emotional life, to take a grip of the dual mind of Salt. Without this dual nature, which is the birthright of Mercury, it could not serve as a guardian of the thresholds between the coldness of Salt and the intense liquid fire of Sulphur.

As the sigil suggests, Mercury is the cosmic healing force, and, in the Three Principles of the alchemists, it stands sentinel between Salt and Sulphur, attempting to establish a balance between them. His function is to ensure that the two remain in their proper domains – Salt in the head, and Sulphur in the sexual parts. As must be evident, Mercury governs the domain of the feeling, and emotions. It is cooled by Salt and warmed (sometimes, over-warmed) by Sulphur.

Whilst it is true that Mercury was the winged messenger between the pagan gods of Roman mythology, it is also true that the power of Mercury brings a sense of unity and harmony to the eternal warring between Salt and Sulphur. Mercury lifts the inert death-tendency of Salt by tempering it with imagination, thus rendering its activity creative. It cools and civilizes the fiery temper of Sulphur. However, should the mercurial power fail, and Mercury himself be dragged into these lower passions, then, literally, all Hell can break out in the personal world of that man or woman. Mercury is often represented as a psychopomp because he has the power to descend into the Underworld, the realm of Pluto, which is the domain of the sulphurous powers.

Whilst Mercury is a sort of arbitrator between Salt and Sulphur, he is by inclination given more to the former than the latter: the gods do not readily give up their places in the upper airs. As Shakespeare recognized, he is more a messenger of thought than of passion:

Be Mercurie, set feathers to thy heeles,
And flye (like thought) from them, to me againe.[26]

Oddly enough, it is the contemporaneous Ben Jonson, rather than Shakespeare, who explores most perceptively the esoteric background to Mercury. Surly, in his speech to Subtle, in *The Alchemist*, refers openly to the Three Principles (of Paracelsus). This may be taken as a mocking speech, ridiculing alchemy itself, yet it contains several grains of esoteric wisdom. Surly reminds us that the Three Principles are:

Your sal, your sulphur, and your mercury...[27]

Four lines later in the same speech, Surly mentions the three again, but this time he uses arcane terminologies:

Your lato, azoch, zernich, chibrit, heautarit.

Lato is latten, a metallic compound rather like superior quality brass, and usually hammered into sheets. *Azoch* is one of the most mysterious of all alchemical words, a form of *Azoth*, which contains the first and last letters of the Roman, Greek and Hebrew letters: it is claimed to be from the Arabic word for Mercury, which is often wrongly confused with an anti-life agent, *azot*, or *azotikos*. *Chibrit* is sulphur, whilst *heautarit* is Mercury, relatively undisguised.[28]

Because they together represented the psycho-spiritual workings of the human being, the Paracelsian Three Principles were susceptible to transmutation. At least one group of Rosicrucians recognized the importance of this triad for the future evolution of humanity. Below, I reproduce a simplified relevant diagram from the *Aurum Seculum Revivum*, of 1621.[29]

Reading downwards, and centrally, we see that this diagram combines, as though in a single structure, the three sigils for Sulphur, Mercury and Salt. The arcane artist who drew the diagram was quite right to link them together, to form from the three a single unit, as, like the Trinity itself, they are a substantial three-in-one. In the diagram, the three are united against a backdrop of the two triangles of Fire $\triangle$ and Water ∇, which are more frequently combined to make the Seal of Solomon ✿ and the alchemical six-pointed star.

One thing which may easily evade notice is that the diagram has been constructed in such a way as to contain precisely the Rosicrucian unit of 33. There are 6 contained spaces within the diagram. There are two large triangles, offering a count of 6. There is one small triangle (3), two crosses (2 × 4 = 8), 1 crescent and 1 circle. There are two semi-circles (or a divided circle) which is numerically 2. There are two V shapes bounding the large triangles, with the combined value of 4. And finally (and certainly more subtle) the sigils for the Three Principles are so drawn as to contain within their bounding lines 2 spaces.

$$6 + 6 + 3 + 8 + 1 + 1 + 2 + 4 + 2 = 33$$

This particular diagram may be regarded as representing the redeemed triad, mainly because the two triangles have separated. They no longer combine to form the alchemical star of the Seal, and have found their own proper level: Fire has moved upwards whilst Water has sunk downwards. The sigil for Salt is now in its more appropriate element of Water, whilst burning Sulphur is now in its own element of Fire. This arrangement suggests that the mediating Mercury has completed its work, and has ensured a separation between the two. For sure, its own circular bowl marks the point of this separation.

For all its simplicity, this extraordinary diagram appears to encapsulate the aspirations that lay behind the activities of all those men and women who contributed to the writing of Shakespeare's *Secret booke*.

Chapter 6

Nostradamus his Codes

Non est quod Dominus noster timeat de ambagibus, aenigmatibus vel
amphibologiis: omnia futura sunt vel ipsa luce lucidiora. Nihil 'εν αίνιγμοις
erit, nihil άλληγορίαις obscurando.

Our master need have no fear of ambiguities, of enigmatic meanings or of
equivocations. All things future are more clear than day itself – none of them
will be set out under an enigmatic or allegorical form.

[From a letter dated 15 July 1561, written by Michel Nostradamus to the
lawyer, Lorenz Tubbe, regarding his own horoscopic readings for their
mutual friend, Hans Rosenberger.[1]]

Without doubt, the most remarkable and enigmatic esoteric work to see
the light of day during the last flowering of the Renaissance, was the
collection of *Propheties* from the erudite pen of Nostradamus.

The astonishing thing about these prophecies, which covered a
futurity stretching from circa 1555 for over two hundred years into our
own future, is that the majority still remain enigmatic. Only a handful
of these curious quatrains (four-lined verses) have been so far understood, even by those commentators who have studied the work of this
remarkable man. The encoding methods of Nostradamus were just as
sophisticated as those used contemporaneously by the Rosicrucians,
and in many cases they have kept his inner meanings concealed.
Nostradamus wrote over two thousand prophetic verses touching upon
the future of Europe and America. He claimed that they extended as far
into the future as 2235 AD.[2]

The predictions did not appear in one fell swoop. The first batch of 353
verses appeared during book form in 1555. Later, Nostradamus wrote
additional verses to produce a complete edition approaching one
thousand quatrains. The finest surviving edition of this complete work
was published in 1568, two years after his own death. Even so, the work
retains the stamp of his own authority, indicating that he must have
personally oversaw the editorial work, though not the actual printing.

D.

We have already seen that clever encoding was highly prized in the sixteenth century, in both art and literature. Artists and writers regarded it as *de rigueur* to incorporate into their works hidden references, of the kind that would be appreciated by only the few. There was nothing democratic about Renaissance art.[3] In studying the Shakespearean and Rosicrucian encodings, we have merely scratched the surface of this intriguing subject: in truth, a great many of the sixteenth- and seventeenth-century writers and artists indulged in codification.

That he worked with the 33 code might at first appear to be remarkable. However, it is already clear that this encoding was part of the general Christian ethos long before it was adopted for the purposes of the Rosicrucian movement.

Overleaf, is a page from the first batch of his prophecies, as they appeared during his lifetime in 1557.[4]

Those not familiar with sixteenth-century French need not despair at the sight of these three verses. We have no need to either understand or translate them here, for we are presently more interested in their structure than in their meanings. In fact, the literary encoding within the three verses themselves is so thorough that their meanings have only recently been unravelled. For the moment, I would like to point to one

PROPHETIES

DE
M. NOSTRADAMVS

CENTVRIE PREMIERE.

I

Estant afsis de nuiæ fecret eftude,
Seul repofé fus la felle d'ærain:
Flambe exigue fortant de folitude,
Faiæ profperer qui n'eft à croire vain.

II

La verge en main mife au millieu de
branches,
De l'onde il moulle & le limbe & le pied:
Vn peur & voix tremiffent par les mache
Splendeur diuine Le diuin pres s'afsied.

III

Quant la liæiere du tourbillon verfée,
Et feront faces de leurs mâteaux couuers:
La republique par gens noueaux verée,
Lors blancs & roges iugeront à l'enuers.

or two examples of the familiar 33 encoding on the page reproduced here.

If you count the number of words within the section beginning PROPHETIES ... to the end of the last verse (ending, *croire vain.*) you will find exactly 33 words (the abbreviation M, for *Monsieur* counts as one word).[5] The number of the verse, the I, must be included in this count.

The first line of verse III (beginning, *Quant la lictiere...*) consists of 33 letters. Furthermore, the last line of this verse also consists of 33 letters, provided one follows the convention of reading the ampersand [&] as the *et* for which it stands.

Quant la lictiere du tourbillon versée,

...

Lors blancs [et] roges iugeront à l'envers.

For the moment, I will translate these two lines of the third verse as:

When the litter is overturned by the whirlwind,

...

Then the whites and the reds will make judgements in reverse.

The middle two lines, by virtue of the misspelling (misspelling, that is, even by sixteenth-century standards) of the word *noveaux*, total 66 letters, thus averaging 33 per line.

Et seront faces de leurs manteaux couvers:
La republique par gens noveaux vexée,

And [when] the faces will be covered by their cloaks:
The republic by new people will be vexed.

At first, it might not be clear why this third verse should have been accorded special consideration. Why should the third quatrain in the series be enclosed (so to speak) in the mystic number 33? The answer to this question is found in the simple fact that, despite all appearances, this is the *first* prophetic verse in the series, which Nostradamus will eventually build to almost a thousand, under this single title. In a sense, there is something holy or sacred about this verse: it is the first to project the reader through the veil of time. It is this alone – this sense of *entrance* – that explains why it should merit this 33 treatment.

The first two verses reproduced (left) are not actually prophecies. They consist of statements about the nature of prophecy in ancient times. In these first two verses Nostradamus has offered a number of references to the writings of the third-century scholar, Iamblichus, concerning the way that the prophetesses of old went about their business of predicting the future.[6] Thus, for example, *la selle d'aerain*, at the end of the second line, is a reference to the bronze seat on which the Sibyl sat, at the oracular centre of Delphi.[7] Iamblichus had mentioned this special tripod in his own account of Delphi. The image, overleaf, depicts a pythoness of Delphi, seated on one of these distinctive tripods.[8]

Another example from the same Iamblichus is found in the final word of the first line of verse II.

La verge en main mise au millieu de branches,

The term, *branches*, is actually a reference to the ancient Greek *Branchides*, who specialised in prophecy.[9] It is clear, then, that Nostradamus did not view the first two verses as belonging to his prophetic series. He was intent merely on showing that, in being a prophet, he was involved in a process of great antiquity, and one that was linked with the ancient mysteries, about which Iamblichus had written.

Only when we reach the third verse, protected by the magical number 33, do we find ourselves thrown into the actual business of prediction proper. The subject of this verse is one concerning what seems to have been Nostradamus' favourite future event – the French Revolution. This is one of the few verses which the more scholarly commentators on Nostradamus were able to 'solve', in the sense of understanding its general meaning.[10] Perhaps they were helped by the fact that Nostradamus had used words of great relevance to the Revolution, but which would have been almost meaningless in the sixteenth century, when he wrote the verse. For example, the words, *La republique*, in the third line, could not have had much meaning in French history prior to 1789, when the Revolution occurred and imposed the first Republic on French Society. The phrase would have had a meaning only in a historical sense, as, for example, in the development of ancient Rome.

I have no wish to discuss this third and opening verse in detail here: the meaning of the quatrain has been discussed by a sufficient number of commentators already.[11] My purpose has been merely to show that Nostradamus, for all his well-deserved reputation as a unique prophet, was working within a numerological tradition used, in his own day, in

England and other parts of the Continent, as part of that literary tradition I have called *Shakespeare's Secret booke*.

One glance at a title-page — the classical doorway into another world — will convince us that Nostradamus, or his printers, were interested in the 33 encoding. The title-page to the 1568 edition of his *Propheties*, printed by Benoist Rigaud in Lyons , contains 33 words (figure 10). To obtain this count, one ignores the single abbreviation, M. (for *Monsieur*) and the numerical date.[12]

Nostradamus seems to have taken especial delight in codes and in obscurantist references. He was one of the greatest exponents of the *Language of the Birds*, an esoteric tongue designated by many titles, including, *The Gay Language*, the *Tongue of the Retort* and the *Green Language*.[13] Of all these names, the most fitting is *The Language of the Birds*. One need only listen to birds, chirping and singing in the still air of the country, to understand why this name is so perfect. Whilst the melody of intermixed bird song is beautiful, one cannot understand it: the song makes sense only to the birds themselves.

Given a reference to what is a virtually unknown language, this is an appropriate place to distinguish the *esoteric* from the *exoteric*. The teachings of esotericism are reserved only for the few, whilst things that are exoteric are available to all. Clearly, Nostradamus was an esoteric writer: in constructing his quatrains in the language of the birds, he evidently intended his prophecies to be grasped only by the few. Nostradamus was not in any sense a democrat, writing for the *hoi polloi*: rather, he was writing for scholars, familiar with several languages and with a knowledge of classical literature.

Whilst touching upon this Language of the Birds, it would be almost sacrilegious to pass by, unnoticed, a hermetic work which takes as its subject a gathering of birds. This is the *Jocus Severus* of Michael Maier — a title which means, an 'Earnest Joke'. Here we see a gathering of 16 birds in a single plate.[14] A count of the long title (figure 11) reveals that it consists of 33 words.[15] As is usually the case, one ignores the single-word abbreviations (here, M.D.)

The birds are gathered, under the control of the phoenix, to determine which among them is the wisest. After much argument, the birds decide that the bird of Pallas is the wisest — that is to say, the owl. The joke, perhaps, is that this bird, the *Ulula* in Latin, the *Eul* in German, is actually the *screech owl*, a bird favoured by the night. In contrast, the

phoenix is the resurrectional bird, the true bird of the Sun and the Ego.

This work is one of the few, published in the seventeenth century, which is dedicated not only to all alchemists (*Omnibus verae chymiae amantibus*) but also to the Rosicrucians. Another little joke – in this case a double joke – is contained in this dedication. Under the law of this kind of numerology, it is possible to discount repeated words: in this short text, the word *Fama* is repeated, and thus may be counted only once. Under these conditions, the dedication itself consists of 33 words:

> Omnibus verae chymiae amantibus, per Germaniam notis et ignotis, et inter hos, Nisis nos Fama fallat, adhuc delitescenti, at FAMA FRATER-NITATIS & CONFESSIONE SUA admiranda & probabili in genere manifestato, ascribo, dico & dedico.[16]

When the ampersand (&) in the capitalized section of the dedication is read as the *ET* that it really represents, then the phrase in uppercase consists of 33 letters:

FAMA FRATERNITATIS [ET] CONFESSIONE SUA...

By the Fame of the brotherhood, and his Confession...[17]

The verses of Nostradamus have not yet been understood – even by those who write about them with such seeming assiduity and glibness. This is mainly because scholars have not recognized that the technique which Nostradamus used while constructing his verses involved a highly sophisticated system of encoding. He would play with language in a way that was virtually unique in his day, and he based a large number of his prophecies on references to classical literature; almost five hundred years after he wrote the verses, this serves to obscure his quatrains even more. Nostradamus was an exponent of what may only be called esoteric language – the language of our *Secret booke* – and if we are to grasp the sophistication with which he wrote his prophetic verses, the most sensible thing we can do is to examine a sample verse in some detail. As we untangle the more or less obscure references in the verse, we will begin to marvel at the brilliance of Nostradamus' ability as a literary encoder.

To illustrate these points, I have selected for special scrutiny quatrain III.3. This proves to be an excellent quatrain by which to explore the encoding techniques of Nostradamus, mainly because, in this verse, his word-play is precisely formulated. So far as Nostradamus was concerned, the clever encoding was adapted in his predictive verses mainly to ensure that his prophecies were not revealed openly to all and sundry. What he had to offer was far too precious to be poured out freely. For this reason alone, great effort and considerable learning are generally required to 'solve' the conundrums hidden in the verses of Nostradamus.

I have given only one example of an encoded verse below, having selected it from the hundreds available for only one reason – because Nostradamus ascribed to it the number 33, by locating it as the third verse in book 3 of his *Propheties*. As we might imagine with such an encoding, Nostradamus has used the French language as an open display of encoding, almost in the manner of a crossword.

Below, I give a copy of the original prophetic quatrain III.3 in the form it was published in 1557, whilst Nostradamus was still alive.[18]

I I I

Mars & Mercure & l'argḗt ioint enſéble,
Vers le midy extreme ficcité:
Au fond d'Aſie on dira terre tremble,
Corinthe,,Epheſe lors en perplexité.

We shall note immediately that this verse, number 3 in book 3, opens with a line of 33 characters – provided we convert the abbreviation signs, as indicated in the line below:

Mars & Mercure & l'argent ioint ensemble,

This version of 1557 makes an interesting comparison with the one (below) published eleven years later, in 1568, by which time Nostradamus was dead. As we have seen, the earlier verse had contained a number of abbreviations (for example, *argēt* for *argent*) as well as a printer's error (two consecutive commas after *Corinthe*, in the fourth line).[19] In the later version, these have been removed, making for an easier read, and, of course, for an easier count.[20]

I I I.

Mars & Mercure & l'argent ioint enſemble,
Vers le midy extreme ſiccité:
Au fond d'Aſie on dira terre tremble,
Corinthe, Epheſe lors en perplexité.

Mars & Mercure & l'argent joint ensemble,
Vers le midy extreme siccité:
Au fond d'Asie on dira terre tremble,
Corinthe, Ephese lors en perplexité.

General readers need not be troubled if they cannot understand this French. First, as will become evident it is not strictly speaking pure French at all. Second, it is quite possible to be familiar with all the words that appear in one of the Nostradamus quatrains without being able to form any intelligent view as to what the quatrain actually means. As we shall discover during our analysis of this verse, all four lines are intended by Nostradamus to be read as a sort of sixteenth-century equivalent of a crossword puzzle, or what Nostradamus himself would have called a *ludus*, or a *Jocus*, a game.[21] As we pursue the hidden clues in this verse, we shall discover how its meaning gradually changes. Meanwhile, however, I offer a fairly literal and provisional translation into English, below:

Mars and Mercury and the Moon joined together,
Towards the midi extreme dryness:
In the depth of Asia they will speak of an earthquake.
Corinth, Ephesus then in perplexity.

Quatrain III.3 was first published in 1555. As we shall discover, it predicts the Battle of Lepanto, which, from Nostradamus' standpoint, will not take place for another sixteen years – that is, in 1571.[22]

The Battle of Lepanto proved to be the most famous naval battle of the sixteenth century. It was fought successfully by the combined force of mainly Venetian and Spanish fleets under the command of John of Austria (above).[23] The exotically framed portrait depicts the Battle of Lepanto in the lower central cartouche.

Their enemies, the Turks, had over 250 galleys in their fleet, under the command of Ali Pasha. The Christian fleet had 208 galleys, but almost a hundred other large ships. At the end of the battle, the Turks had lost around 25,000 men, to the Christians' loss of 8,000. Figures vary, but the historian, Herrera, insists that 20,000 Turks were killed, 2,000 taken prisoner, and that 12,000 Christian slaves were liberated from the Turkish galleys. Over 240 Turkish vessels were destroyed.[24] Caracciolo records that 30,000 Turks were lost, and 6,200 taken prisoner, and that 12,000 Christians were released from their galleys, with a loss of 215 Turkish vessels.[25]

The sea-battle of Lepanto was the last major sea-fight in Western waters, involving ships propelled by oars (overleaf).[26]

This battle is now rightly regarded as the most important victory of the sixteenth century against encroaching Islam.

The first line of quatrain III.3 describes the *time* of the event. It does this astrologically, by reference to the positions of certain planets:

Mars & Mercure & l'argent joint ensemble,

Mars and Mercury and the Moon joined together,

We have no problem identifying Mars and Mercury from this line. *Argent*, which literally means 'silver', is the colour traditionally identified with the Moon. In view of this, we might interpret the line as pointing to a time when Mars, Mercury and the Moon were in conjunction (that is, *ensemble*). Later, we shall seek for a time when this cosmic event took place.

Vers le midy extreme siccité:

Towards the midi extreme dryness:

Despite all appearances, the second line (above) is not intended to direct our attention to the *midi* (the south). Nor is it intent on predicting an extreme dryness in the south. In a similar way, the third line (below) is not really concerned with what is being said in the depth of Asia.

Au fond d'Asie on dira terre tremble,

In the depth of Asia they will speak of an earthquake.

What the earthquake is, we shall examine shortly. As we shall see, *Midi*,

Asia and even the *earthquake* are part of the *ludus*, or game, being played by Nostradamus – part of the encoding he has built into the verse.

Vers le midy extreme siccité:
Au fond d'Asie on dira terre tremble,

Hidden at the beginning of these two lines are two words that take on a distinct and relevant meaning, when considered together:

Vers le midy extreme siccité:
Au fond d'Asie on dira terre tremble,

In this context, the word *Vers* is a proposition, meaning 'towards'. The word *Au* is also propositional, and means 'in', or 'at the place of'. In these lines of the verse, Nostradamus plays cunningly with these two words to create a third word that is essential to his meaning. First, he tells us:

Vers le midy *e . . .* (that is, 'towards the middle e'). . . .

The letter **e** of the word, *extreme*, is towards the middle of the line.

Then, he tells us that this same **e** is found

Au fond d'Asie (that is, 'at the end of the word *Asie*') . . .

In each case, Nostradamus is evidently pointing to the letter **e**, within these lines of the quatrain.

By means of this subtle instruction, he encourages us to locate, in the middle (*midy*) of the two words, **Vers** and *Au*, the letter **e** – thus:[27]

Vers e au

By following the simple directions given by Nostradamus in this little *ludus*, we have obtained the word, **Verseau**. This is the French for the zodiacal sign, Aquarius, reproduced below from a sixteenth-century book on astrology.

If our reading of Nostradamus' little *ludus* is correct, then the event that Nostradamus is intending to predict in this quatrain must somehow be linked with the time when Mars, Mercury and the Moon would be located in the zodiacal sign of Verseau, or Aquarius.

Now, as Nostradamus has hinted, in the year 1571, when the power of the Turks was broken in the Mediterranean, Mars, Mercury and the Moon *were* conjunct (that is, *ensemble*) in the sign Aquarius. It is one of Nostradamus' most common tricks to present incomplete data, which permits us later to confirm our reading when the full data becomes available. In this case, not only were these three planets in Aquarius, *but so also were the Sun and Jupiter.*[28] He had mentioned only three of the five 'planets' in his verse, presumably for economy of space, and perhaps to extend his little *ludus,* and make it more amusing, after the event. Below is a section from a horoscope cast for 4 February 1571 (New Style), showing the gathering of these five planets in Aquarius (♒).[29]

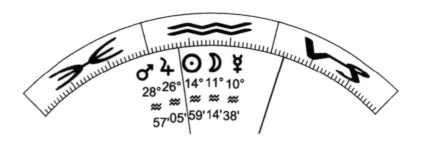

Nostradamus had encoded the year perfectly, and with much less astrological drama than the event itself warranted.

By now, it should be evident that, in order to arrive at this prediction, Nostradamus must have had a vision of some kind which permitted him to see not only the battle of Lepanto itself, but to be aware also of the year in which it would take place. In order to set down his quatrain, in a manner that would permit later readers to analyse its meaning, he had to represent both space and time.

Space, or location, Nostradamus has represented by means of his reference to Corinth and Ephesus. He links these places with an earthquake: Nostradamus has described an event on the seas as representing an earthquake: this is a humorous sort of reversal. The battle of Lepanto was, in a sense, a seaquake — one, indeed, that would have reverberations throughout Europe, and the Anatolia caliphate. It was a sea-battle, yet

Nostradamus has turned the image into another one of his delightful *ludi*. As part of his little game, he hides the place where this earthquake will take place by reference to place-names.

Corinthe, Ephese lors en perplexité.

Corinth, Ephesus then in perplexity.

Taken at face value, the line does not have much obvious meaning. Corinth (*Corinthe*) is in Greece, at the juncture of land where the Peloponnese meets with the main body of the Greek mainland. Above, are the ruins of the Temple of Apollo at this ancient site.[30]

The ruins of Ephesus (*Ephese*) are in Turkey. Although at one time ships could reach this ancient city, it now lies inland from Kusadasi, on the mainland of Turkey, opposite the island of Samos. Overleaf, is a view of the ruins of the imposing ancient Roman theatre at Ephesus.[31]

We are now able to touch upon one of the great Green Language techniques that Nostradamus used, and one that no commentator has so far recognized. This technique involves him representing place-names in such a way that they may be joined together by straight lines on a map, in order to indicate something else, of relevance to the quatrain.

If, with this in mind, we follow the enigmatic final line of this quatrain, we may be inclined to take a map of Greece and draw a straight line from

Ephesus, so that it passes through Corinth. When we extend this line, we discover that it projects into the straits between the islands of Cephalonia and Zante (below).

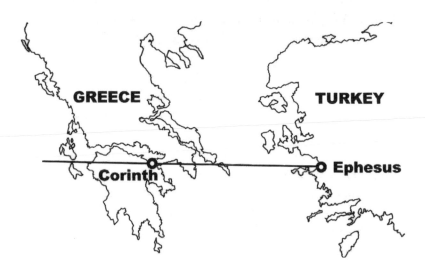

The Gulf of Lepanto lies to the east of these straits. The Christian warships that fought at Lepanto had sailed down the eastern side of Cephalonia, and had entered the sea lanes leading into the Gulf in the very same area as is marked by this line.[32]

Corinthe, Ephese lors en perplexité.

Corinth, Ephesus then in perplexity.

After following the line from Ephesus to Corinth, Nostradamus tells us that we shall be *lors en perplexité*. Once again, he is indulging in *ludi*, or a play on linguistics. One of the Greek words for 'perplexity' is άπορία (*aporia*). This Greek word has a secondary meaning, related to things which prove, at times, to be something of a perplexity for seamen. This secondary meaning is, 'straits'.

Many of the ancient Greek terms are still used in modern map-making. For example, the waters seen from the gardens of the Monastery of the Virgin Mary, on the heights of Corfu's Paleokastritsa (above) are still called the *Straits* of Otranto.

Thus, Nostradamus is telling us that, after following the extended line connecting Ephesus and Corinth, we arrive, not at *perplexity* (as a state of mind) but, rather at the *straits* (άπορία) as a geological reality.[33] Whether we should read this hermeneutic as a reference to the straits between the islands of Cephalonia and Zante, or to those between the mainland of Greece and the Peloponnese, is up to the judgement of the reader.

Either way, the line we have drawn leaves us in no doubt that Nostradamus is intending us to read (in the fourth line of his quatrain) a reference to the future place of the battle of Lepanto. This battle will take place to the east of these straits, which divide mainland Greece from the Peloponnese. In this particular quatrain, Nostradamus did not use the word Lepanto, but he might have been inclined to had he not preferred playing games.

There is a tendency to overlook the importance of his extraordinary book, *Les Propheties*. This is largely due to the nonsense that is written by those soi-disant specialists who write books on the quatrains without actually knowing anything about them, or about Nostradamus. The fact is that this work, whilst it so evidently deals with the future, actually belongs to the past: part of the fascination of this book rests on the fact that, whilst the verses were written almost five hundred years ago, they are still, even at this distance of time, revealing themselves to be accurate predictions. Even in my own lifetime, the predictions which Nostradamus made concerning the Moon landings – the Apollo missions – have been fulfilled. Similarly, so has the prediction he made concerning the destruction by terrorists (he referred to them as being the equivalent of pirates, who were, indeed, the terrorists of the sixteenth century) of the Twin Towers on Manhattan, New York.[34]

As we have seen, a number of encodings in our increasingly commodious *Secret booke* are linked with, or derived from, quotations from biblical texts. This method of encoding became popular in the mid-sixteenth century, after the verses in the books of the Bible were finally given numbers.[35] This system of numeration made for ease of reference in certain encodings. Nostradamus was particularly adroit at using both biblical verse numbers and texts as the basis for his *ludi*. He was helped in this enterprise by the French printer, Estienne, who, circa 1551, began to introduce the useful numeration, with which we are now familiar, into the verses. Below, I shall examine a quatrain which demonstrates his ability as an encoder of predictions by means of references to a pair of unrelated biblical texts.

It has been said that the journals of Pierre de l'Estoile did for the Paris of Henry IV what the diaries of Samuel Pepys later did for the London of Charles II.[36] That is to say, Pierre de L'Estoile, through his vigilance as an observer, allied to his wry sense of humour and feeling for the picaresque, brought details of contemporaneous French history vividly to life.

L'Estoile, admirably placed by his official role as *Audiencier de la Chancellerie de Paris*, recorded his eye-witness observations of day-to-day events in the political circles of the Palais de Justice, the Louvre, and in the streets of Paris, for almost four decades.

From time to time, when writing the diaries which he had begun in 1574, Pierre de l'Estoile makes it clear that he was no supporter of prophets or astrologers.[37] Even so, the interesting truth is that he was really the first to offer posterity an insight into how certain predictions – especially those attributed to Nostradamus – were interpreted in the decades immediately following the death of the great man.

L'Estoile's journals cover a period of 37 years from 1574 to 1611, and offer an eye-witness view of the religious wars of those years, as well as a remarkably complete account of the reign of Henry IV, whom l'Estoile served indirectly as an official in the Palais de Justice, in Paris. From our point of view, what is of immense value in these diaries are the references to the manner in which one or two of the quatrains of Nostradamus were interpreted – wrongly interpreted, one should observe – in terms of contemporaneous events.

L'Estoile was no supporter of prophets, or even of astrologers, yet his own innate sense as a historian prevailed, and he innocently records the effects which one or two prophetic quatrains had on his contemporaries. His insights preserve a feeling of how deeply the prophecies of Nostradamus had entered into the blood-stream of French life, in the decades following his own death, in 1566.

By 1583, when l'Estoile made his first reference to a quatrain (as it happens, a genuine verse), eighteen editions of the *Propheties* had already appeared.[38] However, even by that time the integrity of the corpus of quatrains was under threat, as a number of individuals had already begun to publish pamphlets and books that pretended to continue the work of Nostradamus, taking both his name and visionary genius in vain. This scurrilous activity resulted in an accumulation of quatrains, written superficially in the manner of Nostradamus, which the uninitiated frequently took to be genuine. L'Estoile himself seems not to have doubted that all the quatrains he copied were, indeed, from the pen of Nostradamus, even though this was not the case.

Of the six quatrains that Pierre de l'Estoile recorded as being written by Nostradamus, only two appear to have been genuinely from the pen of the Master. I doubt that l'Estoile knew the other four were forgeries. L'Estoile's writings reveal very little knowledge of Nostradamus, and he does not appear to have made any attempt to check the verses he copied against available editions of the *Propheties*. Indeed, it is unlikely this scholarly idea would even have crossed his mind. Any attempt to check the verses against the ten books of the *Propheties,* or against works that contained references to the so-called *presages,* would have been a drawn-out business that would certainly have obtruded on his busy life. It does seem that these quatrains came to him as manuscript copies, for he never offers a reference by way of book or quatrain number.

In contrast to the rather obvious forgeries, two of the quatrains that he recorded were genuine — in the sense that they may be located in earlier editions of the *Propheties*. One of these genuine quatrains is of particular interest, for it is clear from his diary entry that l'Estoile and his acquaintances read it as relating to an event which they anticipated for 1609 — the very same year in which he copied the quatrain in his diary. Their interpretation of this genuine quatrain led them to presume that the year would see the death of the reigning Pope, who was Paul V. It may come as a shock to us, now we have been permitted a glance into the *Secret booke* of Shakespeare, to realize l'Estoile did not appear to even imagine that the verses were encoded. He, like many of his successors, attempted to read these arcane verses as though they were straightforward descriptive texts.

In view of this, there is no need to ask why l'Estoile assumed that the prophecy must refer to the year 1609, since this is the year recorded in the first line of the quatrain. However, Nostradamus was an arch-obscurantist, and the dates he gives in his verses may hardly ever be taken at face value. Before looking into the meaning of quatrain X.91, let me set it down in the form that l'Estoile himself recorded it, in his diary entry for 10 February 1609.

> Clergé romain, l'an 1609,
> Au chef de l'an, fera élection
> D'un gris et noir, de la campagne yssu,
> Qui onc ne fut si malin.

The prophecy, l'Estoile tells us, was circulating in the Palais de Justice (where he worked), and even in Rome. Understandably, the reference to 1609, alongside the mention of an *election,* in the second line, led l'Estoile and others to assume that the verse predicted the death of the reigning Pope, Paul V (right). His death, in 1609, would, of course, demand the election of another Pope.

The quatrain, insisted l'Estoile with a literary shrug, was nothing but a *fadèze*, a piece of nonsense. However, when he had finishing copying the verse into his diary, he inscribed an evident warning at the end of the final line: *Tocque Tabourin* – the beating of a warning drum.[39]

The version of quatrain X.91, as printed in the 1568 edition of the *Propheties*, reads:[40]

X C I.
**Clergé Romain l'an mil six cens & neuf,
Au chef de l'an feras election
D'vn gris & noir de la Compagne yssu,
Qui onc ne feut si maling.**

Clergé Romain l'an mil six cens & neuf,
Au chef de l'an feras election
D'un gris & noir de la Compagne yssu,
Qui onc ne feut si maling.

Roman clergy the year one thousand, six hundred and nine,
At the head of the year will make [an] election.
Of a grey and black issued from the countryside.
Which once was not so malign.

We see that, in the version he recorded in 1609, Pierre de l'Estoile reduced the year to figures. This is a pity, for, had he been interested in numerologies, he might have observed that the verse number and the full text of the line were designed to offer an addition of 33 characters. L'Estoile also changed *Compagne* to *campagne*, *feut* to *fut*, and *maling* to *malin*. Perhaps these are not major changes. Probably, they are adjustments to amend a sixteenth-century text, to bring it into a more up-to-date seventeenth-century form – and indeed they change the meaning of the verse only in a minimal sense. The really important thing that l'Estoile missed out was the number of the verse: no doubt this was not provided by the correspondent who sent the verse to him.

The first line, like so many lines of Nostradamus, is not quite what it seems. As we contemplate it, the line turns out to be a clever piece of encoding.

Clergé Romain l'an mil six cens & neuf,

Roman clergy the year one thousand, six hundred and nine,

For all its appearance, the number 1609 is not really a date at all. It is intended to act as an index to the first two words of the quatrain – *Clergé romain*. This is a scarce-disguised reference to Paul's *Epistle to the Romans* (Romains) used by the clergy (*Clergé*) in their readings from the *New Testament*.

If we apply this index (1609 or 16 09) to *Romans*, we discover something of profound importance. Chapter 16, verse 09, of *Romans*, consists of a greeting sent by Paul from Corinth to his followers in Rome. Below, I give the opening of this verse in English, followed (for the purist) in Latin and French.

Salute Urbane, our helper in Christ, and Stachys my beloved.

9. Salutate Urbanum, adjutorem nostrum in Christo Jesu, et Stachyn, dilectum meum.

9 Saluez Urbain, notre compagnon d'œuvre en Christ, et Stachys, mon bien-aimé.

This salute to Urbain leads us to suspect that this particular quatrain by Nostradamus is somehow related to Pope Urban (*Urbanus*). Let us pursue this idea.

Since the time when Nostradamus first published this prophecy in 1557, there have been only two Popes who adopted the name of Urban

(*Urbanus*, in Latin). Giambattista Castagna, adopted the name Urban VII when elected in 1590. However, he fell ill a few days afterwards, and died without having been enthroned. Maffeo Barberini, who would adopt the name Urban VIII, would reign for a substantial period, from 1623 to 1644. Could it be this latter future Urban, whom Nostradamus is saluting by reference to the biblical text?

Au chef de l'an, fera election

At the head of the year, will make [an] election.

Who, or what, was this *chef de l'an*? It is reasonable for us to assume that, within this particular encoding, the chief must be mentioned in the text of *Romans*, from whence we took the reference to Urban. Given this, the 'chief' of the passage must surely be the Apostle Paul, who wrote the letter, and whose name is at the head (*au chef*, in French) of the *Epistle* in the *New Testament* itself.

Epître de Paul aux
Romains

In Latin:

EPISTOLA BEATI PAULI APOSTOLI

AD ROMANOS:

This reading makes perfect sense for, during the stipulated and encoded year 1609, there was a Paul (Paul V) on the papal throne in Rome. Just as Paul was the headlined writer of the letter, so was his name-sake, Paul V, the chief of the Roman Catholic Church, in that 'year' mentioned in the quatrain. The double meaning is delightfully compact, and cleverly encoded, for the date 1609 has taken on a real meaning within the context of 16:09.

It seems then that the quatrain is predicting the election of a future Pope, who will adopt the name Urban. For all Nostradamus has used a simulated date (1609), it is already evident to us that he does not foresee this Urban coming to the throne of Rome in that year. However, instead of offering a future date for the accession of Urban VIII, as we might expect, Nostradamus gives a startling description of this Pope. He devotes the remaining two lines of the quatrain to a startlingly precise description of something uniquely distinctive about this future Pope.

The election will be of one who is...

D'un gris et noir, de la Compagne yssu

Of a grey and black, issued from the countryside.

Obscure as this description is, it certainly made perfect sense once Urban VIII had been elected Pope. Urban VIII was from the Barberini family, who were famous for their heraldic device of bees. As we shall see, the *gris et noir*, the grey and black, is a reference to insects – to bees. In the imagery associated with the Barberini, the bees fly from a garden, and may therefore accurately be said to *yssu de la Compagne* (to issue from the country). Nostradamus had delightfully used the word *yssu*, as though to suggest, onomatopoeically, the sound of bees.[41]

The Barberini were originally from Florence. In consequence, images of the Barberini bees may be seen on the facades of several of the buildings they erected or owned. Later, thanks to the architectural interests of Urban VIII in Rome, one may see, even to this day, fine buildings in the Eternal City displaying the Barberini bees.[42]

The original bee image, associated with the Barberini family, was probably that adopted by Cardinal Antonio Barberini, who imagined the bees collecting honey in a garden, alongside his motto, *Exercet sub sole laborem*: 'It does its work under the sun.'[43] The implication in the device is that the Barberini did all their transactions openly, and without guile, disdaining the cover of corrupting darkness – a corruption then endemic in Italy as a whole.

When Maffeo Barberini was elected Urban VIII, he naturally adopted the device of the bee. He did however change the motto. In future, it was to read, *Sponte favos, ægrè spicula*. This translates, 'honeycombs willingly, stings unwillingly'. The sentiment was supposed to characterize the nature of a merciful ruler, who is by nature more anxious to please than to punish. It was certainly true of Urban VIII that he went out of his way to please his relatives, by giving them easy access to the papal honey-pot. He was, we are told, the last of the great papal nepotists.

An example of these papal bees may be seen in a marble detail from St. Peter's in Rome (below).[44]

Now, it might be argued that the bee is *not* usually grey and black. Even here, however, Nostradamus was being accurate: the Barberini bee was pictured, in heraldic terms, as black and grey, *volant* against an azure background.

The imagery of the Barberini bee is continued, to some extent, in the final line of the quatrain.

Qui onc ne fut si maling.

Which once was not so malign.

This could refer either to the device of the bee or to the personality of Urban VIII.

In respect of the bee, we learn that before the insect was adopted by the Barberini of Florence, their arms were figured by gadflies (*tafani*), and these were later changed to bees. It is possible that Nostradamus was developing the conceit that formerly, or once (*onc*) these gadflies did not sting quite so savagely as later, when they became bees.[45]

I must admit that I have no special knowledge concerning the secrets of the papacy, and I am not qualified to judge the merits of one man against another, let alone one Pope against another. However, it is also possible to read this line as though Nostradamus was implying that Urban VIII would not be *si maling* (so hurtful) as a former Pope.

The immediate former Pope, prior to Urban VIII, was Gregory XV, who reigned for only one full year. I can see no reason why Nostradamus would have considered it necessary to compare Urban with Gregory. Could it be that Nostradamus was inclined to compare Urban with Paul V, who invisibly participates in the quatrain by being on the papal seat in 1609? This seems unlikely, as there is little to tie these two great men together.

It does seem more likely, however, that Nostradamus was comparing one Urbanus with another – that is to say, Urban VII with Urban VIII. At the very least, these two have a papal name in common. As we have seen, Urban VII, who came to the chair of Rome in 1590, reigned for only 13 days, and was not even crowned. In contrast, Urban VIII (below),[46] who was elected in 1621, remained on the papal seat for 21 years.

I suspect that this is what Nostradamus had in mind when he wrote the last line of the verse. Urban VII was *maling* in the sense that, through no fault of his own, he did nothing much as Pope. In contrast, Urban VIII did

a vast amount to augment and improve the Papacy, both in reforms of rituals and in promoting extensive building.

Quatrain X.91 is a remarkably succinct one, if somewhat limited in its application. It identifies a future Pope by name, confirms the identification against his future device, and compares him favourably with an earlier namesake. So precisely accurate is the quatrain in its encoding that it almost persuades us to dispense with our usual caution: we tend to forget that we are reading not history, but a prediction, laid out 66 years before it was fulfilled.

One puzzle about quatrain X.91 is that, whilst Nostradamus ensured that the first line (with the addition of the verse number) gave us 33 characters, he appears to have made no real effort to ensure that the verse itself should consist of 33 words.

XCI.

Clergé Romain l'an mil fix cens & neuf,
Au chef de l'an feras election
D'vn gris & noir de la Compagne yffu,
Qui onc ne feut fi maling.

Even when we include the verse number, we find that the count comes only to 32. However, those who creatively encode such things as numerologies take a particular delight in making use of 'invisible' numbers, if only to ensure that their encoding is not too obvious. In this case, we are compelled to ask, if we must add the quatrain number (in a quatrain that itself specifies four numbers — *mil, six, cents* and *neuf*) then why should we not also add the book number, to obtain the desired 33?

The quatrain is itself a *ludus*, partly playing with sacred scripture, identified by chapter and verse numbers. Further, that quatrain has been built upon an encoding which incorporates two numbers relating to that quatrain — the century number (X) and the quatrain number (XCI). Wheels within wheels, we might say today — *ludi* within *ludi*, Nostradamus might well have said, with a quiet, knowing smile.[47]

Chapter 7

The Ego in Strife: Jacob Boehme and William Law

O Man! Consider thyself, here thou standest in the earnest, perpetual strife of Good and Evil, all nature is continually at work to bring about the great redemption; the whole creation is travailing in pain and laborious workings, to be delivered from the vanity of time, and wilt thou be asleep? . . . Thou hast the height and depth of eternity in thee, and therefore, be doing what thou wilt, either in the closet, the field, the shop, or the church, thou art sowing that which grows and must be reaped in eternity. Nothing of thine can vanish away, but every thought, motion and desire of thy heart has its effect either in the height of Heaven or the depth of hell . . .

[William Law, *An Appeal to All who Doubt*, in G. Moreton's edition of Law's *Works*, 9 vols, (1892), Vol. VI, p. 117.]

In the eighteenth century, the Reverend William Law commissioned an engraved portrait of the sixteenth-century mystic and esotericist, Jacob Boehme, to serve as a frontispiece for the English translation of his *Works*.[1] Law went to some pains to ensure that the 33 encoding was reflected in that picture (right). Boehme was Law's intellectual mentor, his spiritual ideal, his path to understanding Christ. So far as Law was concerned, the introduction of this encoding of the early Rosicrucians was a prerequisite for doing his hero honour.

At the top corners of the engraved portrait are two angels. That to the left is one of the Cherubim with the flaming sword, his form bathed in an aura of flames. Above the angel's head is a triangle, with its apex upwards $\triangle$ – symbolic of elemental Fire in the alchemical tradition. It was a symbol that Boehme had adopted as part of his personalized symbol for the Ego.

The angel to the right, who is probably Gabriel, is bathed in an aura of radiant light: he holds a branch of mixed flowers, among which we may discern roses. Above his head is the triangle, with its apex pointing dowwards $\triangledown$ – the symbol of elemental Water and, again, one that Boehme had adopted to figure in his own symbol of the Ego.

We have already noted that the combination of these two triangles produces the Seal of Solomon, and is a nominal expression of the 33 encoding. It seems to have been partly in this spirit of encoding that Boehme made use of this symbol in his illustrations.

Boehme viewed the Seal as being pre-eminently the spiritual sign of the human Ego. So far as the symbolism in the portrait is concerned, Boehme is represented as viewing the human Ego as a composite part of the angelical Fire of the Cherubim. The Ego was also — perhaps incidentally — being linked, here, with the flaming sword that kept the Ego out of Paradise. At the same time, Boehme viewed the human Ego as possessed of a cooling Water that mystically conjoins with that Fire. This Water is represented in the halo-form of the angel, who brought the news of the coming of Jesus Christ to Mary and the world.

This link, drawn between the element Water and the archangel Gabriel, is deeply traditional.[2] The archangel is depicted blowing a trumpet, perhaps announcing a message for humanity. From the bowl of this instrument, issues a banderol, upon which are written 19 words (this count must ignore the ampersand):

To Christians, Jews, Turks, & Heathens,
To all the Nations of the Earth;
This Trumpet Sounds for the Last Time.

Around the engraved frame of the portrait is an inscription:

JACOB BEHMEN, The TEUTONIC THEOSOPHER, Born at OLD SEIDENBURG, 1575. Died at GORLITZ, 1624.

A count reveals that, when one includes the two dates as the equivalent of two words, the inscription consists of 14 words. The addition of 19 and 14 gives a total of 33.

The tendency of the early Rosicrucians, and other esotericists of the sixteenth and seventeenth centuries to make hermeneutic use of the 33 encoding, is developed to the full in the esoteric writings associated with the sixteenth-century mystic, Jacob Boehme, and his disciples. We shall discuss one or two examples below, particularly that example of the 33 code, which reflects upon Boehme's view of the Ego.

One important text to which we shall refer is Boehme's *Clavis*, which was translated into English by the Reverend William Law in 1764. Law, who was conversant with the 33 encoding, ensured that *The Author's*

Preface to this work should open with a capitalized I, and consist of 33 lines of text.[3]

By now, it must be clear that esotericists only rarely reveal their innermost thoughts concerning the Ego. The Ego is not only the modern Mystery, which few understand — but also a mysterious thing which almost evades definition. However, Jacob Boehme was an exception to most rules and he, perhaps more than any other, seemed prepared to put forward in his works original views concerning the Ego. A good example of this is found in his *Clavis*, which we shall examine on a number of occasions in this present chapter. In this text, Boehme examines the inner meaning of the name JEHOVA, given by 'the Ancient Rabins' as 'the most Holy Name of God'. For Boehme, each of the six letters of the English version of this sacred name had a secret meaning, which he discussed in some detail.[4] Of these, the first letter is of profound interest to our own study, for Boehme quite rightly treated the opening letter J as an equivalent of I. He defined this letter quite appropriately (as we will now recognize) in section 33 of the *Clavis*. Below, I append a translation of what Boehme had to say about the I, for this makes the most immediate sense in English, where the I is the name of the Ego.

J

33. For I is the Effluence of the Eternal indivifible Unity, or the fweet grace and fulineſs of the ground of the Divine Power of becoming ᵇ fomething.　　　　ᵇ Egoity, or felf.

Thus, one of the most influential esotericists of the seventeenth century was prepared to define the word I, or the Ego, as an effluence of the Eternal. Further, he was prepared to add a note to the effect that this effluence was itself nothing other than the equivalent or manifestation of the Ego, or Self. It is interesting that even though the passage number in the book was designed to ensure an hermeneutic link between the 33 and the Ego, William Law took this numerology further. He went to the trouble of ensuring that there were precisely 33 distinct grammatical units in this definition.[5]

To express his views concerning the Ego, and its relationship to the higher spiritual realm, Boehme evolved a uniquely expressive Christianized astrology, and a highly spiritual Christology, neither of which lent itself to clarity of exposition. In spite of this, a number of proficient esotericists, such as Georg Gichtel and Dionysius Freher, who had a profound interest in Boehme's writings, became his disciples and promulgated his teachings. Among these disciples were a number of English mystics, who had been touched by the Christian elements within Rosicrucianism, the most notable of whom were John Pordage and Jane Leade. This pair established the mystical sect of Philadelphians, in 1670. In England, Boehme's teachings were given a new and spiritually creative slant by the writings of William Law, who published a series of engraved plates that set out the ideas behind the Boehmian system.[6] Altogether, Law published thirteen of these engraved plates in a single series. He accompanied these with notes and explanations that were sometimes lucid, at other times opaque, yet always filled with an insightful admiration for the vision of the great mystic.

In his writings, the Reverend William Law was more often than not a poet, for poetry is the true language of mysticism. However, this sense of poetry, of cadency and metre, poured over even into the engravings he devised, to express Boehme's visions. In Law's esoteric engravings, one feels not so much the hard edge of the burin but hears, as it were, the lineaments of music. One is not surprised, as the historian Henri Talon reminds us, that Law famously died singing a hymn.[7]

Although these thirteen engravings are of relatively late execution in comparison with the other images we have examined so far in this present book, I feel that we may discuss them here for a number of reasons. Not only do they incorporate many of the Rosicrucian ideas that colour Boehme's theosophy, but William Law was evidently influenced by such leading esotericists as Mercurius van Helmont and von Welling. Further, the plates from *An Illustration of the Deep Principles* are themselves (particularly so in their coloured states) among the more beautiful esoteric engravings ever to have been published. It is a tragedy that their meanings have been so radically misunderstood, even by esotericists who should have known better.

It will be worth our while examining a detail from one of these plates, in which the Law-Boehme duad set out their view of the nature of the Ego. The entire plate is reproduced in figure 12. As we began with a passing reference to his rather specialist treatment of the name JEHOVA, it is fitting that we continue with a detail from one of his esoteric plates, in which he included reference to this Rabbinic name of God.

The detail (opposite) is from plate 7 of the Law series. As we shall see, this represents a clear exposition of the genesis of the individual Ego: the diagram reaffirmed in graphic terms what Boehme had earlier written in section 33 of his *Clavis*. From an encircled triangle, bearing the Hebrew

name of God, IEHOVA, which has been separated into three segments, reflective of the Trinity, descends the Latin word FIAT. The word means 'let there be' or 'let there be made'. Part of the esoteric power behind this word stems from the fact that it is the *third* word in the *third* verse (hence 33) of the first chapter of *Genesis*, which section, in the Vulgate Latin text, comprises 33 words.[8]

LIBER

GENESIS,

CAPUT PRIMUM.
IN principio creavit Deus cœlum et terram.

2 Terra autem erat inanis et vacua, et tenebræ erant super faciem abyssi: et Spiritus Dei ferebatur super aquas.

3 Dixitque Deus: Fiat lux. Et facta est lux.

This word, *Fiat*, is represented in the engraving as still being linked with the higher Trinity, for its first three letters **FIA** are portrayed in the light, whilst its concluding letter, the T, is plunged into the relative darkness of the lower sphere. It is in this sphere that we find the emergence of the number 1.

Throughout the series of plates, this 1 is drawn in an unconventional manner: the top part is portrayed in the form of an arrow pointing upwards, suggesting that it is designed to indicate its higher origins.

The arrow-like triangular top is partly a visual reminder of the triangle of light from which this numeral has just emerged. The lower part is bifurcated, probably in order to indicate that this 1, which is descended from the unity of the spiritual world, has been dipped into polarity. It must be quite evident, already, that this 1 represents the Ego, the One or Monad, derived from the higher Trinity.

Below this second circle is a larger one that contains a crown, a circle of flames, and the letter A. I shall return to the crown in a moment: meanwhile, it is imperative at this stage that we see the letter A as an extension, or spiritual transformation, of the number 1 in the circle above. This number one, which in our view represents the nascent Ego, is linked with the triad or Trinity. The link is established by virtue of its own upper triangulation, and perhaps by the three points of the associate letter T of FIAT, with which it shares the circle. In the letter A, this graphic notion of Trinity is transformed into the upper triangle of the letter as an Δ. The lower part of the Boehmian 1 is transformed into the lower bifurcation of ascender and descender of the A:

↟ TRANSFORMS INTO A

Thus, the numerological connection between the number 1 and the letter A, as well as its Greek and Hebrew equivalents, *alpha* and *aleph*, is graphically confirmed within the diagram. In his analyses of these images, William Law confirms Boehme's view that the letter A stands for Adam, the first created human being. Adam is therefore number 1 by virtue of his primogeniture, and A by virtue of the first letter of his name. As we have seen, this tradition has extended into occult symbolism, in which the *alpha* is often linked with the beginning, not only of things, but of humanity and the Ego.

The letter **A** of Adam is portrayed in a burning circle to show that Adam still dwells in the Garden of Eden, and is not yet experiencing the consequences of the Fall.[9] In view of this symbolism, it might be tempting to make an assumption. We may be inclined to assume that the crown at the top of this circle points to Adam as the crown of Creation, save for the fact that there is one important hidden element in the design. In the complete print, a wide circular zodiacal band passes behind the area occupied by the crown. I reveal a section of this band in the detail below.

In the complete print (given in this present work as figure 12), the circular band is inset with images of eleven sigils for the zodiacal signs. Only one of the signs is not shown: this is the sign Aries (♈) which, in the natural order of the zodiac, would fall between Pisces (♓) and Taurus (♉) above. Thus, in this case, Aries remains as an unrevealed cosmic force *behind* the crown. As the zodiac is, among other things, a measure of Time, the sign Aries marks the beginning of the seasons: in the spring-time, it marks the beginning of life. Aries is one of the Fire signs, and thus finds greater expression in the fiery circle below, when it is transformed into the letter **A**. Aries is represented by the sigil ♈ which depicts the descent of spirit into the point of matter, or into the point of Time, where matter may become manifest.

Of course, we have already noted that the Elizabethan magus, John Dee, placed great importance on the hermeneutic of this sigil ♈. He assigned to it a fundamental and hermetic role in the structure of his esoteric device, the *Monas Hieroglyphica*. In this sigil, the entire structure of the *Monas* seemed to grow from the fecund symbol of Aries:

It is not at all surprising that in his *Clavis*, Jacob Boehme, used this *Monas* sigil of Dee as a heading for his unconventional and spiritual summary of the seven planetary natures, which lay behind both his graphics and his writings (below).[10]

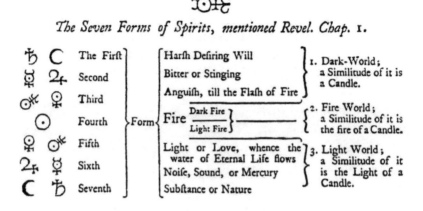

The Seven Forms of Spirits, mentioned Revel. Chap. 1.

In the traditional image of zodiacal man, Aries rules the head. This association reveals the symbolic significance of the crown, which, properly, can only be worn on the head.[11] We see, then, that this crown is the outer form of the Arietan impulse, which strives to begin life. It is as though the sharp point of the sigil for Aries ♈ injects the life-force of spirit into form. This is why it may be said of Aries that it descends into matter by way of Time. The **A** below the Aries-crown, the Adam, is a manifestation of this first descent into matter. At the *Fiat* of God, Light was created. Later, by another creative deed, man and woman were created.[12]

What summary may we offer for this analysis of the remarkable detail from plate 7? First, it is clear that the Ego is conceived as descending from the Trinity, and emerging first in monadic form. It then descends into the archetypal Adam, wherein its own monadic form is transmuted into the letter **A**, which mystically retains the impress of the Trinity. At this point, it seems to turn over, to point its apex downwards, **V**, as it merges with the first sign of the zodiac, Aries ♈. At this point, it may be conceived as having descended into the stream of Time, or into the sub-supernal levels of Creation. Among the deeper levels of esoteric symbolism, the sigil for Aries ♈, the letter A and the related forms for the Greek *alpha* and Hebrew *aleph*, were regarded as conveying much the same symbolic import in regard to the doctrines of beginnings. This idea was wisely used in art and literature.

The lamentable Tragedie

of *Locrine*, the eldeſt ſonne of King *Brutus*, diſcour-
ſing the warres of the *Britaines* and *Hunnes*,
with their diſcomfiture, the Britaines *victory*
with their accidents, and the death
of *Albanact*.

To remain within Elizabethan or Jacobean literature, we may take as an example one design that appeared in a tragedy attributed to the dramatist and Rosicrucian, Thomas Heywood.[13]

One has to be aware of the hermetic importance of the letter **A** to recognize the two forms in the vignette to the opening of Heywood's play, *Locrine*. Fortunately, the numerology within the text is a fairly easy guide to the fraternity of the Rosy Cross, for the expansive title consists of 33 words. However, the vignette heading is what interests us here: hidden within the floriations are two letter forms, one of which is an ornate A, and the other its mirror image. The mirror image is heavily shadowed, indicating that it is the equivalent of what is sometimes called in arcane lore, the *dark aleph*. In terms of cabbalistic teaching, all things in heaven have their counterparts on earth — all entities of light have a reflected equivalence in the dark. In terms of the arcane thought of the seventeenth century, these two letters — one in Light, the other tinged with Darkness — would represent the pure and sullied Ego, the latter darkened by its descent into matter. As we shall see, Jacob Boehme and William Law employed this symbolism of the dual Ego in their illustrations.

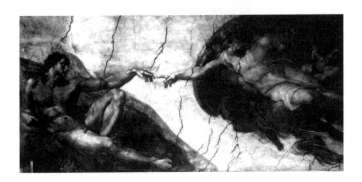

It is not too much to trace a similar hermeneutic, linked with the letter **A**, in God's hand-gesture, in the famous detail of Michelangelo's fresco on the ceiling of the Sistine Chapel (previous page).[14]

We may trace in God's first finger and thumb a resemblance to the letter **A**, reaching out its descender towards the limp hand of Adam, which suggests the shadow A, the *dark aleph*.[15]

Michelangelo has even portrayed the body of the naked Adam in the form of a letter **A**, with one descender in the guise of a leg, the other in the guise of an out-reaching arm (below). Not only does this form contrive to reflect the creative hand-gesture of God, but it also emphasizes the important connection between the form and the name, Adam.

This view of the relationship between the form of the letter **A**, which constitutes the first letter of the alphabet, and the creation, or forming of Adam, the first human being, is expressed in a number of contemporaneous works, with which Michelangelo might have been familiar whilst working on the Sistine Chapel ceiling. A considerable literature existed relating to the nature of the first language, which Adam used to name all the other creatures at the beginning of the world. In view of this, no great leap of imagination was required to link the letter **A** with the name of Adam and also with the world's beginning.

One of the best summaries, contemporaneous with Michelangelo, of beliefs concerning the origin of the Adamic language, was that written by Charles Bovelle of Amiens, who was born close to the time of Michelangelo, around 1475. Bovelle's chief interest in life was the nature of language, and, during many years of research, he came to the conclusion that the language Adam had spoken was Hebrew. In his view, the alphabets used in Europe in the fifteenth century, had been derived from the archetypal Adamic language of Hebrew. Bovelles saw this gradual change from Hebrew, 'from the summit of the archetypal language', as a decline, brought about by the influences of time and place.[16] Although it is unlikely that Boehme himself learned from either Michelanelo or Bovelles, he imbibed this knowledge of the hermeneutic **A** from a similar source.

The detail from the Boehme-Law plate (like the engraving from which it is derived – figure 12) proposes a much richer sequence of esoteric symbolism than I have discussed above: even so, the residue of this descent is found in the lower A, which clearly has many other levels of meaning than merely the name of Adam. Technically, we might be inclined to form the opinion that the Boehme-Law diagram we have just examined deals with Archetypes: this is, of course, quite true. However, Archetypes are themselves eternal, and in consequence the diagram portrays how the Ego emerges into Space and Time contemporaneously. It is a portrayal of how every man and woman comes into being, to become spirit dwelling in material form. One of the tenets, in arcane literature, that the letter **A** is representative of the descended (or fallen) Ego, is intimately woven into Boehme's own insistence that the letter **A** is also an image of God. The argument for this is based on the fact that the German for 'Eye' is *Auge*. God is visualised as the **A** of *Auge*, looking down into the created world and seeing His own reflection:

With the perfect union of God and Man, the two letters form a symbol that may be seen to represent the Three in One:

As Boehme must have recognized, one hermeneutic behind this deification of the A is numerological. In the simple key system of encoding, the word *Auge* is the equivalent of 33:[17]

A   U   G   E

1 + 20 + 7 + 5 = 33

The resultant symbol is not only an echo of the Light and *Dark alephs*, but also an extension of the hermetic doctrine of 'as below, so above'. Further, the symbol intimates that the purpose of Creation was for God to see Himself.

Boehme also combines this simple graphic system with a play on the first two letters of AUge, with the U representing a V, which (Boehme tells us) stands for desire: ... *it is all things, and yet a nothing. It beholdeth itself, and yet finds nothing but an A, which is the Eye.*[18] In *The Clavis*, we learn that the letter **A** is,

> ... that which is proceeded from the power and virtue, *viz.* the wisdom; a Subject of the Trinity; wherein the Trinity works, and wherein the Trinity is also manifest.[19]

So far, we have extracted from this detail something of the secrets (as portrayed by Law) relating to Boehme's view of the Ego. However, we have not yet gone far enough in our exploration of his hermetic symbolism. To do some justice to the importance of Boehme's programme of symbolism, which lies behind his account of the incarnating and excarnating Ego, we should examine another plate from the series. As this particular plate was specifically designed to show the circulation of the Ego through Space and Time, it will throw further light of understanding on the Ego.

There are thirteen inter-related plates in the series, each thoroughly arcane in theme, and all coloured by a Rosicrucian symbolism. For those individuals intent on the study of the Ego and reincarnation, the twelfth of these plates is probably of the greatest interest. I say this knowing full well that the entire series is integrated hermeneutically, and each throws light on the others: they cannot be fully understood out of sequence. The main graphic theme of plate 12 is reincarnation, in that it offers a graphic account of the descent and re-ascent of the Ego, between the spiritual and material realms. It is reproduced below in small, and in a larger dimension in figure 13 of the present work.

In this engraving, the two realms are symbolized by an upper light semi-circle, which encloses a number of symbols. The topmost realm includes an encircled triangle. At the bottom of the image, a dark semi-circle enfolds a large capital **A**, which grips between its ascender and descender an image of the Earth.

A complete analysis of this plate is not possible, here. However, it is important that we study a small number of symbolic graphics within the plate, in order to recognize that it deals with reincarnation, even though this was not one of the words that either Boehme or William used in connection with the plate. The events take place against the background of a central flaming Sun, around which circle the zodiacs and planets. As I have noted, the design is divided by two great semi-circles, the top one of which is light, filled with burning flames, and dominated by an encircled triangle and a crowned symbol.

In the lower regions is the dark realm, symbolized by a monotonous grey sphere. This is not the infernal world, but it does contain (scarcely visible in the darkness, but just below the Sun) the triad of Purgatory, which is linked to the lower serif of the letter **A**.[20]

In an earlier plate (number 9 in the series), these contrasting Light and Dark semi-circles were identified by two **S** symbols. The upper **S** represented Sophia, or Wisdom. Adam is severed from this Sophia, and falls to the outermost borders of the spirit world. This world of darkness is identified by the second **S**, which is the initial of Satan. The opposition between these two worlds, and between Wisdom and Satan, are taken for granted in the later plate 12.

As we have seen, this letter **A**, which we have observed in the lower circle, and into which is inserted a representation of the Earth in the form of a globe, stands for Adam. That is to say, the **A** represents the Adamic state of fallen mankind. The lower parts of the ascender and descender of this **A** are sheathed in darkness, but the upper apex of the letter forms a triangle that imitates the celestial triangle of the celestial world, above. This darkened **A**, which may be associated with the *dark Aleph* of Cabalistic tradition, marks the point where the human Ego descends into birth, and then re-ascends, at death, back into the spiritual realm.

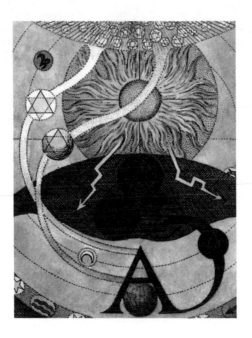

The descent into birth, or, properly speaking, rebirth, starts from the lower curvature of heaven, where we see a myriad of encircled Seals of Solomon. These represent souls awaiting incarnation. Almost certainly, it is this cyclical movement of the Ego that offers one reason why the encircled Seal of Solomon has been adopted as a symbol for this entity.

William Law, following Boehme, actually described this Solomonic Seal as 'the most significant Character in all the Universe'.[21] In a moment, we shall see why it was possible for Law to be so extravagant in his praise of the symbol.

In Law's view (which reflects the view of Boehme) the Ego does not lose its connection with the Trinity. Thus, one triangle within the Seal of Solomon marks its current direction (either towards incarnation, or towards excarnation through the spheres). This emphasis in the engraving is indicated by one of the triangles having being drawn in solid black line, the other in a dotted line: the apex of the dotted line indicates the upper or downward direction. In the following example, the Ego is conceived as moving downwards, into incarnation:

At this point, in order to appreciate more fully the meaning that Boehme and Law ascribed to this symbol, we need to make a digression – though remaining within the context of Boehme's view of symbolism.

The Seal of Solomon had particular significance for Boehme, and this passed into the designs of William Law. Both these mystics recognized that the standard sigils for Fire $\triangle$ and Water $\triangledown$ were mutually antagonistic. Furthermore, since the apex of each pointed in opposite direction to the other, the two symbols could be used to denote opposing forces. This is one reason why both Boehme and Law made use of the combined symbols, in the form of the Seal of Solomon, in order to denote the Ego. The Ego was conceived by them as descending from Heaven towards the Earth, and then ascending back to Heaven. Hermeneutically, the Ego contained within itself a memory of both phases of this journey.

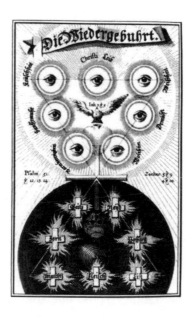

Among the many arcane designs associated with Boehme is one that helps us understand the full depth of these warring, or opposing triangles. The frontispiece to his *Die Wiedergebuhrt* (which refers to a spiritual *rebirth*, rather than to reincarnation) is based on a disjuncted Seal of Solomon, in the form of two triangles.[22] The uppermost triangle of Light joins with the lower triangle of Darkness, only at a single communal point, at their apex. This point of junction is at the centre of the cross, the lower half of which is in darkness, the upper half in light. In the engraving, this triangle of Light ▽ has been separated from the triangle of Darkness, ▲. To both have been added appropriate mirrored symbols.

The seven eyes that determine the triangle of Light are associated with the seven Gifts of Spirit, centred upon the Holy Spirit. These are reflected, in the triangle of Darkness, as the seven Deadly Sins, gathered around an inverted human skull. The skull is close to the bottom of the central and unifying cross, which suggests that it is the skull of Adam, traditionally buried at the foot of the Cross on *Golgotha* ('the place of the skull').

Since the entire design is conceived as a sort of moral mirror-image, reflecting across the horizontal arm of the cross, the reflected heart, visible below the tail of the Holy Spirit, is quite evidently the opposite of this death's-head. It is a human heart — the symbol of purity of soul — which enables mankind to escape death, and be re-born.

The hermeneutics in this interesting plate are easily missed. The biblical reference above the Holy Spirit is to *The Gospel of St. John*, 3:5:

> Jesus answered, Verily, verily, I say unto thee, Except a man be born of water and of the Spirit, he cannot enter into the Kingdom of God.

The disjuncted triangle of Light is, of course, a triangle balancing upon its apex: ▽ This is the traditional symbol of the Element of Water. The implication is that the ▲ triangle of Darkness is the traditional symbol of the *Dark Fire* of occult systems, which may be understood on one level as being the fires, or burning pains of Purgatory. The notion of these dark fires seems to have evolved theologically, on the reasonable assumption that there cannot be light in Hell or Purgatory.

To the right of the page is a reference to *Zechariah* 3:9 and 4:10. These texts offer a clue to the deeper meaning of the imagery:

> [3:9] For behold the stone that I have laid before Joshua; upon one stone shall be seven eyes: behold, I will engrave the graving thereof, saith the Lord of hosts, and I will remove the iniquity of that land in one day.

> [4:10] For who hath despised the day of small things? For they shall rejoice, and shall see the plummet in the hand of Zerubbabel with those seven; they are the eyes of the Lord, which run to and fro through the whole earth.

The seven eyes are therefore more than symbols of the Gifts of Spirit. They constitute the union of Water and Fire which is the nature of the higher world, and which contrasts with the *Dark Fire* and death of the lower world. It is reasonable to presume that the seven Sins are inscribed upon flaming crosses because each human sin is yet another nail in the Cross of Christ.

One interesting near-hidden symbol is the fact that the darkness of the lower encircling consists of a spiral, rather than a series of concentrics.

At the very centre of the spiral, hidden as though it were the tongue of a flame, the tip of a tail emerges. This reveals that the dark spiralling is actually the body of a curled snake – no doubt, the Old Serpent of the Bible, which brought about the Fall of Man.[23] The realization that this is the tip of a serpentine tail enables us to reach into the deeper level of meaning within the engraving. This tail emerges at the very centre of the circle that encloses the Dark triangle, and this offers a correspondence with the higher circle. The mirror image of the centre of the Light triangle, is placed exactly on the eye of the Holy Spirit. The contrast, between the light of the eye and the darkness of the Serpent, lies at the root of the hermeneutics of this plate. Whenever we find, in the designs of Boehme or in those of his disciple William Law, the overlaid triangles of what is usually called the Seal of Solomon, we have to imagine them as carrying the hermeneutic associations set out in this frontispiece.

A further hermeneutic, which we have already discussed, is that the Seal of Solomon makes an excellent symbol of the Ego, precisely because, inherent in its structure is the mystic 33.

Having grasped more fully the underlying significance of the components that make up the Seal of Solomon, we may return to the narrative concerning Fig. 13.

The Ego is conceived as carrying with it both the effects – that is to say, for want of a better word, the *residue* of memories, and the accumulated wisdom gained from its various experiences in both the incarnate and excarnate states. The Ego, descending into incarnation in the above detail from the plate, is the one that follows the curvature that touches the orb of the Moon, and joins with the **A** at its cross-bar. As we may see, in this particular Seal of Solomon, the descending triangle is drawn as a dotted line. It is also portrayed as consisting of both light and darkness:

The Ego ascending from incarnation, back into the spiritual realm after death, follows the other pathway that begins at the apex of the triangle of the letter **A**. This triangle, which points upwards, is drawn as a dotted line.

The soul or Ego is itself represented as a similar Solomonic hexagon, curving down towards the **A** of the Adamic state, with which it unites at the very apex of the letter.[24] We observe that the symbol of the excarnating Ego is depicted without shade. It is pure, having gone through all the stages of purification offered by the planetary spheres.

William Law does not always explain his symbols, and when he does, he does not often explain them clearly. However, it seems likely that the crowned circle, wherein is depicted a **C** and an **I**, drawn over a Seal of Solomon, almost certainly depicts the archetypal Ego. This is the crown jewel of the spiritual realm, with the **IC** being a reference to *Iesu Christus*, with whom the Ego is indissolubly linked. Be that as it may, the Ego is certainly represented in the descending Seal of Solomon, that reaches the apex of Adam, symbolizing the created and fallen humanity. The merging of the Earth with this Adam (whose name meant *Red Earth* — the A is coloured red in the original artwork reproduced here) indicates that the A pertains to the physical body, created by God. So, the descending incarnating soul merges with the apex, with the terrestrial triangle. From that position, at the beginning of earthly life, it has before it two possibilities. It may redeem the darkness that becomes attached to it during this particular lifetime — in which case, at death it begins its return journey to the spiritual realm, sweeping upwards, to pass through the centre of the flaming Sun. In this post-mortem state, the Ego is portrayed as a duality of Light and Darkness, and it is taken for granted that a passage through the spheres is necessary to cleanse away the earthly dross that sticks to it. Of this ascent back to heaven, Boehme wrote:

> Yet is there still a vast Difference between Souls in their Departure from this World: and this Difference wholly depends upon the real State and Condition of that significant Character, which was spoken of before; for those Souls that have attained it in this Life to Perfection, or in other words, those that here have put on the Heavenly Substantiality of Jesus Christ, meet with no Obstacle in their Passage. Those in whom that Character is more or less defective, meet with more or less Impediment; and those that have nothing at all of it, cannot go any further than into that Region, which most significantly is called the Triangle in Nature. O that there were none such at all![25]

The *Triangle of Nature*, symbolized in the dark triangle with three dark circles centred upon the three apexes, is the triad of Purgatory. Yet, as the diagram shows and as Christian theology teaches, there is a pathway from this dark triangle, leading back into the light of the Sun, that is Christ.

Cleansed, the Ego returns once more to heaven, to rejoin the other Egos, symbolized as myriad Solomonic Seals. Those interested in the influence of Egyptian symbolism on European graphic art will recognize that this lower heaven, with its central crowned IC, is in the form of a mighty *vesica piscis* (below).

This thoroughly Christian symbol of spiritual radiance was derived from the Egyptian hieroglyphic *ru*, which denoted a doorway, or a place of birth, and entrance to a higher world.[26] This function as a portal is clearly preserved in this plate, where it is portrayed as the exit and entrance into the higher spiritual realm.

We have frequently observed the propensity for Rosicrucian works to incorporate the mystic number 33 into their structures. In the case of Fig. 12, the 33 is inbuilt into the truncated zodiacal circle and the planets that follow the spiralled circling which starts with Aries and seems to end with the Sun. This count incorporates:

In the zodiacal circle:	18 stars
	9 sigils for the zodiacal signs
Within the spiral:	5 planets
	1 Earth[27]

This 33 numerology is of real importance for figure 13, as it depicts an important moment of opening. William Law insisted that it illustrates that extraordinary moment when Christ opens up the gate, that the children of the first Adam might follow him into Paradise, 'which could not be done by any Soul before that Time'. The graphic theme of the picture may appear to be that of separation of the polarities of dark and light, but the reincarnational movement of the soul and the combined 33 numerology, point to the Christian theme of redemption.

Almost certainly it is this theme-driven need to achieve the 33 numerology that explains why Law should have left out the planet Venus: her presence would have disturbed the count.

Conclusion

Licet enim homo 1000000. annos viveret, nihilominus tamen satis mirari &
initium, quomodo id accidat, satis perpendere non posset, qua ratione
videlicet tam nobilissimus thesaurus ex cinere uratur, & rursus in cinerem
redigatur.

If it were permitted for a man to live for a million years, none the less, he
could never sufficiently marvel at the wonderful manner in which this most
noble treasure is obtained from the ashes, to be again reduced to ashes.[1]

[Anonymous, *Lapidis Nosyri Alia cognitio*, in *Gloria Mundi, Alias, Paradysi*
Tabula (1677)][2]

Perhaps one conclusion to this book may be found hidden in the quotation above, from the alchemical text, the *Gloria Mundi*, which was itself a
glory of that age of the *Secret booke*.

It is unlikely that, prior to studying this present work on encoding, the
general reader would have appreciated the hidden significance or
hermeneutics in this passage. It is only by means of a knowledge of
encodings, and through learning to double-read in search of hidden sense,
that we may wrest from such arcane texts their true meanings. Now,
thanks to a knowledge of the code of 33, and a quick count of the Latin
words, we may recognize that the passage relates to the Ego, the guardian
of the *nobilissimus thesaurus*. By extension, it must relate to a general
theory of reincarnation, as was implicit in the phoenix bird, which
appears so often in alchemical literature, as being periodically reduced to
the ashes. Thus, we have learned something of deep importance about the
literary techniques of the alchemists and esotericists, who buried their
truths in encodings during that late medieval flowering.

That a numerologically-based code was used by Shakespeare and many
of his learned contemporaries is well beyond doubt. Even so, the full
significance of this code has not yet been explored by modern scholars.
Nor, of course, has space allowed me to explore it fully in this present
work. As one or two footnotes to my text have shown, books and studies
dealing with various Elizabethan and Jacobean codes and symbols are
numerous enough — however, none seem to deal exclusively with this
near-ubiquitous encoding of 33. This is a pity, for an understanding of the

33 code permits an entrance to much of the Rosicrucian, alchemical and peripheral literature of those periods.

Some ancient esoteric ideas are not yet sufficiently prepared for general acceptance: others are almost on the point of being accepted. The esoteric proposition that initiates may lay down certain seeds, in the hope that they will flower in five centuries' time, and enrich the culture of the future, may seem entirely foreign to our present way of thinking. Our prejudices about the nature of history, and of the cycles that underlie history, prevent us from countenancing such an idea. For us, the notion behind the mythology of the phoenix is no longer a living one: the fire-bird has become an outlandish symbol, engraved on lapidaries and palimpsests in ancient Egypt, seemingly with no relevance to modern life. However, the notion that initiates, and the poets, artists and scholars schooled by such initiations, may incorporate hidden numerologies into their works, should no longer be quite so foreign to those who have read this work.

What I have here called Shakespeare's *Secret booke* was used by many poets and scholars other than the Bard. It was used by a multitude of writers, over a period of almost three hundred years, which marked the flowering of esotericism in Europe. It was, as I hope I have shown, especially adopted for the high-flown esoteric literature of the Rosicrucians, their brother alchemists, and related fraternities. At times, however, individualistic scholars, such as John Dee and Michel Nostradamus, who cannot easily be categorized in a historical sense, also borrowed it, to add their own unique marginalia and thereby enrich the value of the *booke*.

The pages – some of the pages – have been opened. If this present work helps enthuse other and better scholars to scrutinize these pages further, in pursuit of this fascinating number, then I will have achieved my purpose. We must recall that this magical 33 brings together the Christ with the Ego, and with entries and entrances to a higher world – a notion parodied on the stage and made glorious in many a tomb. That is, indeed, a subject worthy of pursuit.

In brief, then, this *booke* has preserved hitherto unnoticed secret encodings in seventeenth-century works. The majority of these are linked partly with a Christian idea of numerology and partly with the literary and graphic methods of the new Rosicrucians. By analysing a few pages from this *booke*, I hope to have left the reader in no doubt that Shakespeare made use of the same secret codes, constructed around the number 33, as did the genuine Rosicrucian fraternity. However, in spite of both extravagant and well-argued claims about Shakespeare's membership of the Rosicrucians and early Masonry, there is no evidence that such claims are valid.[3]

The Bard was no Rosicrucian — merely a far-sighted genius. It is possible that the one thing the Bard had in common with those of the fraternity is their realization that, for the moral education of mankind to succeed, our inner world had to become more dependable and governed by a more profound sense of morality. The time for treading the confining tracks of a maze was in the past: henceforth, mankind would be called to follow a straight and spiritual road, built by the Ego. They (that is, the Bard and the Rosicrucians) seem to have had in common a spiritual solution to that old dichotomy between blind destiny and individual will.

In that most delicate of all plays, *The Tempest*, Alonso and Gonzalo are, like their companions, being led secretly by magical means towards their destinies. However, Gonzalo, who cannot comprehend the greater plan, sees the journey as one caught in a labyrinth. Alonso's speech, delivered (we note) at the opening of Act 3, Scene 3, of the play, observes:

> ... here's a maze trod, indeede,
> Through fourth-rights, & Meanders ...

The speech above is abstracted from one that is exactly 33 words long:

> *Gon.* By'r lakin, I can goe no further, Sir,
> My old bones akes: here's a maze trod indeede
> Through fourth-rights, & Meanders: by your patience,
> I needes must rest me.[4]

When the party resolve that they should follow this maze no longer, the magician Prospero enters, on cue, yet invisible to them. They have reached a seminal point in their journey — a point where things will change. Under Prospero's command, *severall strange shapes* carry in a banquet, and invite the weary travellers to eat. The party decide that the gift must have been made by people of this island, upon which they find themselves: they fail to recognize that the spiritual world has just been opened to them — that they stand at the entrance to a new world. They fail to perceive the light of spirit, seeing the strange shapes only as denizens of the earth.

The Victorian artist, Gordon Browne, cleverly illustrates this important sense of separation, between the worlds material and spiritual, by dividing the image vertically with the aid of a tree-trunk.[5] On the one hand he has depicted the familiar world of the weary travellers. On the other, he reveals the *living Drollerie* (Sebastian's words[6]) of the Elemental world.

Browne is true to the text, for in his illustration neither world actually penetrates the other.

It is fun to attempt to disentangle this bevy of conjured joyful elementals, in the hope that they total the Shakespearean 33. However, they prove elusive: the highest count I have managed is 22 (figure 14). We may learn something, even from this deficiency, however. By the nineteenth century, when Gordon Browne worked his magical pen, all knowledge of the 33 encoding seems to have been lost, save to a handful of historians held to be near-crazed by their peers. The later scholars and readers seem not to have recognized Shakespeare's fascination with the number 33, and this failure to recognize the number sometimes led to misunderstandings.

Only once did Shakespeare refer openly to the number 33 in his writings. However, it is perhaps not altogether surprising that this reference should be shrouded in mystery and misunderstood by many readers. Indeed, so little has this overt mention of 33 been understood that some editors have excised it from their redactions of the play. It was to the credit of the influential performance of *The Comedy of Errors*, eventually filmed under the direction of James Cellan Jones in 1983, that the original reference to the 33 has been preserved, despite the reasoned opposition of many editorial commentaries.[7]

In the final lines of *The Comedy of Errors*, Shakespeare has the Lady Abbess say,

> Thirtie three yeares have I but gone in travaile
> Of you my sonnes, and till this present houre
> My heavie burthen are delivered:[8]

Precisely why the Abbess should refer to *thirtie three* years is not clear from the chronological details revealed within the plot: strictly speaking, that number could not possibly be accurate. It is certainly not a period of years that could have been derived from either of the known literary sources for the play.[9] Thus, inexplicable as the reference is, it does appear to have been invented either by Shakespeare himself, or by the editors of the 1623 *Folio Edition*, through which the work has descended to us.

In these three lines, the Lady Abbess appears to be twisting a metaphor by speaking of a pregnancy of thirty-three years, as though the 'birth' of her two children has taken place in Ephesus, to an Abbess — that is, to herself — who has evidently taken religious vows of chastity.[10] The Christian metaphor is subtle, and whilst it is meaningful within an esoteric theme, it does not fit the dramatic situation of the play. Within the denouement, which is being unfolded during this speech, the Abbess is restored to her husband, Aegeon, to her twin sons (both of the same Christian name!) and to her son's own twins, the like-named servants.

The Comedy of Errors rests upon an entirely farcical plot, which can only be held together, in dramatic or even humorous terms, by the excellence of its actors and actresses. Just to help this absurd comedy of mistaken identities on its way, the plot involves two pairs of male twins in the play. The first pair are the twin sons of Aegeon and Aemilia (who, by the time of the play's action, has become the Lady Abbess), Antipholus of Ephesus and Antipholus of Syracuse.[11] The second pair — again with identical Christian names — are Dromio of Ephesus and Dromio of Syracuse. These two sets of twins were supposedly born at the same time and in the same place — an astrological nicety that would have been essential for an Elizabethan audience, but fairly irrelevant to the modern world.[12] No explanation is given in the play as to why the two sets of names are the same. Aegeon and Aemilia had purchased the latter pair of con-temporaries as slaves to their own sons. As must be evident, the moment one attempts to apply reason to *The Errors*, the whole plot dissolves into a cloud of absurdities — the premises upon which it is based are too far-fetched, even within the intellectually relaxed atmosphere of comedy theatre. In spite of this, *The Errors* remains one of Shakespeare's most

fascinating works, for it displays moments of insight and human awareness, and has an esoteric sub-plot interwoven with its various themes.[13]

The reference to *thirtie three* years, which I regard as being the esoteric
nexus of this play, has evidently caused difficulties for many editors of the
play. Time and again, they have changed this number of years, set out in
the speech of the Abbess — most usually to twenty-five.[14] These editors
certainly have good reason on their side, but we must remember that true
poetry is not always governed by reason. In this speech, the Abbess is
referring to her two twins, whose identical appearance is seminal to the
confusions in the play. It is relatively easy to calculate their ages (and thus
the period that the Abbess was supposedly in this metaphoric *travaile*)
from details mentioned by her husband, Aegeon.[15] The *Thirtie three yeares*
could not be accurate in terms of earthly time-keeping, yet it happens to be
important as an indicator of esoteric streams within the play itself.

Whilst this reference to thirty-three may come as something of a shock
to anyone who has attended the chronological details of the play with care,
it merely confirms various hints given at other stages of *The Errors*. As
though to dispel the idea that the stipulated years could be an accident,
rather than an encoding, this 33 is not permitted to stand in isolation
within the speech. The 1623 edition — which is the earliest surviving copy
of the play known to us — confirms the number by insisting that the page,
on which the reference appears, should display 33 lines (below).[16]

100	*The Comedie of Errors.*
And we shall make full satisfaction.	Come go with vs, wee'l looke to that anon,
Thirtie three yeares haue I but gone in trauaile	Embrace thy brother there, reioyce with him. *Exit*
Of you my sonnes, and till this present houre	S. *Dro.* There is a fat friend at your masters house,
My heauie burthen are deliuered :	That kitchin'd me for you to day at dinner :
The Duke my husband, and my children both,	She now shall be my sister, not my wife,
And you the Kalenders of their Natiuity,	E. *D.* Me thinks you are my glasse,& not my brother :
Go to a Gossips feast, and go with mee,	I see by you, I am a sweet-fac'd youth,
After so long greefe such Natiuitie.	Will you walke in to see their gossipping?
Duke. With all my heart,Ile Gossip at this feast.	S. *Dro.* Not I sir,you are my elder.
	E. *Dro.* That's a question,how shall we trie it.
Exeunt omnes. Manet the two Dromio's and	S. *Dro.* Wee'l draw Cuts for the Signior, till then,
two Brothers.	lead thou first.
S. *Dro.* Mast.shall I fetch your stuffe from shipbord?	E. *Dro.* Nay then thus :
E. *An. Dromio*,what stuffe of mine hast thou imbarkt	We came into the world like brother and brother :
S. *Dro.* Your goods that lay at host sir in the Centaur.	And now let's go hand in hand, not one before another.
S. *Ant.* He speakes to me, I am your master *Dromio*.	*Exeunt.*

FINIS.

A further confirmation that this number was intentional is found in the fact that, given certain rules, we may count 33 capital letters (of Roman form) in the two columns.[17]

Why the Abbess should have insisted upon 33 in the above-quoted speech remains a mystery. A mystery, save, of course, that the only overt reference to 33 in Shakespeare's writings comes from the mouth of a religious, who happens to be Abbess of a church in Ephesus – the city particularly associated with the development of the Christian cult of the Mother of God.[18]

My own feeling is that Shakespeare has skilfully worked into this play a number of references that introduce a particular esoteric theme. In brief, this theme holds that there were two Jesus Children (in some streams of literature referred to as holy Twins), and that the Christ descended into the body of only one of these in order to fulfil the scriptures by his redemptive death on the Cross.[19] The combined life of this Jesus and Christ was, of course, thirty-three years. Any theological justification for this apparently heretical tradition may be found in the irreconcilable contrasts in the genealogies of the two Jesus children, described in the gospels of Matthew and Luke.

Presently, there is neither space nor inclination to develop other instances within The Errors, where this esoteric theme is touched upon. My purpose, here, has been to show that the only overt reference made by Shakespeare to this number leads to a profound mystery. Whether Shakespeare was referring to his own favoured encoding, or whether he was referring to the Christian tradition that had, a few decades earlier, intrigued such artists as Carlo Crivelli, Leonardo da Vinci, Michelangelo, Raphael, must be left for some future researcher into esoteric history to ascertain. It is perhaps sufficient to repeat that the esoteric theme of the great ceiling in the Sistine Chapel, which Michelangelo completed early in the sixteenth century, is nothing other than that of the two Jesus children, whose story is told within the framework of a span of thirty-three years.[20]

By its very nature, the number 33 has been revealed as an indicator of the spiritual world, of spiritual verities, as a sign of the entrance to a higher world, and so forth. Depending upon the context, it points to Christ, to the Ego, to the post-mortem realm, and the Astral world. It is a number familiar to the magician Prospero, for it commands the spiritual hermeneutics that veil the hidden worlds.

The name of the magician, Prospero, draws us back to the most spirit-filled of Shakespeare's plays, *The Tempest*. The first scene deals with the shipwreck on the magical island. In the second scene, the first speech, delivered within the spiritual haven of the island itself, is delivered by Miranda to her father, Prospero. As we might expect, in this entry into a spiritual region, in a play that deals with the magical realm lying beyond the material, the first line (below) consist of 33 letters. In making the count, one does not include the brackets, which are the equivalent of commas.

   If by your Art (my deerest father) you have

If the first action on the island begins with 33, then it is reasonable to expect the termination of magical action on the island to be linked with that same number. This termination of *The Tempest* is surely the evocative Epilogue, spoken by Prospero in person. This final speech (below) has been most cunningly worked to incorporate the encoded number 33.

> N Ow *my Charmes are all ore-throwne,*
>   *And what strength I haue's mine owne.*
> *Which is most faint : now 'tis true*
> *I must be heere confinde by you,*
> *Or sent to* Naples, *Let me not*
> *Since I haue my Dukedome got ,*
> *And pardon'd the deceiuer, dwell*
> *In this bare Island, by your Spell,*
> *But releafe me from my bands*
> *with the helpe of your good hands :*
> *Gentle breath of yours, my Sailes*
> *Must fill, or elfe my proiect failes,*
> *which was to pleafe : Now I want*
> *Spirits to enforce : Art to inchant,*
> *And my ending is despaire,*
> *Vnleffe I be relieu'd by praier*
> *Which pierces fo, that it affaults*
> *Mercy it felfe, and frees all faults.*
>   *As you from crimes would pardon'd be,*
>   *Let your Indulgence fet me free.*   Fxit.

If you count the number of italic initials in this epilogue (above) you will find that there are precisely 33. One must be careful not to include in this count the initial N that begins the first line, as this is a Roman, rather than italic: one must also be careful not to count the **N** of **Naples**, in the fifth line, for this also is a Roman font.

The sheer brilliance of this beginning and ending encoding takes one's breath away. Needless to say, modern editors have tended to make nonsense of this encoding (as with the majority of encodings in the *Secret booke*), simply because they did not even know that it was there.[21] Contemplating such desecration in so many modern versions of the plays, one recalls the words of that brilliant mid-nineteenth century American, Delia Bacon, who is now enjoying a period of deserved recognition among academics. She insisted that there is nothing superfluous in any of the plays of Shakespeare. The plays are 'the greatest product of the human mind' in which 'Every character is necessary; every word is full of meaning.'[22] Alas, this fundamental truth has not been heeded by many scholars, producers or writers on Shakespeare.

Prospero's Epilogue, where he seems to withdraw from magic, almost brings our own work to a close. Perhaps we may conclude with a masterpiece of this 33 encoding that invites attention to the interface between the familiar world and that where the music of the spheres may be heard: this is surely the interface experienced by all, at the momentous point of death. The lines are from George Chapman, who seems to have dabbled with Sir Walter Ralegh's *School of Night*, in Dorset, but whose poetry, at its best, could rival even that of our Bard.[23]

> He still'd
> All sounds in ayre and left so free mine eares
> That I might heare the music of the Spheres,
> And all the Angels singing out of heaven.[24]

The last of these lines, where the reader breaks through, into the higher realm of angels, is set out in 33 letters. The line reminds us that the title of the poem, from which these three lines are taken, *Euthymiae Raptus or The Teares of Peace*, is also constructed from that same magical thirty-three.

Picture Section

FIGURE 1.   The title-page of Johann Daniel Mylius, *Opus medico-chymicum* (1618). This remarkable work was published by Lucas Jennis at Frankfurt. Little is known about Mylius, other than he was born at Wetter-am-Ruhr, in 1585, was still alive in 1628, and that he was both an alchemist and a Rosicrucian. The signature he appended to his epistle-address to this work (dedicated to God Almighty) was *Ego, Homo*, that is, *I, Man*.

FIGURE 2.   The opening page of Shakespeare's *Loves Labour's lost*, from the First Folio of 1623. Line 33 down, in the second column (marked here with a marginal dot) contains a significant misspelling, linked with a further 33 encoding.

FIGURE 3.   Portrait of Heinrich Khunrath, from his *Amphitheatrum Sapientiae Aeternae* (1602). Some of the various 33 encodings on the page are discussed in the main body of this present text. The open book, in front of Khunrath, contains lines from *Psalm* 71, verse 17. The first page contains 34 letters, the second 32 – when the number is divided equally, they group as two sets of 33. This is a frequently used technique of encoding.

FIGURE 4.   Detail from Robert Fludd's *De Naturae Simia seu Technica macrocosmi historia...* (1618). In this enlarged detail, it is easier to see the erroneous representation of the geomantic shield (at 11:00 o'clock), designed to incorporate the 33 encoding. The 33 encoding on the penultimate line of the title may also be seen more clearly.

FIGURE 5.   The title-page of Edmund Spenser's *The Faerie Queen*, etc. (1611), which is set out in 33 words and abbreviations. The date was not intended to be included in the count. The top-most device of the hog is close to a decorative motive (almost touching its nose) designed to look like a 3. On the opposite side, the same decoration is in mirror image: the pair is, in effect, an encoded 33.

FIGURE 6.   The opening emblem to Michael Maier's *Atalanta fugiens* (1618). The artist appears to have worked two number 3s into the 'clouds' of air – one emerging from his right arm, the other in the billows emerging from his left arm. This was the first alchemical book to combine images, verses and music, so as to cater for the three-fold human being.

FIGURE 7.   Sample page from John Dee's *Monas Hieroglyphica* (1564) to show the standard 33 line-length of the page. Dee introduced a wide range of 33 encodings into this work. A good example on this page (and dealt with in the present work) is in lines 27 and 28, which incorporates 33 letters, in Latin or Greek.

FIGURE 8.   Sample page from John Dee's *Monas Hieroglyphica* (1564) to show something of the lengths that Dee would go to in order to preserve a standard 33 line-length for the pages in this work. The 21 lines of indentation, required to inset the diagram of the *Monas*, is reflected in the diagram of the *Monas*, which contains 21 figures or letters. In this way, Dee reaffirms the importance of the 33.

FIGURE 9.   Engraving of the movable *Collegium Fraternitatis* of the Rosicrucians, from Theophilus Schweighardt, *Speculum Sophicum Rhodo-Stauroticum* (1618). The sighting line, from the figure in the bottom right, is marked with the Latin IGNORANTIAM MEAM AGNOSCO IUVA PATER, which consists of only 31 letters. However, the line continues through the E of FRATERNITATIS, and up to the second *Vau* of the name of God, giving 33 letters in all.

FIGURE 10.   The title-page of Nostradamus' *Propheties* of 1568. This seems to have been the earliest edition in which the complete set of his 940 predictive quatrains was published. Provided one ignores the date in a count, there are 33 words on the page. The first register of the title, up to the fleuron, contains 33 letters.

FIGURE 11.   Title-page of Michael Maier's *Jocus Severus* (1617). The upper register of this title contains 33 words, though the abbreviated M.D. is not included in the count. During his stay in England, from 1612 to 1614, Maier appears to have introduced Robert Fludd to some of the mysteries of the Rosicrucians. Part of the Joke (of the title) is that the 16 birds symbolize the *Language of the Birds*, the secret tongue of alchemy.

FIGURE 12.   Plate 7 from William Law's *An Illustration of the Deep Principles of Jacob Behmen* ... (1764). The plate illustrates the conditions pertaining to the creation of Adam. The FIAT descending into the realm of being creates 33 symbols: 11 zodiacal symbols, 8 planetary (including the Earth), 7 numbers, and, above the single A with its ring of fire [2], the crown [1], and the four letters of the FIAT [4]. The arcs of overlapping circles between 1 and 2, 2 and 3, and 3 and 4, create 11 *vesica pisces* – that is, 33 in all.

FIGURE 13.   Plate 12 from William Law's *An Illustration of the Deep Principles of Jacob Behmen* ... (1764). This plate is said (by Law) to illustrate the moment when Christ opens the Gate, to permit the children of the first Adam to follow him into Paradise. In this image, Law openly uses the encoded 33 of the Seal of Solomon to represent the excarnating and incarnating soul.

FIGURE 14.   Detail of a drawing by Gordon Browne, depicting the elemental denizens of the spiritual world of Prospero's island, in *The Tempest* (Act III, Scene 3 – a classical 33). The picture appeared in the Henry Irving & Frank A. Marshall edition of the play (circa 1889, in the first edition), *The Works of William Shakespeare*, Vol. XIII–XIV, p. 227. Browne has illustrated the opening of the spiritual world that remained unrecognized by Alonso, Sebastian, Antonio and Gonzalo and their companions, all of whom fail to realize that they are on an enchanted island.

Fig. 1

122

Loues Labour's loſt.

A ctus primus.

Enter Ferdinand King of Nauarre, Berowne, Longauill, and Dumane.

Ferdinand.

Et *Fame*, that all hunt after in their liues ,
Liue regiſtred vpon our brazen Tombes,
And then grace vs in the diſgrace of death:
when ſpight of cormorant deuouring Time,
Th'endeuour of this preſent breath may buy :
That honour which ſhall bate his ſythes keene edge ,
And make vs heyres of all eternitie.
Therefore braue Conquerours, for ſo you are,
That warre againſt your owne affections ,
And the huge Armie of your worlds deſires.
Our late edict ſhall ſtrongly ſtand in force,
Nauar ſhall be the wonder of the world.
Our Court ſhall be a little Achademe ,
Still and contemplatiue in liuing Art.
You three, *Berowne, Dumaine,* and *Longauill,*
Haue ſworne for three yeeres terme, to liue with me :
My fellow Schollers, and to keepe thoſe ſtatutes
That are recorded in this ſcedule heere.
Your oathes are paſt, and now ſubſcribe your names:
That his owne hand may ſtrike his honour downe,
That violates the ſmalleſt branch heerein :
If you are arm'd to doe, as ſworne to do ,
Subſcribe to your deepe oathes, and keepe it to.

Longauill. I am reſolu'd, 'tis but a three yeeres faſt:
The minde ſhall banquet, though the body pine,
Fat paunches haue leane pates : and dainty bits,
Make rich the ribs, but bankerout the wits.

Dumane. My louing Lord, *Dumane* is mortified,
The groſſer manner of theſe worlds delights ,
He throwes vpon the groſſe worlds baſer ſlaues :
To loue, to wealth, to pompe, I pine and die,
With all theſe liuing in Philoſophie.

Berowne, I can but ſay their proteſtation ouer ,
So much, deare Liege, I haue already ſworne,
That is, to liue and ſtudy heere three yeeres.
But there are other ſtrict obſeruances :
As not to ſee a woman in that terme ,
Which I hope well is not enrolled there.
And one day in a weeke to touch no foode :
And but one meale on euery day beſide :
The which I hope is not enrolled there.
And then to ſleepe but three houres in the night,
And not be ſeene to winke of all the day.
When I was wont to thinke no harme all night ,
And make a darke night too of halfe the day :

Which I hope well is not enrolled there.
O, theſe are barren taskes, too hard to keepe,
Not to ſee Ladies, ſtudy, faſt, not ſleepe.

Ferd. Your oath is paſt, to paſſe away from theſe.

Berow. Let me ſay no my Liedge, and if you pleaſe,
I onely ſwore to ſtudy with your grace,
And ſtay heere in your Court for three yeeres ſpace.

Longa. You ſwore to that *Berowne,* and to the reſt.

Berow. By yea and nay ſir, then I ſwore in ieſt.
What is the end of ſtudy, let me know ?

Fer. Why that to know which elſe wee ſhould not
know.

Ber. Things hid & bard (you meane) frō cōmon ſenſe.

Ferd. I, that is ſtudies god-like recompence.

Bero. Come on then, I will ſweare to ſtudie ſo,
To know the thing I am forbid to know :
As thus, to ſtudy where I well may dine ,
When I to faſt expreſſely am forbid.
Or ſtudie where to meet ſome Miſtreſſe fine,
When Miſtreſſes from common ſenſe are hid.
Or hauing ſworne too hard a keeping oath,
Studie to breake it, and not breake my troth.
If ſtudies gaine be thus, and this be ſo,
Studie knowes that which yet it doth not know ,
Sweare me to this, and I will nere ſay no.

Ferd. Theſe be the ſtops that hinder ſtudie quite,
And traine our intellects to vaine delight.

Ber. Why? all delights are vaine, and that moſt vaine
Which with paine purchas'd, doth inherit paine,
As painefully to poare vpon a Booke,
To ſeeke the light of truth, while truth the while
Doth falſely blinde the eye-ſight of his looke :
Light ſeeking light, doth light of light beguile :
So ere you finde where light in darkeneſſe lies,
Your light growes darke by loſing of your eyes.
Studie me how to pleaſe the eye indeede ,
By fixing it vpon a fairer eye,
Who dazling ſo, that eye ſhall be his heed,
And giue him light that it was blinded by.
Studie is like the heauens glorious Sunne,
That will not be deepe ſearch'd with ſawcy lookes :
Small haue continuall plodders euer wonne,
Saue baſe authoritie from others Bookes.
Theſe earthly Godfathers of heauens lights,
That giue a name to euery fixed Starre,
Haue no more profit of their ſhining nights,
Then thoſe that walke and wot not what they are.
Too much to know, is to know nought but ſame :
And euery Godfather can giue a name.

Fer. How well hee's read, to reaſon againſt reading.
Dum.

Fig. 2

Fig. 3

Fig. 4

Fig. 5

EMBLEMA I. *De secretis Naturæ.* 13

Portavit eum ventus in ventre suo.

EPIGRAMMA I.

Embryo ventosâ BOREÆ *qui clauditur alvo,*
  Vivus in hanc lucem si semel ortus erit;
Unus is Heroum cunctos superare labores
  Arte, manu, forti corpore, mente, potest.
Ne tibi sit Cæso, nec abortus inutilis ille,
  Non Agrippa, bono sydere sed genitus.

B 3   HER-

Fig. 6

MONAS HIERO-

vt Videtis:Ex Recta enim, Circulo & Semicirculo,Verã il-
lius,Mysticáque iã nos primi docemus, Symmetriam (licet
supra etiã monuimus ex Circulo & Semicirculo eandẽ fieri posse:omnia tamen in idẽ recidunt propositũ Mysticum)
At ,λ.& δ:Primũ quidem,aliorũ sunt Vasorum quasi Ima-
gines:(λ,quidem Vitrei: δ autẽ,Terrei.)Sed,secũdo in
loco,λ, & δ, nos memores reddere possunt, cuiusdam Pi-
stilli & Mortarij,ex Materia(verè)tali præparandorum, Vt
cum eisdem Margaritas Artificiales non perforatas, Lami-
nas chrystallinas, Beryllinasq̃.: Chrysolitos,Rubinos deinde pretiosos:Carbunculos & alios Rarissimos Lapides Artificiales in Puluercs subtilissimos Conteramus. Denique
quod cum ω notatum videtis, Vasculum est,Mysteriorum
Plenissimum:& ab ipsa Vltima Alphabeti Græci litera,(ad
suam primam institutam Mystagogiam nunc restituta) vel
sola partium manifesta Metathesi locali discrepās: ex duo-
bus & illa quoque constante Semicirculis. De Vulgaribus
præterea Necessarijs Vasorum, tum figuris, tum (vnde fieri
debent)Materijs, non est necesse hoc loco, vt verba facia-
mus. Hoc tamen erit considerandum,α,sui Muneris ob-
eundi captare Occasionem,ex Secretissimo breuissimoque
Spiraculi ARTIFICIO : Et (·סרב נשׂירה שׂשׂב תמירי תמלה
(נמׂ;ג בׂמׂעׁל אהׂר litro/Vinium אן] Tyronibus OPERIS
expeditissimum eliciet Primordiale Specimen : Interim dũ
SVBTILIORA Præparandi, artificiosior illis innotescat
Via.At in λ,vitreo (In præcipui sui officij functione,) Aër
omnis externus, Ventusúe damnum adferret magnum.

   ω,autem, OMNIVM est HORARVM Homo.

                        Πόρισμα.

Tῆς ἡρᾶς Τέχης,Quis iam non potest suboderari , suauissi-
     mos & saluberrimos Fructus:vel ex istarum(dico) dua-
rum tantùm literarum enascentes Mysterio? Quorum ali-
quos quasi in speculo videndos, propius aliquantulum ex
                                              nostris

Fig. 7

que, ad fufficientem producta Lõgitudinem (in Infinitum, folent dicere Geometræ; bene, incõmmoda præcauentes) Quæ admittatur effe D A E. Iam in A K: accipiatur Punctum, vbi libet: & fit B. Habita primùm nunc A, B, (noftri fcilicet operis cõmuni Menfura) huius, Tripla capiatur, ab

A verfus C: & ponatur effe A C. Ipfius A B, Dupla fiat A E. Et Dupla ipfius A B, fit A D. Ita quòd tota D E, fit ipfius A B, Quadrupla. Sic ergo noftram CRVCEM ELEMENTALEM cõ fecimus. Ex A B, A C A D, & A E. Linearum Scilicet QVATERNARIO. Nunc, ex B K, refecetur recta, equalis ipfi A D: & fit B I. Centro I, & Interuallo I B, defcribatur Circulus; qui fit B R: fecans rectã A K in puncto R. A puncto R, verfus K, refcindatur recta æqualis ipfi A B; & fit R K. Ad punctũ

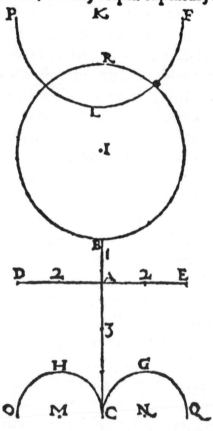

K, educatur vtrinque, (ad angulos rectos, cum ipfa A K) Sufficientis longitudinis linea recta: quæ fit P, K, F. Ab ipfo K, puncto, verfus F, refecetur recta, ipfi A D æqualis : Et fit K, F. Centro deinde K, & Interuallo K F: defcribatur Semicirculus F, L, P, ita quòd F, K, P, fit eiufdem Diameter. Tandem ad punctum C, ipfi rectæ A, C, ducatur Perpendicularis, vtrinque, ad longitudinemfufficientem extenfa: & fit

Fig. 8

Fig. 9

LES
PROPHETIES
DE M. MICHEL
NOSTRADAMVS.

Dont il y en a trois cens qui n'ont encores iamais esté imprimées.

Adioustées de nouueau par ledict Autheur.

A LYON,
PAR BENOIST RIGAVD.
1 5 6 8.
Auec permission.

Fig. 10

JOCVS SEVERVS,
HOC EST,
TRIBVNAL
ÆQVVM,
QVO
NOCTVA RE-
GINA AVIVM,
PHOENICE ARBITRO
POST
VARIAS DISCEPTATIONES ET QVE-

relas Volucrum eam infeſtantium pronunciatur, & ob ſa-
pientiam ſingularem , Palladi ſacra-
ta agnoſcitur:

AVTHORE
MICHAELE MAIERO COM. PAL. M. D.

FRANCOFVRTI
Typis Nicolai Hoffmanni, ſumptibus Theodori de Brij,
ANNO M.DCXVII.

Fig. 11

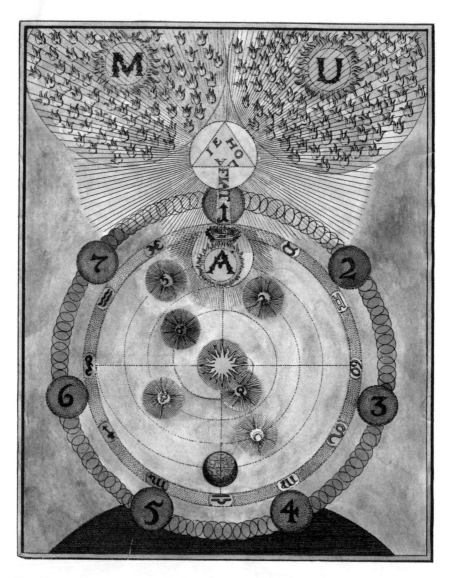

Fig. 12

Fig. 13

Fig. 14

Notes

Introduction

1. A good reliable work, which includes notes on the 33 encoding, but extends the Shakespeare encodings considerably, is Frank Woodward, *Francis Bacon's Cipher Signatures* (1923). See also, William F. Friedman and Elizabeth S. Friedman, *The Shakespearean Ciphers Examined* (1957), which offers an overview that I shall have occasion to criticize later.

2. See Henry Peacham, *Minerva Britannia* (1612), p. 33. Frank Woodward, *op. cit.*, pp. 11–12, offers an interesting analysis of some of the encoding within the verse: he sees this and the adjacent page 34 as an encoded reference to the notion that Shakespeare was Bacon.

3. A marginal note in the work refers to this emblem as *Hugonis Capeti Symbolum* – the symbol of Hugo the Capetian. This must be Hugues, the founder of the Capetians, the third race of French kings, who reigned towards the end of the tenth century.

4. Shakespeare, *The Tragedie of Hamlet*, Act III, in the 1623 Folio Edition, p. 265, col. 2, lines 17–18.

5. The words, reading from left to right, in descending order, are:
AD ÆTHERA VIRTUS . EX HIS . ORI-UNTUR (Set as two words) . DOCUIT QUÆ . OVID'S (two words) METAMORPHOSIS ENGLISHED BY [G.S. (ignored as single-letter abbreviations)] . IMPRINTED AT LONDON MDCXXVI CUM PRIVILEGIO . AMORE . FORMANTUR ET . SAPIENTIA . AFFIGIT HUMO DIVINÆ PARTICULAM AURÆ . CUNCTA . To these, we must add the signature of the artist, [T] CECILL SCULTQ. LON.

6. This is a parable of life itself, as indeed is Ovid's poem. In *Metamorphoses*, Book XIV, line 281, Macareus tells how, *et in terram toto procumbere vultu* (I snouted around with my face turned wholly towards the earth). The full force of this motto and illustration may be seen only in the context of the title-page as a whole. Here, Macareus and his companions no longer breathe the air in a manner befitting men. At the very top of the title-page, we see the hero, Hercules, driving the chariot of the Sun in the higher and godlike spiritual air, which was, in ancient times, called the *Aether*. The earth-breathing swine and the aether-breathing god were, of course, the two extremes of the human being. In making this comparison, Sandys may have intended a play on the *ad auras aetherias* of Virgil's *Georgics*, II. 291–2.

7. This distinctive lettering must be distinguished from the italic upper case lettering of the uppermost motto, *AD ÆTHERA VIRTUS*.

8. The phrase (in a variety of forms) is found in the so-called Emerald Tablet attributed to Hermes Trismegistus, and located textually in the *Poimandres*. It is said, on somewhat dubious grounds, to express the quintessence of alchemical and arcane doctrine.

9. Edmund Spenser, *The Fairie Queene*, Book III, Canto III: in the Everyman Library edition, with an Introduction by J. W. Hales (1912), p. 366.

10. C. H. Josten's view, that the text of the *Monas Hieroglyphica* (for which he has provided a lack-lustre and inaccurate translation) is alchemical in spirit is totally unsustainable.

11. There is an excellent facsimile reprint of this Philalethese work of 1652, issued by the Societas Rosicruciana in Anglia, in 1923, under the title, *The FAME AND CONFESSION of the Fraternity of R: C: Commonly of the Rosie Cross*.

12. The word Fama is often used by scholars to denote the Rosicrucian text associated with Philalethese, set out in note 11, above.

13. See Lucien Febvre, *Le Problème de l'incroyance au XVIe siècle: la religion de Rabelais* (1968 edn.).

14. Rudolf Steiner, *Macrocosm and Microcosm* (1968), p. 159. This is the English edition, based on the German text, *Makrokosmos und Mikrokosmos. Die grosse und die kleine Welt. Seelenfragen, Lebensfragen, Geistesfragen.* No. 119 in the *Bibliographical Survey*, 1961.

15. The series of concentrics is at the top of the title-page of Johann Daniel Mylius, *Opus Medico-Chymicum* (1618) – see figure 1.

Chapter 1

1. *The Tragedie of Hamlet, Prince of Denmarke*, in the First Folio edition of 1623, Part III, p. 152. Act I, scene 1, col. 2, line 3. We note that one of the latitudes that Shakespeare permitted himself with this 33 encoding is that he, at times, required us to include in the count the abbreviated name of the actor or actress, whilst at other times he requires us to ignore the name.

2. *Ibid*, p. 152. Act I, scene 1, col. 2, line 6. For Latin as the language of converse with spirits, we need only look to the Church, whose official exorcism (albeit directed against evil spirits) was and is in Latin. The belief that the demons wrote backwards (as evinced in a number of surviving diabolical pacts) seems to have entered the stream of exorcist thought in respect of both exorcism and conjuration. The famous exorcist hexameter may be excused for its Latin by the fact that it was intended as a palindrome, to be understood by the exorcist and the demon at one and the same time:

   Signa te signa, temere me tangis et angis

   Needless to say, this dual injunction, signalling, as we might suppose, that the demon should neither touch nor cause pain to the exorcist, and issued at the very interface of the demonic world, was expressed in 33 letters.

3. *Ibid*, p. 152. Act I, scene 1, col. 2, lines 17–18.

4. *Ibid*, p. 153. Act I, scene 1, col. 1, lines 28–30.

5. The wood engraving by Gordon Browne is from the Henry Irving and Frank A. Marshall edition of *The Works of William Shakespeare*, (1905 printing), Vol. IX–X, *Hamlet, Prince of Denmark*, p. 147.

6. *The Tragedie of Hamlet, Prince of Denmarke*, in the First Folio edition of 1623, Part III Act I, scene 3, col. 1 line 14, p. 157 (there is an erroneous saltus of 100 in the pagination at this point).

7. *Ibid*, p. 257, Act I, scene 3, col. 1 line 54.

8. Shakespeare, *The Tragedie of Julius Caesar*, in the First Folio of 1623: III, page 126, lines 56–7 in second column, Act 3, Scene 3.

9. *Ibid*, line 60.

10. *Ibid*, lines, 61–4.

11. Kent Hieatt, *Short Time's Endless Monument: The Symbolism of the Numbers in Edmund Spenser's 'Epithalamion'* (1960), and Alastair Fowler, *Spenser and the Numbers of Time* (1964).

12. From the *First Folio* 1623 edition of *The Tempest*, I, Act. III, Scene II, line 1492 in the Doug Moston reprint of 1995. The reader will observe that the general convention requires one to ignore in a count the letters within the persona (here, *Cal.*, for Caliban): this is a general rule that is not always observed by Shakespeare, as we have seen already.

13. *The Tempest*, Act III. Scene II, line 123, in the Frank Kermode edition of The Arden Shakespeare series, 1966 reprint.

14. Kermode, *op. cit.*, quotes Robert Graves, *The White Goddess*, p. 374 concerning this illogical sequence of tenses, which Graves wisely recognized helped create a perfect suspension of time. This suspension between two worlds is, of course, the very essence of the 33 encoding.

15. Abraham Cowley, *Essays, Plays, and Sundry Verses*, (ed. A.R. Waller, 1906), p. 396.

16. The number 8 is weak because it is divisible by other numbers: it is also an even number. The 7 is neither divisible nor even.

17. I quote from the Henry Irving and Frank A. Marshall edition, *Love's Labour's Lost*, in *The Works of William Shakespeare* (c. 1905, but in the 1922 edition), Act 1, Scene 1, line 88.

18. Shakespeare, *Loves Labour lost*, Act 1, Scene 1: in the 1623 First Folio, I, p. 122, col. 2, lines 44–48. In this 1623 edition Biron is represented as Berowne.

19. It is not certain that any of the four belonged to the fraternity, though there is no doubt that they each showed familiarity and even support for the Rosicrucians.

20. Try as one might, one cannot derive a count of 33 from this portrait engraving, nor from the combined six portraits of reputable arcanists of which this is a part, on the frontispiece to Causaubon's book. The reason for this is that the secret of the 33 is found not in the engraving, but in the title-page itself, which folds over the portraits (see below). This title-page consists of 33 lines of print. As if this were not enough, the printer has picked out, from this title-page, a number of words in red: there are precisely 33 such rubricated words.

A True & Faithful

RELATION
OF

What paffed for many Yeers Between

Dʳ. JOHN DEE
(A Mathematician of Great Fame in Q. Eliz. and King James their Raignes) and

SOME SPIRITS :

Tending (had it Succeeded)
To a General Alteration of moſt STATES and KINGDOMES in the World.

His Private Conferences with Rodolphe Emperor of Germany, Stephen K. of Poland, and divers other Princes about it.
The Particulars of his Cauſe, as it was agitated in the Emperors Court; By the Popes Intervention: His Banishment, and Reſtoration in part.

As Also

The Letters of Sundry Great Men

and Princes (ſome whereof were preſent at ſome of theſe Conferences and Apparitions of Spirits:) to the ſaid D.Dee.

Out Of
The Original Copy, written with Dʳ. Dees own Hand: Kept in the LIBRARY of

Sir THO. COTTON, Kᵗ. Baronet.

WITH A

PREFACE

Confirming the Reality (as to the Point of Spirits) of This RELATION: and ſhewing the ſeveral good Uſes that a Sober Chriſtian may make of All.

BY

Meric. Casaubon, D.D.

LONDON,
Printed by D. Maxwell, for T. Garthwait, and ſold at the Littl. North door of S. Pauls, and by other Stationers. 1659.

21. The count of 33 in Khunrath's portrait is derived from the capitalized words within the oval surround to the portrait (the abbreviated UTRIUSQ. counts as one word, the numerals are excluded from the count), and in the twelve-line Latin poem, below (one must remember to include in the count the two words, CONSILIUM DEI, formed from the initials of these lines).

22. *E millibus vix uni* — 'for scarcely in one out of a thousand.' The date of printing is, in some ways, misleading, as the manuscript of this work is known to have circulated for almost five years before publication. The portrait, and possibly the masterly fold-out plates in the work, was engraved by Jan Diricks van Campen. Oddly enough, the most famous plate from this work, the circular portrayal of the interior of an alchemist's laboratory and prayer-room, was executed by Paullus van der Doort, seemingly for the 1604 edition, and in the first complete edition of the work, which saw the light of day in Hannover, during 1609.

23. To demonstrate this point, I have reproduced this title-page, below. The title, up to the *E millibus vix uni*, consists of 33 words (one must discount the abbreviation *Doct*, and the abbreviated *que of utriusque*).

24. The count for Maier's portrait is rather obviously derived from the capitalized words in the lower register. This count gives 31 words, the lower case *etceteras* and the words abbreviated to single letters being excluded from the count. This 31 is supplemented by the two words AETATIS SUAE in the portrait itself, giving 33 words in all. In passing, I should note that Maier was born in 1566: thus, the data recorded on the engraving is incorrect, for in 1617 he was not 49 but 51. Perhaps there is some private numerology built into this confusion, or perhaps (as I believe) the 1617 was inserted because the numbers 16 and 17 conveniently add up to 33.

25. This portrait of Robert Fludd incorporates the most complex of the 33 encodings, which is based on the distinction made by Fludd (or, of course Merian) between the

quotation in Latin in the sunburst, ascribed to *Psalm* 18:29, and the Latin text from *Psalm* 18:29 in the Vulgate version of the *Old Testament*. The Vulgate text reads:

Quoniam tu illumines lucernam meam, Domine: Deus meus, illumine tenebras meas.

The text quoted on the sunburst, allegedly from *Psalm* 18:29, reads:

Si tu illustres lucernam meam, Iehova Deus Splendentes efficies tenebras meas.

If we abstract from this latter version all the words that appear in the Vulgate, we end up with the following:

Si illustres Iehova Splendentes efficies

This abstract consists of precisely 33 lower-case letters.

26. The illustration marks Plate 70 in William Blake's poem, *Jerusalem, The Emanation of The Giant Albion*. Written and etched 1804–1820.
27. Bacon was 1561–1626, Locke was 1632–1704, whilst Newton was 1642–1727.
28. Robert Fludd, *Tractatus Secundus de Naturae Simia Seu Technica macrocosmi historia....* (1618).
29. Robert Fludd, *Utrisque Cosmi Maioris scilicet et Minoris Metaphysica....* (1617), p. 90.
30. On the dark side of the instrument, and scarcely legible even in the original engraving, are a series of words relating to the tones and semi-tones. As these are in darkness, they are evidently not regarded as participating in the numerology of the instrument.
31. The anonymous writer seems to have been the Shakespearean scholar, W. F. C. Wigston: see his *Bacon Shakespeare and the Rosicrucians* (1888).
32. Anonymous, *A New Study of Shakespeare: An Inquiry into the Connection of the Plays and Poems, with the Origins of the Classical Drama, and with the Platonic Philosophy, Through the Mysteries* (1884), p. 351.
33. Nicholas Rowe, *Some Account of the Life, etc., of Mr. William Shakespear* (1709). I have borrowed the detail of Rowe's engraving from Edwin Durning-Lawrence, *Bacon is Shake-Speare* (1910), p. 77.

34. The quotation is from Edward Bulwer Lytton, *Zanoni* (1842). I could not bear to re-read this turgid nonsense, merely to locate the quotation cited here.

Chapter 2

1. The memorial has been redesigned at least once, and has been restored at least twice since photography began, in the mid nineteenth-century. An undated photograph, used as frontispiece to the anonymous, *A New Study of Shakespeare: an Inquiry into the Connection of the Plays and Poems, with the Origins of the Classical Drama, and with the Platonic Philosophy, Through the Mysteries*, (1884), reveals several interesting differences between the memorial of circa 1850 and the modern one.

2. A copy of the Grant of Coat-Armour proposed for John Shakespeare, drawn up by the College of Arms, is given in full, in J.O. Halliwell-Phillipps, *Outlines of the Life of Shakespeare*, (1889), II, p. 56. There is some doubt whether the grant was confirmed; however, a second attempt was made by the Shakespeare family to obtain a grant of arms in 1599 (see Halliwell-Philipps, I, p. 178).

3. Essex, the Earl Marshall, was chief of the Herald's College, and was installed as Clarenceux, King of Arms: according to Durning-Lawrence, it was he who permitted Shakespeare's petition for arms to be granted. See Edwin Durning-Lawrence, *Bacon is Shake-speare*, (1910), p. 139. Durning-Lawrence sees this grant as being part of the plot to establish Bacon with the mask of Shakespeare.

4. This was *The first part Of the true & honourable history, of the Life of Sir Iohn Old-castle, the good Lord Cobham.*

5. See the list of 'Life-Time Editions' in J.O. Halliwell-Phillipps, *Outlines of the Life of Shakespeare*, 1889 ed., I, p. 405 ff., (esp. p. 407).

6. For a thorough survey of the history of these changes, see C. C. Stopes, *The True Story of the Stratford Bust*, (1904).

7. Nicholas Rowe, *Some Account of the Life of Mr. William Shakespear*, (1709).

8. See Edward D. Johnson, *The Fictitious Shakespeare Exposed*, (1949). In this work, Johnson demolished Sidney Lee's *Life of Shakespeare*.

9. It is true that W. Salt Brassington has shown that some of the engravings in Dugdale's *History of Warwickshire* were not altogether trustworthy; however, the discrepancies in the Shakespeare memorial are altogether too remarkable to be explained in this way. See Richard Savage and William Salt Brassington (eds) *Stratford-Upon-Avon. From 'The Sketch Book' of Washington Irving*, (1900).

10. Johnson, *op. cit.*, is very forthright, and calls the supposed birthplace 'a sham and a fraud' (p. 19). In fact, there is no evidence that Shakespeare's father even owned the birth-house until eleven years after Shakespeare's birth. The tradition that Shakespeare was born here seems to have begun in 1759 (see p. 18 of Johnson).

11. J. Green (Master of Stratford Grammar School), writing in 1746, quoted by Alfred Dodd, in *Shakespeare Creator of Freemasonry*, (1910), pl. xi, between pp. 176–7.

12. For a brief study of the portraiture, see William Sharp Ogden, *Shakspere's Portraiture: Painted, Graven and Medallic*, (1912). A longer survey is continued through various editions of *Shakespeariana*, from 1883–1884: the Droeshout engraving is dealt with in the December 1883 (Vol I, no. 2) edition. This gives the verse by Ben Jonson.

13. See however, the anonymous, *A New Study of Shakespeare: an Inquiry into the Connection of the Plays and Poems, with the Origins of the Classical Drama, and with the Platonic Philosophy, Through the Mysteries*, (1884), p. 349 ff.

14. Anonymous, *Gloria Mundi, Alias, Paradysi Tabula* (1677) in *Musaeum Hermeticum*

Reformatum (1678), p. 235. This quotation is abstracted from the longer quotation, given at the chapter head.

15. I took this picture with the permission of the Church of the Holy Trinity, circa 1990.

16. See Brassington, *op. cit.*, pp. 56–7. Irving's story held no credence in Holy Trinity Church, whose custodians claim there would have been a record of a nearby burial: see Edward Betty 'The Exhumation', in *Shakespeariana*, Vol. 1, No. 1, November, 1883.

17. The story may be apocryphal. If it is not, then it does at least dispense with the theory that Shakespeare's body was buried fully seventeen feet deep. The digging of a contiguous grave shaft would rarely have been continued to that depth, but, in this particular church, the depth would have plunged well below the water table of the nearby Avon.

18. Arthur Penrhyn Stanley, *Historical Memorials of Westminster Abbey*, 1911, p. 255. According to Edward Betty (*op. cit.*), Ben Jonson's tomb was also broken into twice – once in 1849, and again in 1859.

19. The quotation is from the preliminary Argument, which prefaces the play. See Elizabeth Cook, *The Alchemist. Ben Jonson*, (1991 edn.), p. 6.

20. As is evident, the count of words does not include the Roman-style publication date. One further piece of wit, so typical of Jonson (who seems to have had a hand in the page design) is that the second line of the Latin quotation from Lucretius consists of 33 letters. I am certain that the double meaning in the author's abbreviation, B.I (The author be I), was also intended to raise laughs among those who were familiar with the arcane associations behind the 33 encoding, and its connexion with the Ego.

21. C.M. Ingleby, *Shakespeare's Bones. The Proposal to Disinter Them, considered in Relation to Their Possible Bearing on his Portrait*, (1883), p. 33.

22. Dr. Ingleby, *op. cit.*, p. 31.

23. C. Le Poer Kennedy, *Notes and Queries*, 2nd Series, ix, February, 1918, p. 132.

24. Thomas Fuller, *The Worthies of England*, (1662) – pt. II (unmarked), p. 243.

25. J. Parker Norris, *American Bibliopolist*, April 1876, vol. viii, p. 38.

26. For Blavatsky, see *The Secret Doctrine*, (1888), II, p.161. There is no evidence that Blavatsky had studied Shakespeare: she quoted freely from his plays in her chapter-heads to *Isis Unveiled*, but the quotations were almost certainly suggested by Southeran, whose role as co-author and researcher is so often ignored by commentators.

27. See for example, George V. Tudhope, *Bacon-Masonry. Revealing the Real Meaning of That Mystic Word and The True Name of that Lost Word with Evidence Showing Francis Bacon to be the Original Designer of Speculative Freemasonry*, (1953).

28. See, *Swan of Avon Lodge No. 2133. The First Hundred Years 1886–1986*, p. 2. On p. 17, there is a photograph of Lord Ampthill laying the foundation stone of the present Memorial on 2 July 1929.

29. The original Vertue sketch is in the British Library, but was reproduced in Frank Simpson, 'New Place. The Only Representation of Shakespeare's House. From an Unpublished Manuscript', in Allardyce Nicoll (ed), *Shakespeare Survey. An Annual Survey of Shakespearian Study and Production*. 5. (1952), p. 55. Simpson refers to Samuel Ireland's work, but seems not to have read it carefully.

30. Halliwell-Phillipps – quoted from a memorial to the Mayor and Corporation of Stratford-upon-Avon, written prior to their meeting on 4 September, 1883, quoted in *Shakespeariana*, November, 1883, p. 21.

31. Francis Bacon, *De Dignitate et Augmentis Scientarum*, book VI, p. 306.

32. Bacon, *op. cit.*, book VI, in vol. ix – p. 264 of the 1882 edition.

33. Bacon, *op cit.*, book VI, in vol ix – p. 115 of the 1882 edition.

34. This example of the *Biliterarie Alphabet* is from Bacon's Latin version of *De Augmentis Scientiarum*, (1882 edition), p. 306.
35. Samuel Ireland, *Picturesque Views on the Upper or Warwickshire, Avon*, (1795), p. xiv. The typographic copy of the curse-stone is given in the text on p. 212. The purpose of this drawing has been misunderstood by scholars – it is clearly intended to record the extraordinary curse-stone, for the monument itself is not accurately represented – even though in many respects it is more accurate than that sketched by Vertue.
36. These two versions of circa 1792 differed from the one used by the American, Ignatius Donnelly, in his unreliable study, *The Great Cryptogram*, (1888) and were almost certainly the basis for that which Malone mis-copied for his own book of 1823.
37. Samuel Ireland, *op. cit.* The print is mounted between pages 212 and 213. The letter-press version of the curse-stone epitaph is on p. 212.
38. It is interesting to see what deviant forms were carried over from this biliteral version into the modern. FREND, the ligatured THE (in a different form), ENCLOASED. The vertical YE and YT (for THE and THAT) have been carried over from the earlier cutting. HEARE on the modern form is different from the HERe of the original. The ligatured TE of BLESTE on the modern stone seems to have been *Blese* originally.
39. William F. Friedman & Elizabeth S. Friedman, in their excellent work, *The Shakespearean Ciphers Examined*, (1957), are rightfully critical of Donnelly and his method, but fall into the error of rejecting the cipher. The sources they quote in this context are frequently inaccurate: for example, on p. 62, their Johnson-Steevens is actually George Steevens, while they get the title of Samuel Ireland's own important work wrong, which suggests that they have not examined the book. This is a pity, for if they had done, they would have come to very different conclusions.
40. Of course, it is likely that these two bottom lines are also encoded, but they form no part of my present investigation, which is concerned only with the identity of the body supposedly buried beneath the stone.
41. I am aware that the basis for this bilateral coding may not be traced beyond Ireland's version of 1795 – see note above. However, even if this version had been invented by Ireland (and there is no reason whatsoever to suppose this) it was still a valid representation of the Baconian bilateral code.
42. W.G. Thorpe, *The Hidden Lives of Shakespeare and Bacon and Their Business Connection...* (1897).
43. For something of the background to the Scrivenery, see Thorpe, *op. cit.*, p. 41ff.
44. See Thorpe, *op. cit.*, p. 42.
45. See Thorpe, *op. cit.*, p. 50.
46. See for example, Frank Woodward, *Francis Bacon's Cipher Signatures* (1923), p. 11.
47. I have borrowed the illustration of the title-page of *Baconiana* from the articles by Appleton Morgan and Isaac Hall Platt, 'Shakespeare and Bacon: Can They be Reconciled?' in *New Shakespeareana*, Vol. II, Nos. 2–3, April–July 1903. This learned exchange certainly makes the case for Bacon being involved in the writing of certain Shakespearean plays. I should note that neither Morgan nor Platt appear to have noticed the encodings, to which I refer here.
48. These words are: Latine, London, Anno, Bacon's, Roman and Italic.
49. We are so required because the apostrophes indicate an elided letter.
50. For this, I have used the Daniele Mattalia (ed.) edition of *Dante Alighieri, La Divina Commedia* (1975 edn.), III, *Paradiso*, p. 654. I observe that some editions give *muove* instead of *move*, which disturbs the count. However, no matter what the editors do

to this final line, the fact remains indisputable that Dante made the last of his cantos in *Paradiso* number 33 in the series – *Canto Trentesimoterzo*. As a matter of fact, he also made *Purgatorio* end at 33 cantos, and evidently believed that *Inferno* did not deserve this sacred number. Even with such reservations, he proved more of a poet than a theologian by ending each of his three books with the near-sacred word *stelle*, 'stars'.

51. The possessive *England's* must be counted as one word. The date, as a number, must not be included in the count.

52. See Alastair Fowler, *Spenser and the Numbers of Time* (1964).

53. For example, Frank Woodward, *Francis Bacon's Cipher Signatures* (1923), pp. 24–25, traced in the inscription the encoding 157 which is an important number-code within Woodward's own system.

54. For something of the background, see Arthur Penrhyn Stanley, *Historical Memorials of Westminster Abbey* (1911), pp. 253–4.

55. Shakespeare, *The Tempest*, Act IV:1.

56. For example, R. E. Latham, *Revised Medieval Latin Word-List from British and Irish Sources* (1973 edn.), pp. 116–7, gives the legal term, *cornu sub cornu*, for 'sharing pasturage equally'.

57. At the end of this little joke, the page (in the 1623 text, rendered *Pag.*), speaking to Armado then introduces a word that many Shakespearian commentators trip up over, in the line:

> Ba most seely Sheepe, with a horne: you heare
> his learning?

The word *Seely* meant, among other things 'blessed' or even 'holy'. It thus proposed yet another reference to Bacon, whose numerical equivalent was 33 – the sacred or holy number of the Christian tradition. The early form of *seely* was 'happy' or 'blessed', and was from the Old-English *saelig*. For details, see C. T. Onions, *The Oxford Dictionary of English Etymology* (1966), p. 827. Evidently, those modern editors of Shakespeare who substitute the modern *silly* for *seely* have missed the point.

58. This magical square is from Israel Hiebner, *Mysterium Sigillorum Herbarum et Lapidarum*, (1651).

59. For this and the standard solar-number associations, see Cornelius Agrippa, *De Occulta Philosophia* (1534). p. cxlviii. Here we find an explanation for the *He*, written above the magic square of the Sun – this is claimed by Agrippa to be the *He extensum*, associated with the number 6. In fact, Agrippa is in error, as he has already pointed out on this page of his work, the *Vau* of the Hebrew alphabet is associated with the number 6. The number 111 is revealed as the number of Nachiel, the Intelligence of the Sun, whilst 666 is the number of Sorath, the *Demonium Solis*, or Demon of the Sun.

60. *The Tragedie of Hamlet*, in the Folio edition of 1623, III, Act II, Scene 2. The speech is reproduced on p. 265. Unfortunately, it is broken at the foot of column one, following the line 'The Heart-ake, and the thousand Naturall shockes', and reprised at the top of column two, with the following line. This break is evident in the passage reproduced, here.

61. This became one of the most important and most interesting of the Shakespeare-Bacon controversies in the early twentieth century. However, see W.H. Smith's set of parallels in *Notes and Queries*, 2nd series, No. 52, 27 December, 1856, p. 503.

62. Thomas Fuller, *The Worthies of England*, 1662, pt. II (unnumbered) p. 126.

Chapter 3

1. For the 'self-regeneraton note', see Clarke E. Johnston, quoted by Manly P. Hall in the Introductory Preface to the reprint of Hitchcock's seminal work, under the abbreviated title, *Alchemy and the Alchemists* (1976). Hitchcock's published works include, *Remarks Upon Alchemy and the Alchemists* (1857), *Remarks on the Sonnets of Shakespeare* (1865), *Swedenborg as an Hermetic Philosopher* (1865), and, *Notes upon the Vita Nuova and Minor Poems of Dante* (1867).

2. There was something altogether marvellous happening in that decade in the mid-point of the nineteenth century. In the United States, Major-General Hitchcock began to fight on behalf of the true nature of alchemy. At the same time, in England, the youthful Mary Anne South, who would later be married, and carry the name Mary Anne Atwood, had published her amazing work on the true nature of alchemy. Her anonymous *Suggestive Inquiry into the Hermetic Mystery* saw the light of day but solicited few buyers, in 1850. It is one of the unexplained mysteries of nineteenth-century esotericism why the first editions of this brilliant book should have been purchased from the publishers and privately burned on the extensive lawns of Bury House in Gosport, Hampshire. Hitchcock and Atwood are stylistically different, and one suspects that Atwood is the greater scholar, yet it is astonishing how often they quote from the same alchemical texts. It seems almost as though they had a communal literary avatar, anxious to set things straight before Blavatsky began to wreak orientalizing havoc on the world.

3. The quotation, from *The Tempest* Act IV, Scene 1, is given on p. 132 of Hitchcock's *Remarks Upon Alchemy*.

4. One or two infelicities in his version of the three lines suggest that Hitchcock was quoting from memory.

5. I have spirited away Hitchcock's awful *Yes*, which was an error for *Yea*, – the change introduced no amendment to the count.

6. Ignatius Donnelly, *The Great Cryptogram: Francis Bacon's Cipher in the so-called Shakespeare Plays* (1888).

7. He discovered the principle of the Baconian encoding when he chanced to glance though a book belonging to one of his children, *Every Boy's Book*, which had a section on cipher-writing and included the bilateral code of Francis Bacon. See Donnelly, *op. cit*, pp. 506–7.

8. I have taken the artwork version from J.O. Halliwell-Phillipps, *Outlines of the Life of Shakespeare* (1889), Vol. I, p. 284.

9. The Latin almost painfully departs from convention to produce the requisite 30 characters. Instead of AD, we are given an abbreviated ANO DO. Instead of the short OBIT, we are given the (acceptable) long form, OBIIT.

10. The fifteen capitalized letters are:

    IVDICIO   PYLIUM   SOCATEM   MARONEM   TERRA   OLYMPUS   STAY
    PASSENGER   DEATH   SHAKESPEARE   TOMBE   FAR   SIEH   HE   LEAVES

The thirteen dipthongs are:

    AE MAERET   TH THOU   TH THOU   TH HATH   TH WITH   TH THIS
    ME MONUMENT   TH WITH   ME NAME   TH DOTH   TH THEN   TH HATH
    AE AETATIS

The five abbreviations are:

    Ys [THIS]   Yt [THAT]   AÑO ANNO   DOi DOMINI   AP APRILIS

11. For interesting notes on the *Liber M*, in the context of the *Fama*, see Paul M. Allen (ed), *A Christian Rosenkreutz Anthology*, (1974 ed.), p. 676–7.
12. The engraving is from the frontispiece to Boehme's *Mysterium Magnum*, from the *Theosophische Wercken* (1682).
13. See the Ezechiel Foxcroft translation, *The Hermetick Romance: or the Chymical Wedding*, (1690). As the Foxcroft titling was designed to encapsulate the 33-letter code, it is likely that Foxcroft was himself aware of the numerological significance of the abbreviation.
14. See Fred Gettings, *Dictionary of Occult, Hermetic and Alchemical Sigils*, (1981), p. 279.
15. The publication history is complicated: see Stanislas Klossowski de Rola, *The Golden Game. Alchemical Engravings of the Seventeenth Century*, (1988), p. 29.
16. It was called 'The Cosmic Rose' by Adam McLean, *The Amphitheatre Engravings of Heinrich Khunrath*, (1981), p. 48.
17. I should observe that different traditions (no doubt ones that began at different times in the evolution of mankind, when reincarnational periods were different) ascribe 1000 years, 800 years, 500 years and even 540 years to the life of the phoenix. It seems that reincarnational periods are speeding up with the passage of time.
18. From an esoteric standpoint, this 5-letter name of Jesus has been seen by the French occultist, De Guaita, as representing the Fall into matter, because the central *shin* is pulled down into the fourfold elemental world of the severed pairs of letters. See his *Essais sur les Sciences Maudites* (1897). A summary in respect of the mystic word is given by Adam McLean, *op. cit*, p. 53ff.
19. Esoterically, this numerology is involved with the in-breathing and out-breathing of incarnation (the lunar number 28, which is a number of materialization) and love (the Venus-number is 5).
20. The Latin *solius verae* takes on a subsidiary meaning within the context of the design, for Christ is the true Sun (*Sol Verus*), and the contrast between the sole centre of the design and the tenfold periphery becomes even more poignant in its symbolism: the ten gates of perception contracted into the grave of matter.
21. In the *Gospel of St. John*, I, 12, it is promised that all who receive Christ will have the power to become *sons of God*.
22. The portrait is from a loose print in the author's collection. Below the print is a laudatory Latin poem, entitled *In Effigiem D. Authoris*, which suggests that it served at one time as the frontispiece to one of the editions of Fludd's *De Naturae Simia Seu Technica Macrocosmi Historia*, (1618).
23. For an example translation (of which there are many) see that of Steele and Singer, given by E. J. Holmyard, *Alchemy* (1957), p. 95. For a reference to the seven levels and seven keys, see H.P. Blavatsky, *The Secret Doctrine*, II, p. 109.
24. Michael Maier, *Atalanta fugiens, hoc est, Emblemata Nova de secretis naturae chymica*, (1618).
25. I have not included, at the bottom of these pages, the printer's sheet continuation directions and folio guides (here, EMBLE-, HER- and B 3, on the grounds that these would not have been conceived as playing a part in the hermeneutics.) The fifteenth line down has clearly been designed to read as one line, although it incorporates two distinct sets of material:

   rans. Embryo ventosa Borì qui clauditur alvo,

Chapter 4

1. The full stop after *liquebit* seems to have been inserted in error (or perhaps as an occult blind), for the following sentence continues and makes sense without need for any

other break than a comma. It is worth pointing this out, for when this full-stop is removed, the sentence is found to consist of exactly 33 words. The quotation is from the address, made by John Dee to the Roman Emperor, Maximilian, King of Hungary and Bohemia, at the beginning of Theorem XXII in the *Monas Hieroglyphica*, (1564), p. 22.

2. The translations into English from the Latin and Greek of Dee's *Monas Hieroglyphica* in this chapter are my own.

3. The short rope is intended to link the letter-form with the horizontal bar, which is the traditional sign of abbreviation. This means that the letter form A must be read as *alpha*, whilst the letter-form ω, which has a similar armature arrangement, must be read as *omega*.

4. The symbolism, in a less concentrated form, is found in many earlier sculptures and biblical illustrations. A good example is the Agnus Dei page of the tenth-century *Codex Aemilianesis*, in the Escorial. The Sun and Moon are represented in small on the upper marginal decoration. The Cross itself is the main divisor of the page, its four spaces being occupied by the four Evangelist symbols.

The *alpha* and *omega* (above) are represented within a central *vesica piscis*, ranged vertically, with the *alpha* on top, the *omega* at the bottom, between images of the lance, cross and sponge-rod of the Passion.

5. Gertrud Schiller, *Iconography of Christian Art. Volume 2: The Passion of Jesus Christ*, (1972), pp. 878–164. For the specific reference, see p. 109. This work is the English translation of *Ikonographie der christlichen Kunst* (1968).

6. *The Book of Revelation*, 22:13.

7. *The Book of Revelation*, 1:8.

8. Dee's chart, for 04:02 PM on 13 July 1527, is preserved in the Bodleian at Oxford, Ashmole 1788, f. 137r. Mercury was in 10.50 Cancer, with Jupiter conjunct, in 9.18 Cancer. The chart is reproduced in Benjamin Woolley, *The Queen's Conjuror: The Life and Magic of Dr. Dee* (2002), opp. p. 78. Nostradamus' chart, for a few minutes after midday, on 14 December 1503, is given in David Ovason, *The Secrets of Nostradamus* (2001), figure 16, and pp. 377–395. His Jupiter was in 10.57 Cancer.

9. The engraved portrait of Dee is from the frontispiece to Meric Casaubon, *A True & Faithful Relation of What passed for many Yeers Between Dr. John Dee ... and Some Spirits...* (1659).

10. John Dee, *Monas Hieroglyphica* (1564), p. 25.

11. The *omega* is associated with Fire simply because the symbol is linked by Dee with the sigil for Aries ♈ which is the first Fire sign.

12. I give one example, derived from the writings of the Rosicrucian, Jacob Boehme, on page 173.

13. In those cases where interlinear diagrams, corollary headings and heorem headings are inserted, this number is usually disturbed, but the potential within the page design is for 33 lines.

14. *Monas*, p. 24. See figure 8.

15. Dee has cleverly counterpoised the final *que* (and) of *Habilitatemque* with the abbreviate q, also for *que*, of *Laboresq*, no doubt to indicate that this latter be ignored.

16. For an account of this 72, see David Ovason, *The Secret Symbols of the Dollar Bill* (2004) pp. 102-4, and notes 70-71 on pp. 183-4.

17. Dee's data, for 4:02 PM on 13 July 1527, is also given in the British Library manuscript, Sloane 1782, f.31.

18. I write this fully aware that, for the Elizabethan astrologer, the year 1564 was, in theory at least, filled with threat. At the solar eclipse on 8 June 1564, the four planets, Saturn, Jupiter, Mars and Venus, would be in the same sign (Leo). Perhaps it was in the light of this threat that Dee mentioned his own undertaking had ended peacefully.

19. The fact that the letters I T L of IɴTᴇʟʟᴇᴄᴛᴜs are so distinguished suggests that they stand for a Latin phrase, relevant to the device. Since we are dealing with both the Ego and the eye, there is good reason to suspect that the ITL stands for IN TENEBRIS LUX: There is Light in the Darkness. Just as light penetrates the dark ball of the eye, so light from the world penetrates into the Ego, returning, as it were, 'Light to Light', as in the *Credo*.

20. Milton was born on 9 December 1608 – the very month in which some historians believe John Dee died. However, Dee seems to have had the last symbolic laugh in this, as in so many other matters. In his diary for 26 March 1609, we find a marginal drawing of a skull, with the truncated signature, **Jno** △, alongside. It is reasonable to take this as a reference to Dee's death, as does Benjamin Woolley in *The Queen's Conjuror: The Life and Magic of Dr. Dee* (2002), p. 322.

21. A good reproduction of this print is in Gertrud Schiller, *Iconography of Christian Art*, (1972), Vol. 2, *The Passion of Jesus Christ*. See print 529, with descriptive text p. 160.

22. See Peter Green, *The Argonautika. The Story of Jason and the Quest for the Golden Fleece. Apollonios Rhodios*, (1997) pp. 188–89.

23. The *golden fleece* is an idea derived from the magician, Cornelius Agrippa, who transmutes the fleece into a vellum, on which was written an alchemical text. The story relates to the *Argonautae*, who accompanied Jason on the ship, *Argo*. Jason was aided by the enchantress, *Medea* (mentioned by Jonson in this passage). The story is one that crops up again and again in alchemical literature. The tale of *Pythagoras' golden thigh* and *Pandora's box*, as alchemical agents, have been traced to Martin Delrio, *Disquistiones Magicae* (1599), by Elisbeth Cook (*op. cit.*). The dragon's teeth were the teeth of the dragon that *Cadmus* had killed. When these were planted, there grew from each tooth a fierce warrior. As they threatened the life of Cadmus, he threw into their midst a precious stone: they fought for it, leaving only five survivors. Here, Jonson links them with *mercury sublimate* because this is white, like teeth, and, like the teeth of the dragon, might 'bite' corrosively. Jonson twists the legend to liken *Jason's helm* to an alchemical alembic or glass receptacle. The *Hesperian garden* is the same story, hi-jacked by alchemists, with which Dee plays here. Jove, appearing to Danae as a *shower of gold*, was a mythological tale hijacked by the alchemists – see for example, the plate captioned AER in Barent Coenders van Helpen, *Escalier des sages* (1689). The *boon of Midas* was no boon, but a bane: he had been granted a wish that everything he touched should turn to gold – the wish being granted, everything he tried to eat turned into the splendid metal. *Argus' eyes* relates to the story of how Mercury slew the hundred-eyed dog, Argus, in consequence of which Juno put the eyes on the tail of the peacock. This iridescent tail figures frequently in alchemical works: see, for example, the *Triunum Bonum* plate in Khunrath, *Amphitheatrum sapientiae aeternae* (1602). *Boccace* is, of course, Boccaccio, who, in his *Genealogica Deorum*, mentions a god name

Demogorgon. In earlier literature, it is recorded that it was forbidden to pronounce the name of this god: in doing so, the fourth-century Christian, Lactantius, is supposed to have released its terrible power on the world. In his *Faerie Queene*, (IV. Ii, 47) Spenser portrays Demogorgon living in the deep abyss with the three *Fatae*. Jonson seems to have had in mind the notion that some things should not be said, but this is not a prerogative of alchemy.

24. The image of the Hesperides is from the top register of the title page of Michael Maier *Atalanta fugiens* (1618).

25. The *Monas* itself is counted as 4, as it contains the four elements of Sun, Moon, Cross and Aries. The diagram below it, which is a reconstructed mortar and pestle, consists of 3 graphic units. The exploded *Monas* within the rectangle consists of 8 units (crescent, sun, four armatures of the cross, and two arcs of the Aries sigil). The two vase reconstructions together consist of 5 units. So far, then, we have $4 + 3 + 8 + 5$, which gives 20. The internal rectangle makes 21. There are 12 identifying letters within the whole diagram, bringing the total to 33.

26. Andreas Libavius, in his *Commentariorum Alchemiae, Partis II, De Lapide Philosophorum* (1606), provides a large number of woodcuts of alchemical vessels, not one of which even resembles the *alpha* drawn by Dee.

27. The following intertextual notes relate to the difficulties one encounters in translating this passage.

[1] In medieval Latin, a *spiraculum venti* is a blast of air, but in a theological context it is also an *afflatus*, the breath of the Holy Ghost. Thus, one who is *spirativus* is acting upon such holy inspiration. It is reasonable to assume, therefore, that Dee is writing of skilful or ingenious blasts of air that induce inspiration.

[2] The Hebrew does not appear to have any meaning, and may be concerned with an arcane numerology. On page 47 of his own rather banal (and sometimes inaccurate) translation of Dee's *Monas*, C. H. Josten tells us that the Hebrew words that appear in this section cannot be translated. He further tells us that Professor Scholem, of the Hebrew University of Jerusalem, had informed him that such elements as were unintelligible seemed to suggest a chemical process. In a similarly inadequate translation into French of the *Monas*, Grillot de Givry in *La Monade Hiéroglyphique* (1975), p. 47, also notes the poor quality of the Hebrew, but then uses this as an excuse for translating it in alchemical terms. In his own translation, set out by J.W. Hamilton-Jones in *The Hieroglyphic Monad* (1947), there is no doubt that the Hebrew relates to an alchemical process, for (without distinguishing that Dee had moved from Latin to Hebrew) Hamilton-Jones derives from the Hebrew an incorruptible salt and a substance that floats within the vitriol after dissolution... The Latin, *Litro Vinium* could not possibly mean 'a litre of wine', as Josten suggests (see Josten, *op. cit.*, p. 197). The measure we now call a litre was not determined until during the French Revolution, circa 1793. The Greek *litra* was equal to an English pound in weight, and it may have been to this that Dee was referring. Bearing in mind that *vinum* can also mean 'grapes', it is possible that Dee was referring to the fruit, or even to the fruit-wine of those fruits he had described earlier. Beyond that suggestion, I must confess that I cannot understand the reference.

[3] *Tyro* (here, *Tyronis*) is another Latin word that does not appear in the standard dictionaries. However, in the fifteenth century, the word was used of a squire who was aspirant to knighthood, and may perhaps, therefore, be used in a general sense to mean an aspirant. The word would certainly have been known to Dee, who was a genealogist.

[4] Given the context, the *Primordiale Specimen* must be the original *afflatus*, or inspiration: accordingly, I have translated it in this way.

28. The diagram is from the *Monas Hieroglyphica*, p. 23.
29. The detail is from Johann Daniel Mylius, *Opus medico-chymicum*, (1618): *Basilica Chymica*, from the series of roundels depicting the stages in the Creation of the World and Man.
30. Whilst the Latin version of *Luke* mentions a birth in a *praesepio*, Dee has mentioned specifically the birth in a *stabulo*.
31. A good bibliography for this esoteric programme is found in the notes to David Ovason, *The Two Children: a Study of the Two Jesus Children in Literature and Art* (2001).
32. The woodcut is reproduced from David Ovason, *The Two Children* (2001), p. 78: it is from Franciscus de Retza, *Defensorium inviolatae virginitatis Mariae*.
33. The woodcut is by Albrecht Dürer, circa 1500, from *Revelationes Sancte Birgitte*.
34. Reproduced from Ovason, *The Two Children* (2001), p. 103, the drawing is based on an illumination in the Reichenau Egberti mss.
35. Krause-Zimmer, *Die zwei Jesusknaben* (1969). My own work, *The Two Children* (2001), deals in a general way with art and the genealogies, and includes a study of certain forms of art that touch upon the theme, from pp. 271 to 408.
36. I list here only those artists for whom I have reproduced a picture illustrating their approach to the theme in my work on the subject, mentioned above.

Chapter 5

1. The engraving, designed by Theophilus Schweighardt, and called *Collegium Fraternitatis*, is from the frontispiece to his *Speculum Sophicum Rhodo-Stauroticum* (1618).
2. The fabric held by the hand of God is blowing in the wind. This is a conventional way of showing that the hand must be conceived as being in motion. A present, the hand is lowering the temple into a valley, near (as it seems) Mount Ararat, but it could be withdrawn and moved elsewhere at any moment.
3. The drawbridge is marked out with the words *Si Diis Placet*.
4. The 27 words in capital letters are: ORIENS, OCCIDENS, MERIDIES, SEPTENTRIO, VIDEAMINI, COLLEGIUM FRATERNITATIS, FAMA, CAVETE, JESUS NOBIS OMNIA, NOTA, VENITE DIGNI, MOVEAMUR, SI DIIS PLACET, PUTEUS OPINIONUM, IGNORANTIAM MEAM, AGNOSCO, IUVA PATER, and CRF.
5. This period is too close to the present reincarnational period to be accidental. Were the Rosicrucians preparing the ground in order to facilitate their work during their next important personal reincarnational period?
6. I cannot ascribe this extraordinary work to the eighteen-year-old Protestant, Andreae of Tuebingen, who had been born in 1586. As with most Rosicrucian works, the authorship of this work remains shadowy, and was certainly intended to be so. The work was published anonymous under the German title, *Chymische Hochzeit Christiani Rosencreutz*, in 1616, and went into at least three editions in that same year.
7. The Latin in *Matthew* VII:6 reads *neque mittatis margaritas vestras ante porcos*.
8. The original title of this second-century AD work seems to have been *Metamorphoses*, but it was generally known in the late medieval tradition as the *Golden Ass*. There is an excellent Latin edition available in the parallel text translation of William Adlington, in the revised edition by S. Gaselee: *Apuleius. The Golden Ass, being the Metamorphoses of Lucius Apuleius* (1535).
9. The woodcut is from, *L'Asino d'Oro di Lucio Apuleiosa volgarizzato da Agnolo Firenzuola* (1863). p. 246.
10. I quote here from the William Adlington translation of 1566 (see his *The Golden Asse of*

Apuleius, with the introduction by E. B. Osborn (1923), p. 277). This is the most vital and enjoyable of the translations I know.

11. The *carbuncle* (now a variety of the garnet) was in former times supposed to be a solar stone, which had the property of emitting its own light. In Shakespeare's *Antony and Cleopatra*, (Act IV, Scene 8) we have a compelling image of this fabled link with the Sun, when Cleopatra offers Scarus, the brave friend of Antony, a military reward:

> I'll give thee, friend,
> An armour all of gold; it was a king's.

It is a gift that Antony approves:

> He has deserv'd it; were it carbuncled
> Like holy Phoebus' car.

12. The first performance of *Antony and Cleopatra* seems to have taken place shortly before 20 May 1608. The earliest known surviving copy of the play appeared in the first Folio of 1623. *The Chymical Wedding* was published in 1616, but may have circulated in manuscript prior to this time. Shakespeare had mentioned a carbuncle on the wheel of Phoebus' chariot in *Cymbeline*, Act 5, lines 189–90.

13. The alchemical symbolism attached to this sepulchre, which may indeed be interpreted as a reference to the physical body of Man (often termed 'Venus' in esoteric literature) is not relevant to our present inquiry.

14. For example, this detail of Rosicrucian mythology played a role in the rites and symbolism for the 5 = 6 initiation ritual that MacGregor Mathers created for the Second Order of the Hermetic Order of the Golden Dawn. See Ellic Howe, *The Magicians of the Golden Dawn. A Documentary History of a Magical Order 1887–1923* (1972), pp. 79–88.

15. Richard Kienast, *Johann Valentin Andreae und die vier echten Rosenkreutzen Schriften* (1926).

16. The equivalent terms used by the early Rosicrucians, in the post-Paracelsian phase, were (for the Etheric) the *Vegetabilis*, or the *Ens Veneni*, and (for the Astral), *Ens Astrale*. For discussions of these terms, see E. Wolfram, *The Occult Causes of Disease, being a compendium of the teachings laid down in his 'Volumen Paramirum' by Bombastus von Hohenheim, better known as Paracelsus* (1911).

17. The number refers to the second book of Daniel Mylius, *Philosophia Reformata*, (1622), this engraving being the eleventh in the series. Although this delineation points unequivocally to the developed seven-fold Man, the image is merely one of a series of 61 engravings, which depict a coherent sequence of spiritual events.

18. In some contexts, the alchemical *Rubefaction* seems to be linked with the mythological tale, told by Ovid, of the suicide of the Greek hero, Ajax. When he thrust the sword into his breast, the flowing blood rubefacted or ensanguined the ground to produce a purple flower, its petals bearing the letters of his name, and a word of lament. In this account, the rubefaction is of a hero, rather than a king, but Ajax was the bravest of the Greeks.

19. This has been the received wisdom in theology and esoteric literature for centuries, but I believe the notion that the word Adam is derived from the Hebrew אדם meaning 'to be red' is now disputed by modern scholarship. If the word is actually derived from the Hebrew אדמה, then Adam is the 'Earth Man'.

20. The Sanskrit, *Atman*, means 'breath of life', and is often used as though it denotes the universal superconsciousness. For a fuller definition, see Powis Hoult, *A Dictionary of Some Theosophical Terms* (1910), pp, 17–18. The Sanskrit, *Buddhi*, has been translated

as meaning 'The bliss aspect of the Trinity', but it is also part of the self, and linked with spiritual discernment: see Hoult, *op. cit.*, p.29. The Sanskrit, *Manas*, means 'Mind': for a Theosophical account, see Hoult, *op. cit.*, p. 79. In his work, *The Mental Body* (1927), p. 237, the Mason and Theosophist, Arthur E. Powell, claims that the name given to the Atma-Buddhi-Manas triad, 'the three higher principles of a man' is the Greek term, *Augoeides*, or Radiant Body. In this respect, however, see G.R.S. Mead, *The Subtle Body*, (1919), in the 1967 edition, pp. 56–81.

21. Shakespeare, *Romeo and Juliet*, Act III, Scene 5, in the Irving and Marshall edition, line 136.

22. One has to be careful, here, for in Elizabethan England the word Salt referred also to the seasoning, or enlivening property of the substance – as for example in the expression, 'The salt of youth'. In this sense, salt is different from the Salt or *Sal* of the alchemists.

23. Shakespeare, *The Tragedie of Hamlet*, Act IV, Scene 5, quoted from the First Folio of 1623, III, p. 274, second column, line 20.

24. For want of some other explanation for this image, I must presume that it is alchemical, and refers to sevenfold distillation. An application of numerology seems to take us nowhere: the number of salt (that is, *Sal*) is 30, and seven times 30 is 210, but there seems to be no significant correspondence to this last number.

25. Shakespeare, *The Tragedie of Othello, The Moore of Venice*, Act V, scene 2, in the First Folio of 1623, III, p. 338, col. 1, lines 37–41.

26. Shakespeare, *The life and death of King John*, Act IV, Scene 2, in the First Folio of 1623, II, col. 1, lines 8–9.

27. Ben Jonson, *The Alchemist*, Act II, Scene 3, line 186.

28. *Zernich* is trisulphide of arsenic.

29. The diagram, shorn of the Latin and German texts, is from the parallel translations of the *Aureum Seculum Redividum*, reproduced by Paul M. Allen in *A Christian Rosenkreutz Anthology* (1968), pp. 270–1.

Chapter 6

1. The complete letter to Tubbe may be seen in Jean Dupèbe, *Nostradamus. Lettres Inédites*, (1983), pp. 85–89.

2. This rare portrait of Nostradamus is a woodcut after a lithographic drawing by the French artist, Honoré Daumier. It is from *Almanach Prophétique, Pittoresque et Utile pour 1848*, p. 78, which was edited by the Nostradamian scholar, Eugène Bareste, who knew Daumier.

3. See, for example, E.H. Gombrich, *Symbolic Images: Studies in the art of the Renaissance* (1978 edn.); Edwin Panofsky, *Studies in Iconology: Humanistic Themes in the Art of the Renaissance* (1967 edn.), and Edgar Wind, *Pagan Mysteries in the Renaissance* (1967 edn.).

4. The page is from Nostradamus, *Les Propheties de M. Michel Nostradamus*, published in Lyon by Antoine du Rosne, 1557.

5. Nostradamus was, of course, a qualified doctor, but the appellation *Monsieur* seems to have taken precedence over *Docteur*.

6. The two verses may be understood only against the background of Iamblichus *De Mysteriis*, book III. The scholar, Pierre Brind'Amour, in his *Nostradamus. Les Premières Centuries ou Propheties (édition Macé Bonhomme de 1555)* (1996), pp. 45–51, has argued that the Iamblichus text was known to Nostradamus through the work of Petrus Crinitus, *De honesta disciplina*. One can show that Brind'Amour is not altogether right

in making this assertion, but an examination of his classical arcane text is essential as a preparation for understanding the source of these two remarkable verses.

7. That this phrase was derived from a Latin text is confirmed by the fact that *aeneam sellam* (whence the Nostradamian phrase is derived) is Latin: its equivalent in French, *un siège de bronze*, was not used by Nostradamus.

8. The modern artwork is based on a detail of a fourth-century Greek vase painting, depicting the pythoness with Apollo.

9. In his *De honesta disciplina*, to which Nostradamus had evidently referred when writing this quatrain, Crinitus had written *in Branchis ac Delphis vaticinia*... The *Branchides* were a family of priests of Apollo, probably ancestors of Branchus, from whom the name was derived.

10. Elisee du Vignois, *Notre Histoire Racontée à l'avance par Nostradamus*, (1911), pp. 61–104, examined well over one hundred verses dealing with the French Revolution and the immediate consequences of that Revolution, leading up to the Fall of the Directory in 1799. She included this verse I.3 in that series.

11. An available source is James Laver, *Nostradamus or The Future Foretold* (1942, but with several reprints), p. 39–41. Having recommended this, mainly for its conciseness, I have to say that Laver's scholarship is curious, in that he quotes from Iamblichus in Latin, when *De Mysteriis* is in Greek. However, his views are marred, as his translation of the Latin is not accurate. Even so, by the standards of the majority of popular commentators, Laver is probably as good as you will get. John Hogue, *Nostradamus. The Complete Prophecies* (1997), pp. 67–8, makes an even greater mess of interpreting these two non-prophetic verses. The unspecified source translation of Iamblichus which Hogue uses is of poor quality, and this author has the tendency to attribute to Nostradamus the action depicted in the quatrains that is properly attributed to the prophetesses of Delphi and the Branchides. For a good-quality modern edition of the Greek of *De Mysteriis*, see Emma C. Clarke, John M. Dillon and Jackson P. Hershbell, *Iamblichus: De mysteriis* (2003 in the English parallel text).

12. For this edition (the eleventh edition of the work) see Robert Benazra, *Répertoire Chronologique Nostradamique (1545-1989)* (1990), pp. 84–85.

13. The phrase, *Green Language*, does not make much sense in English translation: originally it was the French, *La Langue Vert*, in contrast to *La Langue Ouvert* – the familiar 'open' language of everyday life. When the phrase was adopted by the French linguist, Alfred Delvau, for his fascinating *Dictionnaire de la Langue Verte* (1883), something of the esoteric content of the language was lost by its applicaton being diverted to a more popular, exoteric usage.

14. Michael Maier, *Jocus Severus, hoc est, Tribunal Aequum, quo noctua regina avivum, phoenice arbitro*... (1617).

15. The full title runs, *Jocus Severus, hoc est, Tribunal aequum, quo noctua regina avium, phoenice arbitro post varias disceptationes et querelas Volucrum eam infestantium pronunciatur, & ob sapientiam singularem, Palladi sacrata agnoscitur: authore Michaele Maiero Com. Pal. M.D.* One must discount the final abbreviation M.D. in the count.

16. The 33 words translate:

> I ascribe, address and dedicate this to all true lovers of alchemy, known or unknown in Germany, and among those (unless Fame does deceive us) one hidden away from this, save by the *Fama* of the Brotherhood and by his admirable and commendable *Confessio*, manifested in this way.

17. The force of this dedication rests upon the fact that the titles of the two most important Rosicrucian works, published up to that date, were the *Fama* and the *Confessio*.

18. The quatrain is from the 1557 edition of the *Propheties*, published at Lyon by Antoine de Rosne, under the title, *Les Propheties de M. Michel Nostradamus*.

19. This may have been a tongue-in-cheek *ludus*, for, if we count the commas and full stops in the line, then we arrive at 33 characters. By this rule, both the first and the last lines of quatrain number 3, book 3 are linked with 33.

20. The quatrain is from the 1568 edition of *Les Propheties*, published at Lyon by Benoist Rigaud.

21. The Latin word *ludus* survives in the English ludicrous, which in late sixteenth-century English meant 'frivolous', or 'witty': it is from the Latin verb, *ludere*, 'to play', and in some contexts can simply mean 'a game'. As we have seen, Maier, writing in the following century, tends to use the equivalent word, *Jocus*. Nostradamus' little *ludi* are certainly more serious than those of Maier.

22. I have selected quatrains III.3 for the following brief analysis only because of its numerological importance. I have dealt with it, at greater length, but from an entirely different standpoint, in an earlier work on Nostradamus. See, David Ovason, *The Secrets of Nostradamus* (2001), pp. 83–87.

23. The portrait of John of Austria is after a print made in Venice at about the time of the Battle of Lepanto, and is from William Stirling-Maxwell, *Don John of Austria, or Passages from the History of the Sixteenth Century 1547–1578*, 2 vols. (1883), Vol. I, p. 401.

24. Fernando de Herrera, *Relacion de la Guerra di Cipro y succesos de la batalla naval de Lepanto* (1572), ch. 27. The data is from the useful tabulation in Stirling-Maxwell, I, pp. 440–1.

25. Ferdinand Caracciolo, *I Commentarii della Guerra fatta coi Turchi da D. Giovanni d'Austria* (1581), pp. 43–51. The data is from the useful tabulation in Stirling-Maxwell, I, pp. 440–1.

26. A fairly exhaustive account of the Battle of Lepanto is given in Stirling-Maxwell, *op. cit.* The picture of the oared galley, reproduced here, is from this work, Vol. 1, p. 89.

27. In fact, the French word *midi* meant both 'midday' and 'South', as in *Le Midi*, in reference to the South of France. However, Nostradamus seems here to have been using it in an archaic sense (from which the notion of midday and the South were ultimately derived) – approximately, 'in the middle', whether in the middle of the skies, or the middle of the day.

28. One question is, whence did Nostradamus obtain his information about the positions of the planets in 1571? He wrote the quatrain sixteen years before the event itself. Tabulations did exist, even if they were not as accurate as those to which we are accustomed today. Nostradamus would have had recourse to the *Ephemerides* of Leowitz, which covered a period of fifty years, and included 1571. See, Leowitz, *Ephemeridum novum atque insigne opus, ab anno Domini 1556 usque in 1606, accuratissimè supputatum. . . .* (1557).

29. The chart (which, of course, is not a chart for the Battle of Lepanto) was cast for 4 February 1571 at 11:00 AM, for Corinth, on the Peloponnese.

30. I took the picture of the ruins of the Temple of Apollo at Corinth *circa* 1975.

31. I took the photograph of the Roman theatre at Ephesus *circa* 1988.

32. For details of how the warships of the League closed in upon, and hemmed the Ottoman warships into the Gulf, see Stirling-Maxwell, *op. cit.*, I, pp. 402–4.

33. For an example of this use of ἀπορία, see Herodotus, *Histories*, I:79.

34. I have dealt with the Space Programme and the attack on Manhattan in my work, *Nostradamus. Prophecies for America* (2001).

35. The verse numbers first appeared in the tri-textual edition of the Bible published in Paris, in 1551, by Robert Estienne. A copy is in the collection of the Bible Society, Cambridge University Library. I have established to my own satisfaction that Nostradamus used this Estienne edition for the Bible-based encodings that appeared in his *Propheties*.

36. See Nancy Lyman Roelker, *The Paris of Henry Navarre as seen by Pierre de l'Estoile. Selections from his Mémoires-Journaux translated and edited by Nancy Lyman Roelker* (1958), p. 3.

37. For these diaries, see Paul Bonnefon, *Mémoires-Journaux de Pierre de l'Estoile* (1889). For a brief summary of the nature of the diaries, see Nancy Lyman Roelker, *op cit.*, pp. 12–14.

38. See Robert Benazra, *Répertoire Chronologique Nostradamique [1545–1989]*, (1990), pp. 89–90.

39. *Tocque Tabourin* denotes the noise made by the beating of a small drum. However, given the supposed interpretation of the quatrain, it is likely that L'Estoile had in mind a drum being beaten to a future dance macabre. It is the equivalent of the *Tocsin*, rung to give an official alarm at the outbreak of a fire, or an insurrection.

40. The quatrain is from *Les Propheties de M. Michel Nostradamus*, published in Lyon in 1568 by Benoist Rigaud.

41. Actually, whilst this is true, the fact remains that this spelling was fairly general in sixteenth-century French texts: Nostradamus used it even in his prose writings.

42. Esotericists have for centuries used the bee and the hive as a convenient symbol for a wide range of arcane truths. The ancients saw *apis* as a celestial creature. Perhaps Urbanus (who was a fine classicist) had this ancient tradition in mind, for the celestial influx is the greatest of all benefits for mankind, and the gods themselves seem ever reluctant to sting even wrong-doers – at least, while they are in their pre-mortem state. It seems possible that Urbanus, the earthly representative of God, was identifying himself with these remarkable creatures that bring to earth the 'divine intelligence'. The phase, *divinae mentis*, is from the long passage in praise of bees in Virgil's *Georgics*, IV.

43. For the Barberini bee and the related mottoes, see Mrs. Bury Palliser, *Historic Devices, Badges, and War-Cries* (1870), p. 40. I have changed some of Palliser's translation and details of her reading of the Latin mottoes, but I have warmly embraced the idea that the Barberini bee was originally a *tafano*.

44. The detail of the Urban arms in St. Peter's, Rome, is from Bernini's *baldacchino*, which was commissioned by Urban VIII.

45. My impression, until I began work on this quatrain, was that the bite of a gadfly was more painful than that of a bee. However, I was happy to learn that the *tafano*, which was the original Barberini device, is a horse-fly (I think, of the *Oestridae*) that does not attack people. In this respect, the bee is more malign than the gadfly. The rich Italian language plays upon this truth, for, figuratively speaking, a *tafano* is 'a bore', with a sting that seems at times near-fatal to humans, but which rarely proves fatal. Even if I am wrong in distinguishing the gadfly and the horsefly, the drift of *Qui onc ne fut si malin* must be clear from this development of the Barberini arms. Needless to say, the question of how Nostradamus knew about these future things is certainly beyond my ken, and probably beyond that of anyone.

46. The portrait of Urban VIII is a detail of a print of the painting by Andrea Sacchi, in the Barberini Gallery, Rome.

47. The little joke for Nostradamus would have been that his own family arms included (*ecartelé* in one and four) a broken eight-spoked wheel – a *roue brisée d'Or de huit raies*. I have been unable to trace the origins of this device.

Chapter 7

1. See the frontispiece portrait to William Law, *The Works of Jacob Behmen, The Teutonic Theosopher*, (1764). Volume I, containing *The Aurora* and *The Three Principles*.

2. I could quote many literary sources, but a striking confirmation of this tradition may be found among the zodiacal and hermetic windows in the cloisters of Chester Cathedral, which windows are arranged in calendrical sequence. The finest lights are those in the West of the cloisters, which depict the Four Archangels with their corresponding elemental sigils and associations. A good literary source is the *Calendarium* attributed to Trithemius, dated 1503, reproduced in Karl Anton Nowotny, *Henricus Cornelius Agrippa ab Nettesheym. De Occulta Philosophia* (1967), Appendix V – Quatuor f. 7, p. 617. As the relevant *scalae* contain errors in the sigillization, I append here a detail from a modern reconstruction of this *Calendarium* that I have made, in which the names of the four archangels [*Angeli*] and their elemental sigils may be studied:

Below the name of Gabriel, is the sigil ▽ for the element of Water.

3. See *The Clavis: or An Explanation of some principal Points and Expressions in his Writings. By Jacob Behmen, the Teutonic Theosopher*, (1764). This work is available in Adam McLean, *The Key of Jacob Boehme* (1981), in the Magnum Opus Hermetic Sourceworks series, pp. 11–31.

4. See, *The Clavis* – 'Of the Holy Name JEHOVA', p. 13 in the McLean edition, *op. cit.*

5. See, *The Clavis: op. cit.*, section 33. p. 13 in the McLean edition. In this count, the heading [J], the passage number [33], the marginal note, the lining letter [h] and the same letter, along with the corresponding marginal note, must be counted.

6. William Law, *An Illustration of the Deep Principles of Jacob Behmen, the Teutonic Theosopher, in Thirteen Figures*, (1764). The plates in this present work are reproduced from a loose complete collection of hand-coloured engravings in my own library, evidently from William Law's *The Works of Jacob Behmen, The Teutonic Theosopher* (1764). I worked from the text and illustrations in the Masonic Library of the Supreme Council (Southern Jurisdiction), in Washington, D.C. A good available treatment of Law's notes (*An Illustration...*) on these thirteen engravings may be found in Adam McLean, *The Key of Jacob Boehme* (1981), in the Magnum Opus Hermetic Sourceworks series.

7. Henri Talon, *William Law. A Study of Literary Craftsmanship* (1948), p. 94. Talon is quoting from Law's *Christian Regeneration. Works*, Vol. V, p. 172.

8. This numerology is not applicable to the English or the Hebrew versions of *Genesis*. However, we are dealing here with the Latin Vulgate text, which Jacob Boehme appears to have used at times in the quotations within his illustrations. The numeration of the verses within the Bible were introduced by the French printer, Estienne, in 1551. Most of the Boehme plates incorporate quotations and terminologies in German, but they make use also of Greek, Latin and Hebrew.

9. The Fall of Adam, which represents the Fall of mankind, is graphically illustrated in plate IX of the series: 'He lies as dead, on the outmost Border of the Spirit of this World', as Law puts it, in his translation of *An Illustration of Deep Principles* (p. 50 in the McLean edition). In this engraving, the A is being pulled down into the realm of S [Satan] by what appears to be a crook. In the heavens, all the stars and planets, and the celestial S (Sophia) radiate urgently towards Adam in order to save him.

10. Jacob Boehme, *The Clavis, or An Explanation of some principle Points and Expressions in his Writings*. Translated into English by William Law, Section 132.

11. Undoubtedly, as Boehme was conversant with the Cabala, it is likely that the sephira *Kether* (the Crown) played some part in the symbolism of this plate. However, my aim here, is merely to present a cogent view of the Christian symbolism within the design. A full analysis of even one of these engravings would take up at least the space of this present book.

12. *Genesis* I. 17.

13. That Thomas Heywood was of the 'Fraternity of Rosi Crosse', and author of *Locrine*, has been shown, with numerological proof, by Frank Woodward, *Francis Bacon's Cipher Signatures* (1923), pp. 84–5. As the reader will recognize, this attribution is not relevant to my own argument relating to the vignette.

14. The reproduction is from a photographic print dated 1908, and reveals cracks in the plaster that have been removed during recent restorations. Personally, I feel that these cracks help intensifty the dramatic frisson of the moment.

15. Magically, the creative act depicted in this detail was being performed between the two fingers of Jupiter (as the index fingers were called in Renaissance palmistry). Jupiter was the leader among the pagan gods, and here this idea was being yoked into Christian service.

16. Charles Bovelles [Caroli Bovilli], *Liber de Differentia vulgarium linguarum, & Gallici sermonis varietate* (1533), cap. LII and LIII.

17. The 'simple key' proposes that the 26-letter alphabet may be expressed numerically by a consecutive series of numbers. As the two groups I and J and U and V are treated as being the equivalent of one number, the simple key alphabet really consists of 24 letters. The Greek and Hebrew methods of letter numeration are, of course, entirely different.

18. For an account of this combined letter-form of Boehme, with example sigils, see, F. Gettings, *Dictionary of Occult, Hermetic and Alchemical Sigils* (1981), p. 141, under HOLY DEITY.

19. Boehme, *Clavis, op. cit.*, number 38, p. 13 in the McLean edition.

20. The 'triads of Purgatory' is scarcely a theological term. However, this domain might properly be represented as a dark and inverted triangle, or triadic arrangement, for Purgatory must, by its very origins and redemptive purpose, reflect the triadic celestial realms of the Trinity. It is clear that, since Boehme allows for escape from this triadic prison, his threefold dark symbolism points to Purgatory, and not to Hell itself. To my mind, the most clearly defined description of Purgatory is that given by Dante, in his *Divina Commedia*. Here, we find a triadic form, with Ante Purgatory, separated from Lower Purgatory by Peter's Gate, with the well-defined steps of contrition and confession. Lower Purgatory, where the first three cornices are located, is separated from Upper Purgatory (cornices 5–7) by the Cornice of the Slothful, or Middle Purgatory. This argument, in favour of Purgatory, as against Inferno, is to some extent supported by the fact that the form of Mount Purgatory is echoed in the form of the letter A, whilst that of Inferno is not.

21. See, *An Illustration*, Number X, p. 52, in the McLean edition.

22. The engraving is the frontispiece to book six of Boehme's *Der Weeg zu Christo*, in his *Theosophische Wercken* (1682). This design appears to have been done by Boehme's disciple, Georg Gichtel.

23. The German, *fleisch*, actually means 'flesh' or 'meat', but the fact that it is written upon a Cross suggests that Boehme was wishing to convey the notion of the mortification of the flesh (the German, *das Fleisch kreuzigen*, means precisely that).

24. The nature of this Seal of Solomon, the two triangles of which (as Law tells us) were divorced from each other at the Fall. This is described in Law's text on illustration Number X, in his *An Illustration*.

25. See Law, *An Illustration ... op. cit.* On plate number XII.

26. The hieroglyphic *ru* is sometimes given the sound value *re*: for the meanings 'mouth', 'entrance', 'gate', 'speech', etc., see E. A. Wallis Budge, *An Egyptian Hieroglyphic Dictionary* (1920), Vol. 1, p. 416a.

27. We do not count the huge Sun at the centre of the spiral because this forms the link between the upper and lower registers of the picture – Law has carefully ensured that it is enclosed within a circle, to distinguish it from the spiral.

Conclusion

1. *Mirari & initium* mean more than merely 'sufficiently marvel', as I have rendered them here. However, whilst I understand the relevance of *initium* (which refers to the sacred mysteries) I simply did not know how to turn the phase into acceptable English. I have to say that the nineteenth-century scholar, Arthur Edward Waite, whose grasp of medieval Latin was well ahead of my own, also failed to translate this word, in his own version of the text. Typical of the man, he simply ignored the word, leaving his more perceptive students to flounder.

2. I have taken the Latin from the *Musaeum Hermeticum Reformatum* edition of the *Lapidis*, dated 1678, p. 218.

3. I am perhaps sticking my neck out here, as some scholars have argued forcibly for Shakespeare as Mason and Rosicrucian. See, for example, Alfred Dodd, *Shakespeare Creator of Freemasonry. Being a Remarkable Examination of the Plays and Poems, which proves incontestably that these works were saturated in Masonry, that Shakespeare was a*

Freemason and the Founder of the Fraternity, (1923), and W. F. C. Wigston, *Bacon Shakespeare and the Rosicrucians* (1888).

4. William Shakespeare, *The Tempest*, Act III, Scene 3, quoted from the 1623 First Folio.
5. Gordon Browne's illustration seems to be dated [18]89: however, the edition from which I have taken the image was published circa 1905, and again in 1922: see Henry Irving & Frank A. Marshall, *The Works of William Shakespeare: Volume XIII–XIV* (c. 1905), p. 227.
6. William Shakespeare, *The Tempest*, Act III, Scene 3, line 31.

> Seb. A living Drollerie: now I will beleeve
> That there are Unicornes: that in *Arabia*
> There is one Tree, the Phoenix throne, one Phoenix
> At this houre reigning there.

We observe that the mention of the Phoenix (the symbol of the Ego) comes on line 33 of the 1623 First Folio printing of *The Tempest*.

7. James Cellan Jones' broadcast direction of the play was filmed on 24 December 1983, and seems to be still available in *The Shakespeare Collection*, available through the BBC.
8. First Folio of 1623, Act V, p. 100. In some later editions of the play, not only has the *thirtie three* been changed, but Act V has been apportioned a second scene.
9. The source was William Warner's translation of the *Menaechmi* of Plautus. For the Plautus version, I have used the edition by W. M. Lindsay, *T. Macci Plauti Comoediae*: Vol. I, incl. *Menaechmi* (1904, in the 1963 reprint).
10. In Warner's translation, as in his source, the Latin *Menaechmi* of Plautus: the play is not set in Ephesus, but in Epidamnum.
11. Their names are different in the First Folio of 1623.
12. Astrologically speaking, in Elizabethan terms, only this precision of birth would have enabled the sons and the slaves to have been identical, as pairs of twins.
13. 'The farcical nature of the plot has not debarred Shakespeare from displaying in this work some of his highest qualities.' Henry Irving and Frank A. Marshall, *The Works of William Shakespeare*, Vol. 1, *The Comedy of Errors*, p. 78.
14. For example, Irving & Marshall, *op. cit.*, p. 108, line 400, have changed the number of years to twenty-five.
15. In Act V, Scene 1, lines 320–1, Aegeon says they parted in Syracus seven years earlier. In Act 1, he had said that his youngest boy left home when he was 18 years old. Thus, the boy should have been 25 at the time of the play.
16. One includes in the count the running head and the *Finis*.
17. The first rule is that the I does not come within the compass of the count. The letter I, with its connection with the Ego in the English language, was often used as a sort of encoded disclaimer in order to regulate (i.e., increase or decrease) counts: it permitted a degree of creative latitude for the encoder. The second rule is that one must discount the letter C of Centaur, in the second line from the bottom of the first column. As may be seen from the reproduction on page 193, this is a wrong font – almost certainly a bold face. It may be compared with the Roman capital C that opens the second column. Shakespeare, and those other of his contemporaries who indulged in encodings, would make use of such devices as wrong-fonts to distinguish rejections from certain counts.
18. At the third general Council, held at Ephesus in 431, it was declared that Mary must be known henceforth as *Theotokos*, or Mother of God. In the centuries that followed, Mary increasingly began to receive the honour paid to her Son. In spite of this, the Marian cult reached its most powerful point in the West only in the twelfth century. My point is

that the crucial Council at Ephesus was located at the same place where homage had been paid to the pagan goddess, Diana, in the great Temple of Diana of Ephesus – one of the wonders of the ancient world.

19. Hella Krause-Zimmer, *Die zwei Jesusknaben in der bildenden Kunst* (1969). I have set out the background to this 'heresy' in my book, *The Two Children: A Study of the Two Jesus Children in Literature and Art* (2001).

20. For some notes on this aspect of the Sistine Chapel, see Ovason, *The Two Children*, pp. 339–344. Examples of the two Jesus children theme relating to the other artists listed here may also be found in this work. Needless to say, modern editors have made nonsense of this encoding, simply because the majority of them did not know that it was there.

21. Frank Kermode's edition of *The Tempest*, in the Arden Shakespeare series (*op. cit.*, p. 133) is as guilty as the rest. He has removed almost all the in-line capitals (save, of course, the personal pronoun), and ensured that the two capital N's are represented in italic form. I do not single out Kermode for particular criticism – he is not the only modern editor to have mangled the encodings of Shakespeare with the aim of popularizing the Bard. In passing, however, I should observe that his note on Prospero's charge to Ariel (*ibid*, p. 132, noted 317) is incorrect. Prospero is actually doing the opposite of what Kermode claims: he is *freeing* Ariel to his proper home of the Elements. Kermode, presumably not working with the First Folio of 1623, has merged Prospero's injunction, *That is thy charge.* – which relates to the expeditious voyage, with the following discrete sentence, *Then to the Elements be free* ... which is, of course, Ariel's promised reward. There is lost dramatic potential in Kermode's view: the freeing of Ariel is, of course, paralleled in Prospero's own plea to the audience to let their indulgence set him free.

22. I quote the words from James Shapiro's fascinating study, *Contested Will. Who Wrote Shakespeare?* (2010), p. 99. Shapiro's notes on Delia Bacon, on pp. 326–328 are particularly helpful.

23. See M. C. Bradbrook, *The School of Night. A Study in the Literary Relationships of Sir Walter Ralegh* (1936).

24. See George Chapman, *Euthymiae Raptus or The Teares of Peace* (1609), lines 1110–1112. The lines are examined by Raymond B. Waddington, 'The Iconography of Silence & Chapman's Hercules', in *Journal of the Warburg Institutes*, LXV, (1970).